The Guide to
New York Law Firms

The Guide to
New York Law Firms

Erwin Cherovsky

ST. MARTIN'S PRESS
New York

Library of Congress Cataloging-in-Publication Data
Cherovsky, Erwin.
    The guide to New York law firms / Erwin Cherovsky ; introduction by
Arthur R. Miller.
        p.   cm.
"A Thomas Dunne book."
ISBN 0-312-05870-5
1. Law firms—New York (City)—Directories.   I. Title.
KF193.N4C46 1991   340'.068—dc20   90-26386

First Edition: May 1991

10 9 8 7 6 5 4 3 2 1

To Edith who endured,
To Kim and Karen who wondered, and
To Koko who adjusted at the
feet of her master

Table of Contents

The Next Twenty-Five Leading New York Firms

Foreword

....

The Guide to New York Law Firms is a highly original, Olympian overview of the major New York firms. It provides perspectives we have not seen before in any analysis of law firms or, for that matter, of other legal institutions. The profiles of the firms are well written and perceptive, richly textured and quite fascinating. But they are more than a series of self-contained stories and data sheets. They also detail and bring to life the historical observations and conclusions that the author, Erwin Cherovsky, makes in the Introduction to the book, which comments on a variety of sociological and business aspects of the current New York legal scene. The profiles effectively reveal the essence of big city law practice and in the process track the heartbeat and pulse of these mega-firms—what drives them, what makes them powerful and magnetic, what keeps them on top or near the top of their profession, and what burdens they have faced and may still have to face to avoid toppling from their lofty position in today's highly competitive world of large firm practice.

Based on Cherovsky's extensive discussions with lawyers and non-lawyers who have had substantial contact with these firms, the profiles present a composite portrait of reactions to and outside appraisals of these firms. They also contain summaries of the historical development, ambiance, governance, and direction of the top firms, their relative financial operations and position, the quality of the lawyers and their work product, and the day-to-day environment facing their associates. Finally, each profile and the related data sheet presents a realistic view of each firm, making clear how it is different from others; how, for example, Cravath, Swaine & Moore and Wachtell, Lipton, Rosen & Katz are preeminent but for many different reasons. What emerges from these profiles is a depiction of an important segment of society that heretofore has been shrouded in mystery and only occasionally sketched in isolated and disconnected ways with little or no coherent framework or methodology. Although Cherovsky emphasizes the institutional nature of these firms, he does not lose sight of the important role often played by a single lawyer—or a few lawyers—in both the rise and decline of these firms.

Many will find the *Guide* useful as well as interesting. That especially is true of law school students and younger lawyers who have to make important career decisions. But they typically do not perceive—realistically, they are not in a position to perceive—law firms the way they are described in this book. The experience and perspectives of Erwin Cherovsky's thirty years at the bar, largely in "big" firm practice, together with his discussions with others with firsthand knowledge that is reflected in this book, will make it easier to focus on what counts and what to disregard in the more visible yet often superficial events that occur at all firms. Fortunately, the *Guide* is not a collection of various newspaper or magazine articles or television sound bites. This should help it achieve its purpose of helping students and recent law school graduates by giving a judicious and long-term view of these firms so that they can have a more realistic framework in which to decide whether they desire to devote their professional energies to a particular legal environment.

More experienced lawyers around the country will learn about firms that they only have heard of or merely have had some modest contact with because the *Guide* describes them in sufficient detail to put flesh and blood on the skeleton. Even lawyers who have had more substantial contact with the attorneys in some of these firms will be pleasantly surprised at the more rounded and full-bodied description that the *Guide* provides. There are very few lawyers who will have had enough contact with the fifty leading major firms that they will not profit from the detachment and perspective this book offers.

For readers outside the legal profession, whatever their callings might be, the detailed information should prove extremely helpful in understanding the significance of these powerful institutions and the way law is practiced on the "grand" scale. Law, after all, is a central reality of life for all of us. Thus, understanding the inner workings of the New York legal establishment is a useful exercise for everyone. After reading the Introduction on the New York legal scene and the individual profiles, a non-lawyer will be able to do far more than characterize particular firms with the typically broad brush: "It's just a 'Wall Street firm' or a 'white shoe firm' or a 'legal factory'." The *Guide* will help the reader to discriminate among the firms and give a very good idea of their particular ambiance, quality, and their strengths and weaknesses. It also provides considerable insight into why these powerful groupings are among the "shakers" and "movers" of our society.

Most firms portrayed in Cherovsky's top fifty have stood the test of time. The *Guide,* however, makes it clear that nearly all of them have had their ups and downs. If the *Guide* had been written fifteen or thirty years ago, many of the firms would have been featured but with many differences; others would not have been included; and some that might have been on the list at that time would not make it today! Some firms seem better equipped to adapt and grow; some are more or less stagnant; and some go into eclipse or disappear entirely. Confronted by a major unresolved problem—loss of leadership or erosion of the client base—or a major setback—a malpractice action or legal or ethical improprieties—a firm can decline rapidly from the top or come close to a free fall. One can only wonder who will "make the list" and who won't in the *Guide*'s next edition. And for those who survive it will be enlightening to compare the new with the old "composite assessments" and directions of their firms.

As the *Guide* makes clear, there probably have been more dramatic changes in the practice of law during the last fifteen years than since the emergence of the legal profession in America. Given the volatility of the situation, no one can predict what the future of the profession, let alone that of individual firms, will be. I think it safe to say that the ingredients for success or failure in the fast lane of New York practice—which are identified and delineated in the *Guide*—will be present at all times. But what particular firms and their leaders will do or not do with these ingredients in an attempt to adjust to different circumstances cannot be determined solely by inspecting the past. Nonetheless, part of the fascination of the *Guide* is that it lets us see how these reactions actually have been played out in the real experiences of real firms; the results often are as fascinating as, indeed more so than, those of "LA Law." So, we should be grateful to Mr. Cherovsky for bringing us along with him on this fascinating odyssey through a territory that until now has not been explored with such clarity and insight.

ARTHUR R. MILLER
Cambridge, Massachusetts
January 23, 1991

Acknowledgments

··

The current New York legal scene is replete with legal recruiters (headhunters) and legal consultants of varying sizes and
capabilities. Although it was not possible—or desirable—to
interview a large percentage of this community, I would like
to thank the ones selected (who permitted me to identify them)
for their time, knowledge, and insight: Elaine Dine, Brad Hil-
debrandt, Alan Roberts and K.C. Victor. I also would like to
extend my special thanks to Wendeen Eolis, who, in my mind,
is the guru of legal consultants; she submitted to several interviews and very graciously—and diligently—reviewed and com-
mented on the preliminary manuscript.

For reasons which hopefully are obvious, I will not identify
the practicing lawyers, house counsel and judges who gave me
their views of the law firms and lawyers included in this volume.
The judgments and evaluations of their peers were particularly

helpful in assessing the various capabilities under review. They were selected either because their reputations warranted it or because they were recommended to me by persons in whom I had confidence.

Unless asterisked, the financial information relating to gross revenue, revenue per lawyer and profits per partner in the data sections on the fifty leading firms has been obtained from *The American Lawyer.* Based upon my own review of the methods employed and upon advice from legal consultants, who have compared actual operating results of various firms with the information published in *The American Lawyer,* I believe such information is substantially accurate—certainly accurate enough for the purposes intended in this volume. Nonetheless, some legal consultants believe that there is a greater variance between the actual and reported numbers, particularly in the middle ranges, and that many of these numbers result from disinformation provided by sources.

By way of explanation of the revenue and profit information included in the data sheets, it should be borne in mind that, despite their public significance, the leading New York firms remain private institutions. Until *The American Lawyer* began to ferret out and publish this information in 1983, it was seen only on a need-to-know basis with management of each firm determining who had such a need. While believing that such information is substantially accurate, I leave for others more qualified than I to describe the difficulties and complexities of preparing the financial statements of law firms so that they are in accordance with generally accepted accounting principles consistently applied and comparable to one another, whether on a cash, accrual or modified accrual basis. Although different firms have different fiscal years, I have eliminated the step of making this distinction for ease of presentation and also because it becomes relatively unimportant when each firm is consistent with itself.

The *pro bono* statistics and certain other data were obtained either directly from the firms or from forms completed by the firms for the National Association for Law Placement. No corroboration of this data, other than confirmation from representatives of the law firms, was realistically feasible. The figures concerning numbers of lawyers are as of February 1 of the listed year, and, unless specifically noted, refer to the New York office alone. Much of the information concerning the views held by associates of their firms is taken from annual surveys conducted by *The American Lawyer*. While the methodology, reliability, and validity of the surveys have been questioned by many of the law firms under scrutiny, I thought it was useful to include this information in order to give some sense of certain associate responses and the comparative rankings of the firms.

I want very much to thank my assistant, Robin Fields—my Fran Lebowitz—for her energy, tenacity, and organizational and editorial skills, without which the entire enterprise would have collapsed.

Finally, let me thank Nathan Rosen, who on numerous occasions responded to my calls for library assistance promptly, knowledgeably, and graciously.

Introduction

The Current New York Legal Scene

The genesis of this *Guide* is not the result of a lifelong ambition to write a treatise on New York City's leading law firms. Its origins are more recent and more prosaic. They stem in large measure from reading an "At The Bar" column written by David Margolick in *The New York Times* in December 1988.

In his article, which reviewed recruiting brochures of a number of major American law firms and found them "all unique and in the precisely same way," it was not clear whether Mr. Margolick intended to imply that major law firms and law firms generally are pretty much the same. In my article "All Law Firms Are Not Created Equal," published in January 1989 by *The New York Law Journal* (Appendix C), I concluded that "one should never confuse the outward similarities of firms with their inner reality which, in fact, determines their culture, reputation and destiny."

The *Guide* in many respects is an elaboration of that conclusion. While reciting and acknowledging the value and importance of hard financial and statistical data, the *Guide* attempts to capture and explain the culture and reputation, if not the destiny, of leading New York firms in order to provide a fuller and more realistic portrait of these firms as significant institutions to those who want to be associated with them (law school students and recent graduates and partners and associates in both New York and elsewhere); to those who want to retain them (current and prospective corporate and other clients in the United States and abroad); and to those who in various ways deal with them (other law firms and corporations in the United States and abroad; headhunters and legal and business consultants; investment bankers; accounting firms; federal, state and city agencies, including the judiciary; the press and media; and hardware and software suppliers, among others). Many parties who deal with certain leading New York firms also happen to be clients of other of these firms.

Today, if someone without direct experience wanted to learn about a particular New York firm or its lawyers, he or she would consult the Martindale-Hubbell Law Directory or similar reference. The biographical and other information in those sources is furnished by the law firms themselves. The publishers publish the information as submitted or rearrange it in slightly different form. There are some histories of law firms written either by the firms themselves or by an independent author. Most are out-of-date, of interest only to persons in the firm, and do not pretend to be economic or cultural analyses.

From time to time legal trade journals contain articles highlighting various firms. Although informative, they are designed almost exclusively for lawyers, contain no consistently applied methodology and frequently are not in a position to determine or evaluate critical features. Some books have been published on the subject; they either are breezy and informative primarily to lay readers or sociologically oriented and informative primarily to those with an academic bent. Anyone who truly knows these firms—their personnel, tradition, governance, expertise, and clients—appreciates that they are in key respects very different institutions from the ways in which they have been portrayed.

OVERVIEW
. . . .

Leading New York law firms, however, do exhibit certain similarities. The vast majority, for example, have an extremely broad base of clients and are significant and financially viable institutions by any recognized standard. In 1988 the partners and associates of New York's leading fifty firms (together with those of the next twenty-five) comprised about 16,000 lawyers, which is approximately 2 percent of the 760,000 lawyers in the United States. Based upon available information, the total profit in 1989 for the 4,700 partners of these firms is about $2.25 billion (or $478,000 per partner) compared to the estimated net income of $33 billion for all practicing lawyers, including New York (or $141,000 per lawyer). Although revenues and various tests to determine economic performance (e.g., revenue per lawyer, profits per partner, ratio of revenue per lawyer to net income per partner) are by no means the only measuring rods of success or determinants of partner and associate satisfaction, they surely suggest that these firms are able to attract a wide array of major clients who believe that the services rendered for them are worth the fees paid—whether for persuading third parties, by litigation or discussion, of the correctness or reasonableness of the positions taken; structuring and negotiating transactions; drafting agreements and documents of all kinds; or giving advice concerning the positions to adopt, the people to contact and the strategies to follow. While it may be difficult for clients to change firms in mid-stream, especially after a long relationship, law firms by and large perform in a perfect Adam Smith world where the competition is open to all players, whose selection, particularly on transactional business, is based on merit—or, at least, perceived merit.

Most leading New York firms, to one extent or another, can be considered "full service," running the gamut of departments from corporate to litigation to taxation to trusts and estates with extensive specialties and sub-specialties. They also practice in areas which do not easily fit within traditional departments: labor/management; bankruptcy, reorganization and creditors' rights; insurance regulation and claims; anti-trust regulation; banking and commercial lending; environmental regulation; im-

migration law; intellectual property law; and sports and entertainment law. It was not too long ago when many leading firms
were involved almost exclusively in financial, corporate and
securities matters. Many litigated matters were farmed out to
boutique firms which acted almost like English barristers acting
for solicitors. Over the years and for somewhat different reasons
most litigation as well as déclassé fields such as bankruptcy,
labor/management relations, white collar crime and environmental regulation began to be considered not unworthy of being
cultivated.

Virtually all firms are located in clusters of office buildings
in mid-Manhattan and the Wall Street area and are in a state
of continual motion with shifts of lawyers and staff working
around the clock. Walking through the floors of many firms at
almost any time of the day or night is akin to walking through
a battleship—or perhaps, more accurately, an aircraft carrier—
observing lawyers and staff manning their stations and executing
their particular tasks. Common law lawyers whether in England
or in Colonial America—indeed, lawyers of only a generation
ago—would marvel at the speed, volume, diversity and reach
of the papers churned out by these firms utilizing the most
rapid and sophisticated computerized legal research and word
processing equipment and making, enlarging or reducing and
stapling copies by advanced reproduction equipment for trans-
mission all over the universe by fax or overnight courier. As
marvelous as the technology are the thought processes which
leave intelligent information on the end product—which may
then be indexed, filed and retrieved by other computer technology. Whatever other factors may be involved in realizing a
client's objectives, there is a passionate—some would say ov-
erpassionate—reliance on rationality, clarity and due process.

The expansion of the American and international economy
during the last several decades, including that created first by
corporate and anti-trust litigation and then by mergers and acquisitions (M & A) and unfriendly takeover activity (at least
through 1989), has been a prime cause for the expansion of
many leading New York firms, so that whereas the largest firms
of the 1950s and 1960s had about 150 lawyers, in 1990 the
largest firm had over 1,000 lawyers and the next tier firms were

in the 400-500 lawyer range. For every additional lawyer often about three or four persons were added to the staff, which includes paralegals, daytime secretaries, nighttime secretaries, daytime word processor operators, nighttime word processor operators, internal messengers, outside messengers, directors of administration, office managers, personnel managers, office service managers, employee benefits managers, recruiters, directors of associate programs, librarians, directors of finance, controllers, work-in-process managers, payroll supervisors, administrative coordinators, managers of stenographic services, litigation support directors, file room supervisors, computer training directors, telecopy and reproduction personnel, proofreaders, mail room employees, food supervisors and coordinators, floor coordinators, directors of security, receptionists, maintenance managers and various tiers of assistants. The ship runs on more than fuel.

There is an excellent chance that at least one leading New York firm is involved in the United States or abroad in almost any major public or private offering of equity, debt and hybrid securities, loan transaction, acquisition or merger of a corporation, friendly or unfriendly takeover of a corporation, bankruptcy or reorganization, real estate sale or syndication, labor/management dispute, environmental problem, tax dispute, administrative action, unfair competition or trademark, copyright or patent infringement case, and other litigation spanning all the specialties, including constitutional matters and white collar crime. The clients represented cover the spectrum of major profit and non-profit manufacturing, distribution and service companies (and governmental agencies) here and abroad.

CHALLENGES ARISING FROM INCREASED ASSOCIATES' SALARIES, LATERAL TRANSFERS AND OTHER DEVELOPMENTS

From all available sources, it appears that leading New York firms are currently at the zenith of their financial strength, power and influence.* Almost all of them, however, face serious

*While true when written in mid-1989, this conclusion must be modified by subsequent events, including the substantial decline of M & A activity and hostile takeover work,

challenges to their continued growth and stability. Ironically, the challenges stem in significant measure from the strong and continuing demand by firms over the last decade or so for top law school graduates whose numbers have remained relatively stable to fill the expanded needs of their expanded base of clients. This demand, in turn, has caused first one firm and then others to raise salaries of first-year associates to over $80,000 and those of more experienced associates ever higher (to over $180,000). Other firms were compelled to match the salary scale of these firms or at least increase their own so as not to be placed at a serious recruiting disadvantage. This, in turn, has caused firms to urge, if not require, their associates to work harder and increase their annual billable hours to well over 2,000 hours in order more easily to pay for their increased salaries and maintain an appropriate profit margin for partners. These developments have caused firms to act more and more like businesses in seeking to become more financially sophisticated (e.g., premium pay for highly successful work) and cost efficient (e.g., supervision by professional executive directors) and to expand and market their services both geographically and in terms of specialties. The drive to expand, in turn, has stimulated firms, through headhunters and consultants and direct contact, to acquire laterally, if not whole firms, then key originating partners or whole groups and departments of lawyers to increase revenue and profit, shore up perceived deficiencies or create or enhance desired specialties or capabilities in some respects to keep clients from straying to small boutique firms. (Lateral moves of partners once were a rarity; within the last several years the changes have been so many and so swift that one literally needs a current scorecard to keep track of the

which began in earnest during the second half of 1989 and continued through 1990. A sluggish American economy during the same period aggravated the decline that adversely affected virtually all the leading firms (except to the extent that they maintained viable bankruptcy and reorganization practices). With revenues generally declining, firms have adopted a variety of short-term measures designed to reduce expenses, including hiring fewer summer and permanent associates and eliminating associates already hired (sometimes forthrightly admitting the financial reasons thereof, sometimes disingenuously attributing the decision to their failures to meet firm standards). Many have questioned these cost-saving measures for practical, economic, and moral reasons. Partners themselves have not been immunized from expulsion from their firms for various alleged reasons, but expulsion is fraught with legal complication and consequence. In any event, it is difficult to determine at this writing the duration and extent of the consequences of this economic downturn.

new affiliations.) The increased billable rates and hours and fees have persuaded many corporate clients to retain, when appropriate, small boutique firms or to create or to expand their own in-house legal staffs, siphon off work that their own lawyers are capable of doing efficiently and properly and more closely monitor the special services performed by the leading New York firms which they retain (with the possible exception of the "You-Bet-Your-Company" matters later discussed). Indeed, house counsel staffs of major corporations are today not overly different in size from those of leading New York firms.

Lateral mobility has brought lawyers into firms who do not fit neatly into the established mold of partners and associates seeking to become equity partners (i.e., partners who vote on firm matters and share in the distributive profits and retirement benefits). In addition, new or revised categories of lawyers have been created or emphasized in order to maximize profits: associates who are hired at lower salaries on a full-time or part-time basis with the understanding that they never will be considered for partnership; senior associates who have been "passed over" for partnership but whose value is great enough for firms to ask them not to leave; "contract partners" who are admitted into a firm under contract for a defined time and compensation before a determination is made whether to make them equity partners; and lawyers who are "of counsel" to the firm, whose clients are serviced by lawyers in the firm and who receive by contractual formula with the firm a portion of the fees charged by the firm. Some lawyers are retained on a permanent or ad hoc basis as "special counsel" or "consultant." There is even an incipient movement to hire, on a temporary, job-for-job basis, "specialty" lawyers affiliated with personnel agencies which lease them to firms. Only a continuing dispute until mid-1989 with bar groups concerning prohibited "fee splitting" with laymen (the agencies) prevented these ventures from growing at a much faster pace.

New York firms also have sought within the last decade or so to increase the number of branch offices in the United States and abroad either by using its own lawyers or by acquiring or associating with an existing firm or group of lawyers. There are various reasons to seek this growth: to respond to economic pressure for greater revenue and profit; to go to areas where clients are conducting business to better service them; to expand the firm's client base and capabilities; to anticipate the needs of both the firm as well as its clients by staking out new territory; and to diversify a firm's "portfolio." Some branches parallel the home office to a reasonable degree in depth and diversity of lawyers, while some are mere outposts with one partner or a few partners in charge, hoping to respond to local needs or to act as business conduits for the home office. Keeping branch offices an integral part of any firm when they often are located thousands of miles distant from the home office is a difficult task. Supervising them so as to make them profitable is even more difficult.

The new office technology, the rising cost of doing business (including associates' salaries), the *Bates* v. *Osteen* Supreme Court decision in 1977 which, in effect, gave lawyers the right to publicize themselves and market their services within reasonable bounds, the heightened importance of non-repeat, purely transactional legal business, the increasing significance of professional executive directors with broad financial and personnel powers, the loosening bonds of loyalty between clients and their firms and between lawyers within firms, the vigorous growth of leading New York law firms both by internal and lateral means and the concomitant decrease in intimacy and collegiality and erosion of distinctive cultures, the related expansion and significance of headhunters, consultants and public relations agencies and the parallel rise of trade journals emphasizing the business, office management and personnel aspects of law practice have created a substantially new environment for leading New York firms—one which until the mid-1970s had not changed to any marked degree for generations.

PROFESSIONALISM V. BUSINESS CONSIDERATIONS

All these developments have provoked oftentimes heated criticism by lawyers—and some non-lawyers—that lawyers have sacrificed their professionalism, including their roles as draftsmen, craftsmen, counsellors and scholars, on the altar of Mammon. The basic solution of those who find fault with the trends described is to exhort lawyers to return to some prior unspecified Golden Age of professionalism—in reality, to times which were more economically tranquil and less complex but which nonetheless had their own peculiar problems on how to practice law profitably and act within the confines of legal ethics while discharging their obligations to advance the many causes of their clients. The question, however, is not whether the genie can be returned to the bottle or whether firms should opt for professionalism as opposed to business objectives, including what some have categorized, in a pejorative sense, as adventurism; the real question is how lawyers are to continue securing and representing clients in a new economic and political environment without giving the financial calculus of various matters excessive weight and thereby undermining their calling in the process. Within this new environment, each firm seeks solutions (at least initially) which do not disregard or violate its own traditions and culture. Alas, the goal is difficult to achieve, and no success realistically can be considered permanent.

The accusation that leading New York firms are run like a business—or run *for* business—is nothing new; it is a recurring theme since post-Civil War days. Nonetheless, the distinctive features of leading New York firms separate them from sole practitioners and small and even medium-size firms. Smaller firms contain many excellent lawyers which, however, do not have the institutional framework and longevity which give leading firms their special position and advantage to set their own agendas and solve their own problems. The institutional framework includes not only institutional clients but also the necessary lawyers to furnish, on a continual basis, the "finders" (who originate business), the "minders" (who maintain the business and supervise associates) and the "grinders" (who grind out the paper and documents).

THE NEED FOR COMPETENT GOVERNANCE

What is key to the history of success of any New York firm is the guidance provided by its leaders. After all, a firm is not a collection of umbrella stands under which various departments and partners practice. What happens in and to a firm does not occur by happenstance. The heads of firms, whether on the executive committee or by common acceptance of the partners, are the persons to whom the firm turns for judgment and direction on a myriad of significant matters for which the leadership is, directly or indirectly, responsible: partnership selection from within the ranks; compensation of individual partners; the extent of capital contributions; the amount and terms of debt financing; financial control and oversight directly and through executive directors; lateral acquisition of partners and their compensation; selection of managing directors of the staff; selection of facilities and equipment; establishment and management of branch offices; marketing; oversight of departments and firm committees; etc. A firm could have many distinguished partners and a decent base of clients and still flounder or decline because it lacks people of vision, energy and fortitude at the top with the ability to understand and direct the affairs of a major institution. A firm also could be stymied or damaged by disputes between warring factions of key partners, e.g., between finders themselves or between finders and minders. The demise within the last decade of many leading New York firms comprised of many talented lawyers is testimony to the critical need for effective leadership whose method of selection is acceptable to the partnership as a whole.

THE WORLD OF ASSOCIATES

New York firms do not live by top management alone. Summer and full-time associates of these firms are energetically and, indeed, lavishly recruited from the top—or near the top—of their law school classes throughout the country and provide the necessary man- and woman-power to perform the myriad tasks customarily handled by associates at various levels. Since leading New York firms in many respects are akin to teaching hospitals, it is clear that the quality of associate performance is an important—if not distinctive—factor in delivering those services in a professional and competent manner.

Ideally, partners are expected to provide associates with appropriate delegation of responsibility, guidance, collegial relationships, loyalty, continuing education, evaluation of their performance, adequate and fair compensation, and a fair opportunity to become a partner. Associates, in turn, are expected to give the firm their full-time working energy, maintain the confidences and secrets of clients, strive for excellence, conduct themselves with integrity, dignity and self-respect, enlarge themselves both as lawyers and as persons, be loyal to and integrated in the firm, and continually communicate with partners, clients and associates as part of a team effort. It is unrealistic to expect under the unremitting stress and demands of an active practice, particularly where there are hundreds of lawyers with a large number in any given department, that these reciprocal duties consistently will be discharged by all concerned with grace and without friction. However, the tone and temper of each firm is determined in large measure on how easily partners and associates who are inextricably linked by common matters interrelate and give each other their due.

While it is arguable that first-year associates are not worth $80,000 + per year on any basis (other than supply and demand), those who are able to pass through the associate review net clearly earn their pay. (It is sobering to note that in 1980 the "going rate" was about $36,000, that in 1968, about $18,000, that in 1958, about $5,000, and that in the Great Depression and earlier some associates paid firms for the privilege of obtaining the requisite experience.) Second-, third-, and fourth-year associates who have become disgruntled with their firms are prime targets for other firms—and their headhunters—as well as for house counsel of major corporations. Those who stay on do so primarily because they believe they have a realistic opportunity to "make partner."

Despite all the selection involved before and after a law student becomes an associate, the bell-shaped curve somewhat mysteriously remains operative; only about 15% of all associates, including laterals of the same class, are ever selected as partners. There are many reasons for this result other than lack of talent (however narrowly or broadly defined): the vagaries of particular assignments, the supervision of and relationship with individual partners, the choice of specialty, fortuitous (or non-fortuitous) assignments of clients, the particular needs of a firm, the quality of other lawyers in the class, and firm management policies and decisions concerning partnership opportunities, including the selection of lateral partners. Also, many associates along the way decide for many reasons that they really want to do something else, such as entering the family business, becoming an author, literary agent or business consultant, joining an investment bank, entering politics, becoming a professor of law, joining the government, starting a business, becoming house counsel to a corporation, etc. There is a decent chance that those who survive the burden of approximately eight years in the trenches will have demonstrated an exceptional degree of intellectual strength, legal learning, writing and acuity, initiative, commitment, maturity, sensitivity, judgment, thoroughness, perseverance, creativity, character, and personality—traits that were continually tested and reviewed by many different partners in many different contexts. Those associates who leave a firm with favorable experiences become part of a large alumni group who over the years do not lose touch with the firm. Indeed, it is not uncommon for these loyal alumni in their new positions to retain the firm to do legal work for them or their new organizations.

WOMEN AND MINORITY GROUP ASSOCIATES

Women and minority associates are subject to the same pressures and concerns of other associates as well as to those which are peculiar to them.

The skeptical view of women's ability to be lawyers—expressed in the mid-fifties by the bromide that they were accepted in fact but not in theory—is fast disappearing from the New York scene. Where there were a handful of women lawyers at that time, approximately 40% of first-year associates are now women. Their accomplishments in the 1970s and 1980s speak eloquently of their acceptance, at least as associates, by both lawyers and clients. Indeed, in some perverse way, a competent woman lawyer in many situations can be more effective

some favorable experience with that firm. It is not uncommon now for prospective clients to interview, on a formal basis, several law firms before selecting one. Of course, firms frequently lose clients for reasons which are purely extraneous: the client goes into bankruptcy, or is reorganized, or merges under someone else's control. A client may be taken over in a friendly or unfriendly tender offer or there may be other changes in management control (e.g., a proxy contest; the death or retirement of the CEO; etc.).

Unlike smaller firms, the most significant clients of leading New York firms are relatively large American and foreign corporations of both the profit and not-for-profit variety. Corporate clients are either institutional, the origins of which are lost or not particularly significant, or non-institutional where a definite link exists between the firm and a particular originating partner. Broad representation of one type of institutional client—a significant commercial or investment bank—is frequently the major differentiating feature among firms that otherwise would be comparable. In any event, all clients—once they have cleared a firm's internal procedures designed to preclude conflicts of interest with pre-existing clients—are under the aegis of a particular partner who is responsible for directing and managing their work within the firm mainly, but not exclusively, with the help of associates.

PARTNERS

All partners are not equal. Senior partners frequently utilize middle-level partners, and middle-level partners utilize junior partners to help service particular clients. The terms "senior," "middle-level" and "junior" refer either to age or to the extent of compensation or both.

Whatever the compensation, most partners dwell in relative obscurity, except to the extent they have achieved a reputation with a base of significant clients or with peers outside the firm. It is at least comforting to know that one can dwell in relative obscurity on $200,000–$400,000 per annum. If one's annual compensation is beyond the $400,000 figure, there is a good chance that the lawyer is not so obscure, particularly under the spotlight of an aggressive and expanding trade press. The compensation of partners who become unproductive because of age or other reasons is a continual problem for almost every firm. And the various responses of firms to this problem reveal much about them.

STAFFING AND SUPERVISION

Regardless of the partners involved, all matters need to be staffed. Depending on the client and the matter, a particular matter could involve only one department, one partner and a first-year associate; another matter, a senior partner, a middle-level partner and several associates, all in the same department; still another matter, one senior partner from one department, another from another department, and middle-level associates in each department; larger matters, a number of departments and a number of partners and different levels of associates; etc. Depending on the partner in question and internal firm procedure, decisions on drawing on the expertise of particular departments and particular lawyers for various matters are made by the partner in charge, sometimes with and sometimes without the consultation of other partners or department heads. In some firms associates are permanently assigned to particular clients; in other firms, associates are divided into groups within departments and work on matters within the group.

Whatever administrative procedure is used, the matter of proper staffing—neither overstaffing nor understaffing—and supervision is critical to the success of any matter. Overstaffing and oversupervision obviously are inefficient and unreasonably increase the charges. Understaffing and undersupervision leave the client vulnerable to delay and the inability to identify and properly resolve the legal problems involved in a situation.

Because it is often very difficult to determine at the outset how complicated or time-consuming a particular matter will be, the question of staffing is not one that can always be immediately determined. However, an experienced partner can, within a reasonable time, determine the nature and extent of the staffing required efficiently to accomplish a particular objective. In situations where, for example, there are major claims against a company or it is threatened by a hostile takeover, the matter can be realistically described as "You Bet Your Company." In those situations, where in all probability the chairman of the board or the chief executive officer of the client is directly involved, neither management nor the firm is overly concerned with having a perfect fit between staffing and the matter at hand. Exclusive of this kind of situation, firms continually wrestle with the problem. Wrong decisions in this area can be as bad as wrong advice, as the firm will end up losing the confidence of the client and, sooner or later, the client.

Whether institutional or not, all clients expect fast, expert and thorough service by the firm, department and partner in charge. Although clients apparently seem to focus on selecting the right partner, the group of lawyers directly involved and the reputation of the firm are also necessarily involved. Clients also expect that the partner in charge will discuss with management or house counsel or both, depending on the nature of the matter, the major thrust of the strategy involved at important intervals and that they will be informed of key events as they occur. While some tasks may be delegated to various associates, the client basically is relying on the talent, experience and dedication of the partner in charge to direct the matter both as a specialist and a generalist.

RELATIONSHIPS

The success of any relationship between a client and a law firm turns on there being a proper fit between the parties. This depends, in part, on whether the partners and associates of the firm are able to work with various management representatives in relative harmony. However, as the stakes become larger and the law continues to proliferate and raise numerous new and unresolved issues (despite the numerous issues which apparently have been resolved by litigation and otherwise), clients cannot afford the luxury of turning their matters over to kindred spirits who may not have any real idea of what the issues are or, at best, only a modest idea. Their adversaries, more often than not, are other leading New York firms which are able to address these issues. What clients demand in today's environment is real—not illusory—expertise. If it is not available from a particular firm in a given area, clients, sooner or later, will appreciate the inadequacy of the services rendered and will look elsewhere.

As a result of World War II, when many lawyers of the leading firms served in the armed forces, firms were compelled to utilize the services of lawyers not traditionally hired by them. During previous years the predominant WASP or white shoe firms simply did not hire Jewish lawyers, except for those few assimilated or court Jews of almost exclusively German ancestry who had access to significant banking or industrial business. In reaction to this condition, firms were founded which were almost exclusively Jewish and almost exclusively from the very top of their law school class. Because the performance of Jewish lawyers in white shoe firms during World War II exceeded their employers' expectations, the prevailing views against hiring Jewish (and other minority) lawyers diminished, and with the spread of increasingly democratic and egalitarian views generated by the war, this rigid division gradually was disregarded and diminished. Now, more than two generations later, the days of "white shoe" firms or "Jewish" firms or "Democratic" or "Republican" firms are fast fading from New York City which, with its built-in competitiveness and hustle and bustle, continually stimulates and challenges the energies of all who are engaged in its context. Whatever remnants exist of these old social, economic and political prejudices will be replaced, sooner or later, by a system of pure unadulterated merit. Attorneys will come from many firms and in many packages but will be concerned only with solving real problems effectively and in a timely manner. One also suspects that leading New York firms, while continuing to have their cyclical ups and downs, will continue to have the ability to make the necessary adjustments to respond to new times and circumstances.

Some comments are in order concerning the methodology of preparing the *Guide.*

A firm is considered a leading New York law firm if from 1986 through 1989 it was determined to be one of the first seventy-five firms in terms of average gross revenue for the period. Various financial and statistical data on all these firms are included. Also included is a profile on the first fifty firms. Although many firms based outside New York have established branch offices in New York, they are not covered here but instead are listed in Appendix B. Also not covered in the first fifty firms are those firms exclusively or primarily involved in a customs practice or in the practice of patents, trademarks and copyrights, and unfair competition. The policy concerning these exclusions may be reversed in future editions.

Although information was elicited from the detailed questionnaire sent to all firms, substantially more information was obtained from interviews of key headhunters, legal consultants, house counsel, judges and lawyers in different fields who over the years have had the opportunity to experience and observe these firms in very different contexts. The persons interviewed continue to have dealings with these firms and have requested anonymity. In order to accommodate their request and to encourage them to be open and forthright and not be concerned with whether or not they are in accord with one another or firms and lawyers, none have been identified in the text and no attribution is made to any particular person of any observation, evaluation or verbatim quotation. There also were numerous interviews of partners and associates of each of the leading fifty firms. *The American Lawyer Guide to Leading Law Firms* (1983-1984), *The National Law Firm Guide* (1982-1983), *The American Lawyer* and its affiliate *The Manhattan Lawyer*, *The New York Law Journal* and its affiliate *The National Law Journal* and *Of Counsel* have been consulted and attribution for particular information is noted. I also read *Lions of the Eighties* by Paul Hoffman (Doubleday, 1982) and *The Partners* by James Stewart (Simon & Schuster, 1983), which present anecdotes on a number of the firms covered by this book. All this information has been filtered through my mind for better or worse. As I have been a practicing lawyer in New York City for the past thirty years and had information about many of these firms before commencing this project, I hopefully have been able to separate the wheat from the chaff and produce a reasonably balanced account of what is being described and analyzed.

As earlier mentioned, the profile on each leading law firm attempts to portray realistically the firm's history, tradition, culture, etc. The profiles also attempt to assess the quality of each firm's clients, lawyers, work product and office governance and environment. With some trepidation (as the procedure can be abused by third parties), I have summarized each such assessment, also taking into consideration the relative strength of the firm's most recent annual revenues per lawyer and profits per partner, by assigning each firm one of the following symbols:

—top of the line
—superior
—good
—fair
—unsatisfactory

Several caveats are in order. First, the symbols are not intended to substitute for the more detailed comments in the profile and in the related financial and statistical data; each is an abbreviated summary of my sense of the overall assessment made by sources of how a particular firm measures up to the previously noted criteria which are customarily utilized in evaluating law firms. Second, different firms could receive the identical symbol and have quite different compositions and blends. For example, a firm would not be substantially downgraded if it had a very strong corporate department (which is by far its most significant division) and a relatively weak and small trusts and estates department (which is its most insignificant department). Also, for example, a firm could have relatively strong financial numbers which could be adversely affected by a relatively weak or inconsistent work product or office governance and environment. Third, as the symbols represent a particular range within an assessment spectrum, firms could be assigned the same symbol but not have received identical assessments. Fourth, all the firms analyzed are quite large, whether by number of lawyers, revenue or profit, and quite prestigious; the assigned symbols compare these firms with one another and not with substantially smaller New York firms. If those comparisons were to be made, the evaluations would necessarily be different. Under the circumstances, it should not come as a surprise that the actual range of the assessments turned out to vary from 💼💼💼 to 💼💼💼💼💼 and intermediate positions.

As the portrayal of each firm represents a snapshot in time, I also have indicated by readily understandable symbols (↑ , ↓ , ↔ and **?**) whether or not my sources believe that the firm is in the process of succeeding to improve itself.

In reviewing individual New York law firms it will become readily apparent that they are not mere extensions of law schools, legal aid societies, the courts or governmental agencies. Still, the work of these firms cannot be understood without an appreciation of law schools and legal education, the size and extent of *pro bono* work and the litigation and other business before courts and agencies. And, regardless of the different institutions which are reflected by individual firms, their functioning and direction turns on lawyers who have dedicated themselves to the practice of law.

Lawyers in leading New York firms are a special breed. Except for their *pro bono* activities, they represent clients who most assuredly have the resources to retain them. Although their services cover a wide range of human activity, they individually are not viewed as garden-variety generalists, addressing a broad spectrum of legal problems for ordinary folk. They also are not ordinarily looked upon as being very romantic figures (except possibly for participating in transactions involving very large dollar amounts). There are critics who, with good intentions or otherwise, question their social utility and worth. Nonetheless, these lawyers perform very significant work for very significant clients in every significant area of business and governmental activity. While there are those among them who are primarily concerned with the fees that are generated (and the extent of related expenses), there is still a considerable number who derive their greatest reward from performing demanding tasks in a competent and professional manner. Whatever their motivation, they all live and die by their ability to apply their learning, skill and reason in efforts to resolve, or at least cope with, conflicting views and interests in an orderly manner. If a totalitarian or authoritarian regime ever were to seize power, these lawyers would be among the first citizens to be jailed for their unwavering support of and reliance upon due process. I happen to agree with Harrison Tweed, a highly regarded lawyer in his day, who made the following observation:

> I have a high opinion of lawyers. With all their faults they stack up very well against those in every other occupation or profession. They are better to work with or play with or drink with than most other varieties of mankind.

Format and Content of the Information Presented

....

A total of seventy-five law firms are described. For each of the leading fifty firms, which are listed in alphabetical order, there is an initial assessment and data sheet containing various financial and statistical data followed by a profile of the firm. Thereafter, again in alphabetical order, there are data sheets—with no assessments or profiles—for the remaining twenty-five firms. The leading fifty firms are grouped by composite assessments and directions (pages 25–27) and are listed from highest to lowest by selected criteria (Appendix A).

Unless otherwise indicated, the data have been supplied or confirmed by the firm described. The symbol "p" refers to partners; "a" to associates. The symbol "NA" means that the information is not available; it either has not been provided by the firm or has not been able to be ascertained from available published material or other sources.

Each assessment and data sheet for the leading fifty firms provides the following information:

1. The name, address and New York telephone number of the firm.
2. The assessment of the firm (in the manner noted in the Introduction).
3. The direction of the firm (as noted in the Introduction).
4. For 1986–1990 (as of February 1 of each year), the number of partners and associates (including senior attorneys and similarly designated attorneys) in the New York office; persons who are "of counsel" are included in the total number of lawyers but are not separately listed or counted.

5. For 1986–1990 (as of February 1 of each year), the number of paralegals and support personnel in the New York office.
6. For 1986–1990, the number of lateral associate hires.
7. The titular head of the firm (if one is so designated) and his or her title.
8. Representative clients of the firm.
9. Branches located in cities outside New York, the numbers of lawyers in each branch as of February 1, 1990 and the collective number of lawyers, partners and associates outside New York. In the profiles, the number of lawyers at a branch and the year it was opened are frequently included in parentheses after the city in which the branch is located.
10. Average billable hours for partners and associates in 1988 (unless otherwise indicated).
11. For 1986–1990, the number of women who were partners and associates.
12. The minimum number of years of service before an associate can be selected as a partner.
13. Utilizing the classes of 1978–1982, the number of lawyers who recently have made partner, including the number of lawyers in each class at the outset.
14. For 1986–1989, the gross revenue of the firm, subject to the comments made in the Acknowledgments.
15. For 1986–1989, the gross revenue per lawyer, subject to the comments in the Acknowledgments.
16. For 1986–1989, the profits per partner, subject to the comments in the Acknowledgments.
17. For 1986–1990, starting associates' salaries.
18. The percentage of time dedicated to *pro bono* activities in 1989.
19. For 1988 (unless otherwise indicated), the range of hourly rates for both partners and associates.
20. The principal law schools for all associates in the firm (1988).
21. For 1986–1990, the number of associates who are members of minority groups.
22. For 1986–1990, the number of summer associates hired.

Composite Assessments and Directions of the Firms

···

(see pages 20–21 for an explanation of the symbols)

···

↑ Cleary, Gottlieb, Steen & Hamilton
↑ Cravath, Swaine & Moore
↑ Davis Polk & Wardwell
↑ Skadden, Arps, Slate, Meagher & Flom
↑ Wachtell, Lipton, Rosen & Katz

···

↑ ? Cahill Gordon & Reindel
 ↑ Fried, Frank, Harris, Shriver & Jacobson
 ↑ Kaye, Scholer, Fierman, Hayes & Handler
↑ ? Milbank, Tweed, Hadley & McCloy
 ↑ Paul, Weiss, Rifkind, Wharton & Garrison
 ↑ Shearman & Sterling
 ↑ Simpson Thacher & Bartlett
 ↑ Sullivan & Cromwell
 ↑ Weil Gotshal & Manges

↑ Debevoise & Plimpton
↑ Dewey Ballantine
↑ Proskauer Rose Goetz & Mendelsohn
↑ ? White & Case
  ? Willkie Farr & Gallagher

↔Breed, Abbott & Morgan
↑ ? Brown & Wood
  ? Cadwalader, Wickersham & Taft
  ↑ Chadbourne & Parke
↔Curtis, Mallet-Provost, Colt & Mosle
  ? Hughes Hubbard & Reed
  ↑ Jackson, Lewis, Schnitzler & Krupman
  ? Kelley Drye & Warren
  ? Kramer, Levin, Nessen, Kamin & Frankel
↔LeBoeuf, Lamb, Leiby & MacRae
  ? Lord Day & Lord, Barrett Smith
↔Mudge Rose Guthrie Alexander & Ferdon
↓ ? Patterson, Belknap, Webb & Tyler
  ? Reid & Priest
  ? Rogers & Wells
  ? Rosenman & Colin
  ↑ Schulte Roth & Zabel
  ↓ Shea & Gould
  ↑ Stroock & Stroock & Lavan
  ? Thacher Proffitt & Wood
  ? Whitman & Ransom
  ↑ Wilson, Elser, Moskowitz, Edelman & Dicker
↑ ? Winthrop, Stimson, Putnam & Roberts

? Bower & Gardner

? Coudert Brothers

? Donovan Leisure Newton & Irvine

↓ Epstein Becker & Green, P.C.

↓ Hawkins, Delafield & Wood

↔Parker Chapin Flattau & Klimpl

? Phillips, Nizer, Benjamin, Krim & Ballon

↓ Webster & Sheffield

The Leading Fifty
New York Firms

BOWER & GARDNER

110 East 59th Street • New York, New York 10022 • (212) 751-2900

Rating:

Direction:?

*LAWYERS	PARTNERS	ASSOCIATES
1990: 200	82	110
1989: 199	78	121
1988: 184	63	121
1987: 160	49	102
1986: 144	49	91

	Paralegals	Support
1989:	54	NA
1988:	42	NA
1987:	NA	NA
1986:	13	NA

*LATERAL HIRES

1989: 18
1988: 14
1987: NA
1986: 26

*MANAGING PARTNERS: Daniel E. Siff, Mark B. Feinstein

*REPRESENTATIVE CLIENTS:

New York University Hospital, North Shore University Hospital

*BRANCHES: Albany, N.Y. (6)

*AVERAGE ANNUAL BILLING HOURS:

Partners: NA
Associates: NA

*NUMBER OF WOMEN

	Partners	Associates
1989:	NA	NA
1988:	NA	NA
1987:	NA	NA
1986:	NA	NA

*PARTNERSHIP TRACK: NA

*NUMBER OF LAWYERS FROM ENTERING CLASS TO MAKE PARTNER:

1981: NA
1980: NA
1979: NA
1978: NA

*GROSS REVENUE

1989: NA
1988: NA
1987: NA
1986: NA

*REVENUE PER LAWYER

1989: NA
1988: NA
1987: NA
1986: NA

*PROFITS PER PARTNER

1989: NA
1988: NA
1987: NA
1986: NA

*STARTING ASSOCIATE SALARY

1990: NA
1989: NA
1988: NA
1987: NA
1986: NA

*PRO BONO: NA

*HOURLY RATES

Partners: NA
Associates: NA

*PRINCIPAL LAW SCHOOLS
(Associates): NA

*NUMBER OF MINORITIES

	Partners	Associates
1989:	NA	NA
1988:	NA	NA
1987:	NA	NA
1986:	NA	NA

*SUMMER ASSOCIATES

1989: NA
1988: NA
1987: NA
1986: NA

Unlike most leading New York firms, Bower & Gardner demonstrates the virtues of focusing a practice predominantly on one area: the defense of medical malpractice claims. The firm represents such insurance companies as the American International Group and local hospitals, including New York University Hospital, North Shore University Hospital and the Catholic Medical Center of Brooklyn and Queens. Observers consider the firm, in the words of a prominent litigator, "very powerful and very good" in its specialties, an expertise that has powered Bower & Gardner's expansion from roughly one hundred lawyers in the early 1980s to about two hundred today. Still, some prejudice exists among sources against firms which eschew a general practice; Bower & Gardner is often accused of not being involved in "high law." "Bower & Gardner makes a lot of money doing insurance defense work, but everything's the same case," says a senior trial lawyer disdainfully.

They may soon feel like professional politicos. Effective January 1, 1990, the already politically well-connected Bower & Gardner merged with Albany's five-lawyer Condello, Ryan and Piscitelli, lobbyists *par excellence*. Irwin Landes and Stanley Fink, former state assemblymen (Fink also served as speaker of the assembly 1979–1986) who are current Bower & Gardner partners, illustrate the firm's longstanding Democratic political ties. From 1967 to 1978, partner Albert B. Lewis served as a state senator and then as superintendent of insurance.

Bower & Gardner failed to make *The American Lawyer* list of the top 100 firms nationally in gross revenue, revenue per lawyer or profits per partner from 1986 through 1989.

John Bower and Steven O'Connor founded the firm in 1955 under the name Bower & O'Connor. When Allen Taylor joined in 1959, the firm became Bower, O'Connor & Taylor. John Gardner came to the firm and was made a name partner in 1963. The firm adopted its present name in 1971. Since 1982, Bower has been a member of the State Commission on Judicial Conduct, appointed by Fink.

An Executive Committee and two managing partners, Daniel Siff and Mark Feinstein, govern the firm. The Executive Committee decides on partnership draws and, after a vote by the full partnership, makes final decisions on the admission of new partners. The Compensation of Associates Committee, none too surprisingly, sets associate salaries.

Litigation is the firm's primary practice area, with subdivisions of medical malpractice, product liability, insurance, reinsurance and environmental law. In 1988, through the acquisition of partners from a medium-size firm in New York, Bower & Gardner acquired a corporate capability. Observers agree that the quality of lawyers and work are inconsistent. "The people range the extremes," says a judge. The recent merger with Condello, Ryan will provide Kenneth Shapiro, a partner who left the state government at the end of 1988, a base from which to continue his lobbying efforts.

BREED, ABBOTT & MORGAN

153 East 53rd Street • New York, New York 10022 • (212) 888-0800

Rating: 💼💼💼💼

Direction: ↔

*LAWYERS

	PARTNERS	ASSOCIATES
1990: 109	41	74
1989: 103	39	63
1988: 130	47	79
1987: 123	47	76
1986: 114	45	69

	Paralegals	Support
1990:	20	160
1989:	17	144
1988:	17	NA
1987:	21	140
1986:	16	NA

*LATERAL HIRES
1989: 14
1988: 7
1987: NA
1986: 14

*CHAIRMAN: Richard R. Dailey

*REPRESENTATIVE CLIENTS:
Armco Steel, National Distillers, Quantum Chemical, Empire Blue Cross/Blue Shield, Burger King

*BRANCHES: Washington (9)
Total: 9 lawyers (4p and 5a)

*AVERAGE ANNUAL BILLING HOURS (1989):
Partners: NA
Associates: 1800

*NUMBER OF WOMEN

	Partners	Associates
1990:	2	27
1989:	2	30
1988:	1	30
1987:	1	22
1986:	1	23

*PARTNERSHIP TRACK: 8 years

*NUMBER OF LAWYERS FROM ENTERING CLASS TO MAKE PARTNER:
1981: NA of 8
1980: 4 of 10
1979: 2 of 10
1978: 3 of 13

*GROSS REVENUE
1989: NA
1988: NA
1987: NA
1986: NA

*REVENUE PER LAWYER
1989: NA
1988: NA
1987: NA
1986: NA

*PROFITS PER PARTNER
1989: NA
1988: NA
1987: NA
1986: NA

*STARTING ASSOCIATE SALARY
1990: $80,000
1989: $76,000
1988: $71,000
1987: $65,000
1986: $65,000

*PRO BONO: 4–7% of total time

*HOURLY RATES (1987)
Partners: $205–$300
Associates: $85–$195

*PRINCIPAL LAW SCHOOLS
(Associates): NA

*NUMBER OF MINORITIES

	Partners	Associates
1990:	2	2
1989:	2	2
1988:	2	3
1987:	2	3
1986:	1	2

*SUMMER ASSOCIATES
1990: 22
1989: 17
1988: 20
1987: 19
1986: 20

"The words 'white shoe,' " says a headhunter, "were invented for Breed Abbott." This venerable firm has, after a distinguished history, remained virtually static during a time when other New York law firms have exploded. Indeed, in the period between 1986 and 1989, Breed Abbott failed to make *The American Lawyer* list of top 100 firms nationally in gross revenue, revenue per lawyer or profits per partner. Observers disagree what the firm's prognosis will be. A corporate lawyer says dismissively that Breed Abbott is "declining." A legal consultant, however, calls it "a classic case of falling asleep, bringing in a couple of laterals, then going uphill."

William Breed and Henry Abbott, who had attended Amherst and New York Law School together, founded the firm in 1898. In 1903, George Morgan, an ex–New York County assistant district attorney, joined the firm and Breed Abbott adopted its current name. Breed Abbott's practice relied, initially, on its one large client, Murray Hill Bank. In the early 1900s, the firm expanded into the representation of trade associations such as the National Wholesale Grocers Association and the Cotton Textile Merchants. In the 1920s, California Perfume Company—which later would become Avon Products, Inc.—became a client. This relationship continued until the mid-1980s. Other early Breed Abbott clients which have stayed with the firm include J. Walter Thompson (1916), National Distillers (1924) and Armco (1933).

For four decades, former U.S. attorney and failed politician Charles Tuttle headed the firm. He ran for governor against FDR in 1930 and lost by a landslide. In 1952, he represented Armco Steel in an effort to prevent President Truman's seizure of the steel industry. The injunction Tuttle won was upheld by the Supreme Court.

The full partnership chooses a six-partner Executive Committee to govern Breed Abbott. The members of the Committee choose a chairman, currently Richard Dailey. Members' terms are of unspecified duration and the composition of the Committee is changed regularly. The Executive Committee makes recommendations on the admission of new partners based on the suggestions of individual departments. Then the whole partnership votes on a one-partner, one-vote principle.

The Executive Committee also proposes changes in partnership shares, on which the whole partnership votes. The chairman of the Legal Personnel Committee suggests alterations in associate compensation to the Executive Committee, which then makes a recommendation to the partnership.

Breed Abbott is divided into six departments: corporate/banking, litigation/anti-trust, tax, real estate, trusts and estates and labor. Edward Ross, best known for his successful representation of Mark Rothko's daughter in her claim against the executors of her father's estate and the Marlborough Gallery (and the subsequent dispute concerning the firm's fees) heads the litigation department. Observers universally praise Ross and also single out litigators George K.C. Lee and Stephen Lang, who one house counsel calls "superb."

The firm maintains a small branch office in Washington, D.C. (9, 1946). Breed Abbott had a London office from 1930 to 1956 and a branch in Manila from 1946 to 1954.

BROWN & WOOD
· ·
One World Trade Center · New York, New York 10048 · (212) 839-5300

Rating: 💼💼💼💼   *Direction:* ↑ ?

*LAWYERS	PARTNERS	ASSOCIATES
1990: 198	66	128
1989: 195	66	118
1988: 195	63	128
1987: 188	59	147
1986: 176	54	112

	Paralegals	Support
1990:	35	247
1989:	52	310
1988:	49	NA
1987:	37	257
1986:	31	NA

*LATERAL HIRES
1990: 15
1989: 15
1988: 2
1987: 15
1986: 20

*EXECUTIVE DIRECTOR: John Feldkamp

*REPRESENTATIVE CLIENTS:
Merrill Lynch, Warburg Paribas Becker, Bear Stearns & Co., Inc., Puerto Rico Electric Power Authority

*BRANCHES: Washington (7), San Francisco (28), Los Angeles (8), London (3)
Total: 46 lawyers (17p and 29a)

*AVERAGE ANNUAL BILLING HOURS (1989):
Partners: NA
Associates: 1900

*NUMBER OF WOMEN
	Partners	Associates
1990:	8	41
1989:	6	43
1988:	5	42
1987:	5	58
1986:	4	54

*PARTNERSHIP TRACK: 7–8 years

*NUMBER OF LAWYERS FROM ENTERING CLASS TO MAKE PARTNER:
1981: 5 of 22
1980: 4 of 13
1979: 6 of 10
1978: 5 of 7

*GROSS REVENUE
1990: $77,000,000
1988: $64,000,000
1987: $62,000,000
1986: $50,000,000

*REVENUE PER LAWYER
1989: $315,000
1988: $305,000
1987: $255,000
1986: $255,000

*PROFITS PER PARTNER
1989: $395,000
1988: $380,000
1987: $365,000
1986: $365,000

*STARTING ASSOCIATE SALARY
1990: $80,000
1989: $74,000
1988: $71,000
1987: $65,000
1986: $65,000

*PRO BONO: Supports the Council of New York Law Associates; percentage of total time varies

*HOURLY RATES (1987)
Partners: $220–$350
Associates: $115–$215

*PRINCIPAL LAW SCHOOLS
(Associates): Columbia (15), NYU (11), Fordham (10), University of Virginia (9)

*NUMBER OF MINORITIES
	Partners	Associates
1990:	2	11
1989:	1	12
1988:	1	12
1987:	1	8
1986:	1	7

*SUMMER ASSOCIATES
1990: 16
1989: 29
1988: 25
1987: 27
1986: 30

Until recently, Brown & Wood could have been labeled, as one senior litigator put it, "the legal department of Merrill Lynch." The firm still bears the stigma of supposedly not practicing "high law"; one legal consultant dismissively calls Brown & Wood "basically a bond firm" while a senior litigator views it as "an assembly line of paper." The firm has worked hard, however, to diversify its practice. For instance, in 1986, Brown & Wood acquired twelve-lawyer Tufo & Zuccotti, real estate specialists. In 1988 it lured lateral partner William Goldman from a mid-sized New York firm to start its bankruptcy practice. Observers disagree on where the firm stands now. Brown & Wood, says a legal consultant, has "pretty good leadership, good outside acquisitions, good growth" and a solid future. A senior corporate lawyer, however, calls the firm "yesterday's story—the bond firm that didn't make it."

One criticism consistently leveled at the firm is that it over-emphasizes money as opposed to quality. "They're mercenary," says a headhunter. To cut costs, the firm has shaved associates from its payroll in each year from 1987 to 1989. Brown & Wood had 147 associates in 1987. By 1988, that figure was down to 128; by 1989, to 118.

This policy may have been in response to the firm's flagging operations. In 1986, Brown & Wood had gross revenue of $50,000,000 and placed 71st on *The American Lawyer* list of the top 100 firms nationally in this category. In 1988, the firm had gross revenue of $64,000,000, but had fallen to 78th on the list. Even more dramatically, the firm's ranking fell from 22nd to 32nd in profits per partner (with totals of $365,000 and $380,000 for 1986 and 1988, respectively). The only exception to this trend was the firm's modest rise from 51st to 47th place in revenue per lawyer.

Brown & Wood was founded in 1914 by William Chadbourne (cousin of Chadbourne & Parke founder, Thomas Chadbourne), Richard Hunt and Albert Jaeckel. Chadbourne was involved in the theater, backing shows and representing show business clients. He also participated in Theodore Roosevelt's presidential campaign in 1912 and was the campaign manager to Fiorello LaGuardia in 1933. Hunt, the grandson of architect Richard Morris Hunt (designer of New York's Metropolitan Museum of Art), represented Electrolux, Curtiss-Wright and Phoebe Mallory and Co. and several important investment firms.

Jaeckel reeled in the Merrill Lynch business for the firm. This association began one fateful Saturday afternoon in the 1920s when Charles Merrill, a co-founder of the Merrill Lynch companies, could not reach his lawyer about a major deal that was pending. Instead, he called his old fraternity brother Jaeckel, who had the good sense to be home, and the rest is history. In addition to the Merrill Lynch companies, Jaeckel's clients included Western Oil Supply, the Checker Motor Co. and the Checker taxi empire.

In 1920 Howard Brown joined the firm and his name was added to the firm name. Since then, the firm's name has changed to Brown, Wood, Fuller, Caldwell & Ivey in 1955, then to Brown, Wood, Ivey, Mitchell & Petty in 1976 following the acquisition of the eight-partner New York bond firm of Mitchell Petty & Shetterly, and finally to Brown & Wood in 1986.

The firm's principal governing body is the Policy Committee. The Committee has a varying number of members who serve staggered three-year terms. At least one member each year is required to step down. The Policy Committee's chairman determines how many Committee members must step down and who will be nominated to replace them. The full partnership approves the nominations for both first-term and second-term members of the Committee. The Policy Committee recommends partnership shares, candidates for partnership and members to other firm committees. The entire partnership votes on a one-lawyer, one-vote basis on partner compensation; both seniority and productivity are taken into account. To be admitted to the partnership, a candidate must receive at least 75% of the full partnership's votes.

The firm is divided into seven departments: litigation, corporate/securities, public finance, real estate and governmental affairs, tax, banking and trusts and estates. Corporate and public finance are indisputably the central practice areas, and they are basically serviced by the litigation and tax departments. Although there are no real superstars at Brown & Wood, John Quisenberry (corporate), E. Michael Bradley (litigation), Henry Klaiman (tax) and Alexis Gelinas (tax) are key partners and well-regarded in their fields. Both Peter Tufo and John Zuccotti are viewed as experts in New York real estate, zoning and development. Zuccotti recently left the firm to become a key executive with Olympia & York, the Canadian-based real estate development firm. Charles Johnson, now of counsel, represents Donald Regan and was instrumental in advancing the interests of the Merrill Lynch companies over the years.

The firm's principal business is related to various securities offerings. In the private sector, beyond the Merrill Lynch companies, Brown & Wood represents such investment banking firms as Warburg Paribas Becker, Nomura Securities and Bear Stearns, which act for a wide variety of issuers. In the public sector, the firm represents various states and commonwealths and related public authorities, including the Puerto Rico Electric Power Authority; Puerto Rico Telephone Authority; all the public agencies and authorities of North Carolina; Broward County, Florida; Fairfax County, Virginia; and the Dormitory Authority of New York.

The firm has branch offices in San Francisco (28, 1971), Los Angeles (8, 1986), Washington, D.C. (7, 1981), and London (3, 1989).

Brown & Wood's associates have become more unhappy with the firm. In a 1986 *American Lawyer* poll, mid-level associates ranked Brown & Wood 8th of 41 firms; by 1988 the firm had dropped to 32nd of 37 firms; and in 1989 it was ranked 31st of 35 firms. Undoubtedly, the primary cause for this reversal has been the firm's dramatic cuts in the number of associates in the last three years. The dismissals have resulted in low morale and, despite the 1986 survey when a high percentage of associates planned to be at Brown & Wood long term, in 1988 and 1989 few saw a future at the firm.

CADWALADER, WICKERSHAM & TAFT

100 Maiden Lane • New York, New York 10038 • (212) 504-6000

Rating: 💼💼💼💼

Direction: ?

*LAWYERS	PARTNERS	ASSOCIATES
1990: 197	79	129
1989: 210	57	132
1988: 215	59	147
1987: 215	56	144
1986: 209	54	120

	Paralegals	Support
1990:	36	254
1989:	30	284
1988:	41	NA
1987:	39	304
1986:	33	NA

*LATERAL HIRES

1989: 8
1988: 5
1987: NA
1986: 22

*EXECUTIVE COMMITTEE: George D. Reycraft, Rodney Dayan, Courtland Trautman, Jerome Shelby

*REPRESENTATIVE CLIENTS:
Bowery Savings Bank, Apex Oil

*BRANCHES: Washington (59), Palm Beach (10), Los Angeles (13)
Total: 82 lawyers (27p and 55a)

*AVERAGE ANNUAL BILLING HOURS:
Partners: NA
Associates: NA

*NUMBER OF WOMEN

	Partners	Associates
1990:	5	55
1989:	3	57
1988:	3	66
1987:	2	53
1986:	1	42

*PARTNERSHIP TRACK: 7–9 years

*NUMBER OF LAWYERS FROM ENTERING CLASS TO MAKE PARTNER:

1981: 0 of 14
1980: 2 of 17
1979: 3 of 17
1978: 1 of 11

*GROSS REVENUE

1989: $96,000,000
1988: $97,000,000
1987: $93,000,000
1986: $69,000,000

*REVENUE PER LAWYER

1989: $355,000
1988: $340,000
1987: $345,000
1986: $290,000

*PROFITS PER PARTNER

1989: $410,000
1988: $495,000
1987: $505,000
1986: $355,000

*STARTING ASSOCIATE SALARY

1990: $83,000
1989: $82,000
1988: $76,000
1987: $65,000
1986: $65,000

*PRO BONO: 2–3% of total time

*HOURLY RATES
Partners: NA
Associates: NA

*PRINCIPAL LAW SCHOOLS (Associates): NYU (21), Fordham (12), Columbia (6), University of Pennsylvania (6)

*NUMBER OF MINORITIES

	Partners	Associates
1990:	1	7
1989:	1	6
1988:	1	6
1987:	1	7
1986:	1	6

*SUMMER ASSOCIATES

1990: 32
1989: 29
1988: 37
1987: 40
1986: 38

Cadwalader once was an old-line white shoe firm which, though it traces its roots back to the late eighteenth century, experienced its greatest growth between 1974 and 1984. During this period, largely due to the expansion of the litigation department and the Washington branch office, Cadwalader doubled in size and achieved a more representative ethnic balance. Recently, however, the firm's momentum has eased off to the point that it lost at least sixteen associates in 1989 because of a severe slowdown in litigation matters. In 1990 there was a further erosion in the number of associates.

The firm's finances reflect these vicissitudes. Gross revenue shot up from $69 million in 1986 to $93 million in 1987, then crept to $97 million in 1988. The statistics for revenue per lawyer and profits per partner show an even greater fall-off for 1988. The former dropped from a high of $345,000 in 1987 to $340,000 in 1988; the latter dipped from $505,000 to $495,000 in the same period. Cadwalader also slipped in *The American Lawyer* rankings—and thus, lost ground relative to other leading national firms—in both gross revenue and revenue per lawyer between 1986 and 1988, although the firm achieved a modestly higher standing in profits per partner. In 1990 there was a slight decrease in revenue and a continuing decline in profits per partner from $495,000 to $410,000.

Cadwalader's financial success in the mid-1980s was at least partially a result of a series of savvy real estate moves. In the early 1980s, Cadwalader bought two buildings at 100 Maiden Lane for $20 million and renovated them for an additional $27 million. Once the firm consolidated its neighborhood offices in 1985, it very profitably leased the balance of the space. This fiscal rejuvenation has undeniably tailed off, however, and observers agree that this is a bad sign for a firm that has placed ever-increasing importance on financial success. Says one leading litigator, today's Cadwalader "places revenues above all else."

Though Cadwalader was founded in 1792, the firm's modern history begins in 1914 when, after having had nine predecessor firms, the firm adopted its present name. John Cadwalader had become a partner at the firm in 1878, while George W. Wickersham and Henry W. Taft joined the firm in 1914. Wickersham was President Taft's attorney general; Henry Taft was the president's brother. Wickersham also chaired President Hoover's commission to investigate the breakdown in law enforcement and in so doing wrote the "Wickersham Report," which recommended continuing Prohibition. The current head of the firm, George Reycraft, is a former head of the Justice Department's anti-trust division.

Two committees—a four-member Management Committee and a six-member Associates Committee—govern Cadwalader. The Management Committee, elected yearly by the full partnership on a one-partner, one-vote principle, handles overall firm management and partner compensation. The partnership may, by a majority vote, reverse the decisions of the Management Committee concerning partner compensation. The Associates Committee makes all decisions which concern associates except for the admission of new partners, who are voted in by the entire partnership on recommendations from individual practice areas. Cadwalader's management system was created in 1982 and represented a paring down of the previous model.

Cadwalader has four practice areas: corporate/real estate, litigation, tax and trusts and estates. Observers differ in assessing the firm's strengths and weakness. While one legal consultant views both the corporate and litigation departments as "strong" and the tax department as "very strong," another says that Cadwalader has "mediocre everything." The litigation department has represented Long Island Lighting Company, the Bowery Savings Bank and Apex Oil Company, among others, in important litigation. Besides Reycraft, observers praise litigators Earl Nemser, Edwin David Robertson, and Pamela Rogers Chepiga. Recently, the lagging litigation department got a lift when it was retained by several clients embroiled in insider trading disputes. Standouts in corporate include Thomas Russo, whose practice straddles the line between commodities and securities, John Fritts, Jerome Shelby and Rodney Dayan. On the down side, the corporate department lost burgeoning superstar Trayton Davis, a mortgaged-backed securities specialist, in May 1989. Alan Granwell heads the tax department, which, observers say, is top-notch.

The firm maintains a large, powerful office in Washington (59, 1971), and smaller offices in Palm Beach (10, 1980) and Los Angeles (13, 1989). The Washington, D.C., branch opened when Cadwalader acquired its Washington affiliate, Kane Shulman & Schlei. Prominent attorneys such as H. Clayton Cook, Jr., Stephen Shulman—a specialist in equal employment law who represents clients such as McDonald's Corporation, AT&T and Timex Corporation in this type of work—and litigator Ronald Eastman, who has represented the Democratic National Committee and Northwest Airlines have given the Washington office a solid and independent base of clients. The Palm Beach office deals primarily with international tax, real estate and trust and estate matters.

Associates have reacted negatively to Cadwalader's recent changes, particularly about the firm's increasing bottom-line orientation. In 1986 and 1988 *American Lawyer* surveys, associates complained that Cadwalader's allegedly manic emphasis on billable hours—associates claim the firm expects a minimum of 2,000 billed hours yearly from them, while the firm says it asks for 1,900—has undermined both their quality of life and their quality of work. There is "a fair amount of grumbling," confirms a legal consultant. "Cadwalader does not coddle their associates." In the 1989 survey Cadwalader rose to 18th position from 33rd. The interesting work perceived to be done by associates together with their sense of responsibility and control over their work offset their apparent low involvement in pre-trial depositions and similar assignments.

CAHILL GORDON & REINDEL

80 Pine Street • New York, New York 10005 • (212) 701-3000

Rating: 💼💼💼💼💼   *Direction:* ↑ ?

*LAWYERS

	PARTNERS	ASSOCIATES
1990: 273	61	207
1989: 268	61	202
1988: 252	59	188
1987: 247	NA	NA
1986: 235	NA	NA

	Paralegals	Support
1990:	68	464
1989:	72	465
1988:	76	NA
1987:	70	NA
1986:	53	NA

*LATERAL HIRES

1989: 14
1988: 17
1987: NA
1986: 10

MANAGING PARTNERS: Roger Meltzer, Howard J. Sloan

REPRESENTATIVE CLIENTS:

The New York Times, E.F. Hutton, Drexel Burnham Lambert, Inc. (before its bankruptcy), Dillon Reed, Bankers Trust, Prudential Bache, A&P

BRANCHES: Washington (12), Paris (5)
Total: 17 lawyers (3p and 14a)

AVERAGE ANNUAL BILLING HOURS:
Partners: NA
Associates: NA

*NUMBER OF WOMEN

	Partners	Associates
1990:	2	72
1989:	2	69
1988:	2	64
1987:	NA	NA
1986:	NA	NA

PARTNERSHIP TRACK: 8 years

NUMBER OF LAWYERS FROM ENTERING CLASS TO MAKE PARTNER:

1981: NA
1980: 3 of 23
1979: 2 of 15
1978: 1 of 16

GROSS REVENUE

1989: $146,500,000
1988: $139,500,000
1987: $110,000,000
1986: $88,000,000

REVENUE PER LAWYER

1989: $575,000
1988: $545,000
1987: $460,000
1986: $410,000

PROFITS PER PARTNER

1989: $1,515,000
1988: $1,420,000
1987: $1,200,000
1986: $940,000

STARTING ASSOCIATE SALARY

1990: $83,000
1989: $81,000
1988: $77,000
1987: $67,000
1986: $65,000

PRO BONO: NA

HOURLY RATES
Partners: NA
Associates: NA

PRINCIPAL LAW SCHOOLS (Associates): NA

*NUMBER OF MINORITIES

	Partners	Associates
1990:	0	5
1989:	0	2
1988:	0	3
1987:	NA	NA
1986:	NA	NA

SUMMER ASSOCIATES

1990: 59
1989: 52
1988: 42
1987: NA
1986: NA

Cahill Gordon once had a reputation for being an aggressive Irish litigation firm. Today, the firm's practice and its ethnic composition have become more balanced. As a former house counsel viewed the current firm, "Cahill is red hot. It has risen in the ranks in the last five years. They're outrageously successful but nice."

Indeed, Cahill has become one of the country's most lucrative firms. While according to *The American Lawyer* its gross revenues ranked 22nd in 1988 ($139,500,000), the firm had a revenue per lawyer of $545,000—fifth highest in the country—and profits per partner of $1,420,000, second only to Cravath's $1,595,000.

Notwithstanding, the demise in 1989 of Drexel Burnham, one of Cahill's key clients, has had a substantially adverse impact on the firm's revenue and cash flow and raised questions about the firm's continued success.

William Gibbs McAdoo, Woodrow Wilson's secretary of the treasury and the first chairman of the Federal Reserve System, founded the firm in 1919. Since then, however, it has changed its personnel, personality and name a number of times. Joseph Cotton, whose firm merged into Cahill at its inception, was initially the dominant partner in the firm. John T. Cahill, the U.S. attorney for the Southern District of New York—in 1939 he prosecuted and convicted Court of Appeals judge Martin T. Manton for corruption in office—put together the present firm after World War II. In 1972, the firm added Thurlow Gordon and Harold Reindel, two of its original lawyers who remained for over fifty years, to its name. Gordon died in 1975 at the age of 91 and Reindel in 1979 at the age of 84.

In its early years the firm's main areas of practice were corporate, financial and international law. In 1928 it opened a Paris office and, in 1935, a Washington, D.C., office, where it still maintains a relatively small staff. When Cahill became the dominant partner, the firm changed its emphasis from corporate work to litigation. Cahill's success in 1971 in the *New York Times*–Pentagon Papers case before the Supreme Court (roughly a month after the *Times*'s prior counsel, Lord, Day &

Lord, advised against publication and was replaced) helped to thrust the firm—and partner Floyd Abrams—into the top ranks of First Amendment and media law.

A four-member Executive Committee made up of William Haggerty, Immanuel Kohn, Denis McInerney and Irwin Schneiderman—a group that surely reflects the firm's broadened ethnic and religious base—manages Cahill Gordon. The committee determines partnership shares based on a poll of all the partners. The full partnership votes on a one-lawyer, one-vote principle to approve new partners. The Salary Committee makes recommendations for associate compensation which are then voted on by the partnership.

Cahill is divided into six departments: corporate, securities, litigation, tax, anti-trust and real estate. Litigation is the largest practice area, and its star attraction is indisputably Abrams. Observers also single out litigators Dean Ringel, David Hyde and Denis McInerney. Although most emphasize the litigation department's strength and effectiveness, one leading litigator found the firm too rigid. Cahill's methods seemed to him "linear, almost militaristic."

Cahill's incredible financial success is attributed not to the litigation department but to the firm's dramatically expanding corporate and securities practice. Since Irwin Schneiderman brought Drexel Burnham Lambert, Incorporated and E.F. Hutton into the fold, Cahill has been an M & A powerhouse. And despite the demise of Drexel and nagging questions from critics, the firm remains a key corporate player. Observers laud Immanuel Kohn, Joseph Conway and Gerald Tanenbaum for their work in this area.

The somewhat frenetic nature of Cahill's practice makes associate life there a mixed bag. In *American Lawyer* surveys from 1986–1988 associates criticized the firm's partners for being too busy to bother with training and reported that they were overworked and that matters were understaffed. Moreover, the 1988 associates surveyed found that the odds on making partner were positively grim. On the up side, associates at Cahill receive a high degree of responsibility and the firm remains strongly committed to *pro bono* work. Still, the loss of Drexel and its consequences (loss of business, decrease in perceived opportunities for advancement, sagging morale) have dropped the firm from 11th position (out of 37) in 1988 to 29th (out of 35) in 1989.

CHADBOURNE & PARKE

30 Rockefeller Plaza • New York, New York 10112 • (212) 408-5100

Rating: 💼💼💼💼

Direction: ↑

*LAWYERS

	PARTNERS	ASSOCIATES
1990: 215	60	143
1989: 213	58	142
1988: 183	45	127
1987: 154	40	105
1986: 121	35	80

	Paralegals	Support
1990:	40	341
1989:	50	307
1988:	46	NA
1987:	37	258
1986:	25	NA

*LATERAL HIRES

1989: 3
1988: 13
1987: NA
1986: 17

*CHAIRMAN: None

*REPRESENTATIVE CLIENTS:

American Brands, TWA, American Hoechst, Belgian Airlines, Renault, American Paper Institute, Unysis

*BRANCHES: Washington (31), Dubai (4), Abu Dhabi (2), Sharjah (3), Los Angeles (18)
Total: 57 lawyers (15p and 42a)

*AVERAGE ANNUAL BILLING HOURS:

Partners: NA
Associates: 1944

*NUMBER OF WOMEN

	Partners	Associates
1990:	7	64
1989:	7	56
1988:	4	38
1987:	5	36
1986:	4	27

*PARTNERSHIP TRACK: 7–8 years

*NUMBER OF LAWYERS FROM ENTERING CLASS TO MAKE PARTNER:

1981: 2 of 12
1980: 4 of 12
1979: 1 of 17
1978: 4 of 11
1977: 1 of 17

*GROSS REVENUE

1989: $95,000,000
1988: $75,000,000
1987: $55,000,000
1986: $39,000,000

*REVENUE PER LAWYER

1989: $405,000
1988: $350,000
1987: $320,000
1986: $255,000

*PROFITS PER PARTNER

1989: $505,000
1988: $460,000
1987: $405,000
1986: $365,000

*STARTING ASSOCIATE SALARY

1990: $83,000
1989: $80,000
1988: $76,000
1987: $65,000
1986: $65,000

*PRO BONO: 2–5% of total time

*HOURLY RATES

Partners: NA
Associates: NA

*PRINCIPAL LAW SCHOOLS
(Associates): NYU (15), Fordham (13), Columbia (8), St. John's (5)

*NUMBER OF MINORITIES

	Partners	Associates
1990:	0	13
1989:	0	7
1988:	0	4
1987:	0	2
1986:	0	3

*SUMMER ASSOCIATES

1990: 28
1989: 21
1988: 28
1987: 29
1986: 17

Chadbourne & Parke, a firm built on American Brands, Inc. and aviation clients, was in disarray by the mid-1980s. Since then, however, the firm has become aggressive, expanding its practice through lateral acquisitions and diversification. "It died, then came back," explains a senior corporate lawyer. "It got the good part of Barrett Smith . . . and hired competent people out of law school."

Chadbourne's financial picture between 1986 and 1988 largely reflects this change in course. In 1986, the firm was still floundering with gross revenue of $39,000,000, which ranked the firm 96th among *The American Lawyer* list of top 100 firms nationally. By 1988, the firm had gross revenue of $75,000,000 and had moved up to 57th on the list. Similarly, revenue per lawyer grew from $255,000 (51st place) in 1986 to $350,000 (30th place) in 1988. Only in profits per partner did the firm experience absolute but not relative growth; profits per partner increased from $365,000 to $460,000, but the firm's rank dipped from 22nd to 24th. Results for 1989 demonstrated its continued growth: revenues increased $20,000,000 (27%) to $95,000,000; revenue per lawyer increased $65,000 (19%) to $405,000; and profits per partner increased $55,000 (12%) to $505,000.

Thomas Chadbourne founded the firm in 1902 when he relocated his Chicago practice to New York. The firm underwent six name changes before settling on Chadbourne & Parke in 1984. The low point in the firm's early history came in the mid-1930s, when then-name partner Louis Levy was disbarred. Levy acted as a middleman in obtaining a $250,000 loan from American Tobacco's advertising agency for federal judge Martin Minton when American Tobacco was a defendant in a $6 million stockholders suit pending before the judge. More positively, that decade was marked by Chadbourne's high-powered aviation law practice. The firm represented Eastern Airlines, TWA and North American Aviation (which after a merger became Rockwell International).

One of the most intriguing stories within the story of the firm is that of former Chadbourne associate John Samuels, III. In 1971, while on assignment in London, Samuels organized a company called International Carbon and Minerals. This company fortuitously acquired a West Virginia coal mine and, because of the dramatic rise in the price of coal due to the OPEC-induced oil crisis, Samuels became a multi-millionaire. He then left the firm, and until his bubble burst in the late 1970s, played a central role on the New York cultural scene as chairman of the City Center, the Vivian Beaumont Theater, the New York City Opera and the New York City Ballet.

An eight-member Executive Committee, which appoints members to the firm's other committees, sets the standard billing rates for individual lawyers and makes recommendations to the full partnership on partner compensation, governs Chadbourne. The Executive Committee's members also suggest their own successors. All major policy decisions, including partnership shares and the admission of new partners, require approval by 80% of the firm's partners.

The firm is divided into eight practice areas: corporate, litigation, tax, real estate, energy, trusts and estates, employment and reinsurance. There are also over twenty lawyers unassigned to a specific department who essentially float. Observers direct most of their praise at the tax department. "They are phenomenal tax lawyers," generalizes a headhunter. A tax lawyer at another leading New York firm calls tax department head Donald Shapiro simply "super." In litigation, the key partners are Donald Strauber, a lateral hire from Cravath, and Whitney Gerard, a 1984 lateral hire from Alexander & Green. In 1986, Gerard's client American Hoechst purchased the Celanese Corporation for $2.72 billion and thereby became the world's largest chemical company. Gerard also represents Belgian Airlines and Renault SA. Energy department leader Rigdon Boykin also receives plaudits.

The firm's most important institutional clients are American Brands, Inc., a client since the 1920s, and TWA (although the work has diminished since Carl Icahn assumed control). Chadbourne also represents American Paper Institute, Unysis and International Paper Company.

The firm maintains two larger branch offices in Washington, D.C. (31, 1941) and Los Angeles (17, 1984) and three small offices in the United Arab Emirates (Dubai, Abu Dhabi and Sharjah, 9, 1979). Edmund Muskie, the former senator from

Maine (1959–1980) and secretary of state (1980–1981) who ran for the presidency in 1972, is in charge of the Washington office.

Associates had become increasingly unhappy with Chadbourne. In a 1988 *American Lawyer* survey, they ranked the firm only 25th of 37 firms in New York; by contrast, in 1986 the firm placed 12th among 41 firms. The most significant reasons for the drop are rockier partner-associate relations and inadequate facilities. Nevertheless, in 1989 the firm rose to 14th position, based in large measure on the overall impression that "a younger, more open-minded group is grasping the reins of the partnership and it is . . . more sensitive to trends in the business of law and a little more sensitive to associates' concerns."

CLEARY, GOTTLIEB, STEEN & HAMILTON
One Liberty Plaza · New York, New York 10006 · (212) 225-2000

Rating: 💼💼💼💼💼

Direction: ↑

*LAWYERS

	PARTNERS	ASSOCIATES
1990: 243	64	170
1989: 219	59	153
1988: 207	58	143
1987: 197	54	137
1986: 194	49	118

	Paralegals	Support
1990:	65	497
1989:	44	465
1988:	62	NA
1987:	41	400
1986:	48	NA

*LATERAL HIRES
1989: 7
1988: 4
1987: 0
1986: 4

*MANAGING PARTNER: Ned B. Stiles

*REPRESENTATIVE CLIENTS:
Salomon Brothers, Fleet/Norstar,
Northern Telecom, Michelin

*BRANCHES: Washington (57), Paris (36),
Brussels (29), London (10), Hong Kong (4),
Tokyo (4)
Total: 140 lawyers (NAp, NAa)

*AVERAGE ANNUAL BILLING HOURS:
Partners: NA
Associates: 2000

*NUMBER OF WOMEN

	Partners	Associates
1990:	5	58
1989:	4	49
1988:	4	46
1987:	3	48
1986:	3	39

*PARTNERSHIP TRACK: 8 years

*NUMBER OF LAWYERS FROM ENTERING CLASS TO MAKE PARTNER:
1981: NA of 26
1980: 3 of 18
1979: 3 of 15
1978: 8 of 23

*GROSS REVENUE
1989: $181,000,000
1988: $155,000,000
1987: $130,000,000
1986: $100,500,000

*REVENUE PER LAWYER
1989: $530,000
1988: $490,000
1987: $445,000
1986: $400,000

*PROFITS PER PARTNER
1989: $775,000
1988: $650,000
1987: $580,000
1986: $470,000

*STARTING ASSOCIATE SALARY
1990: $83,000
1989: $77,000
1988: $76,000
1987: $66,000
1986: $66,000

*PRO BONO: 3% of total time

*HOURLY RATES
Partners: NA
Associates: NA

*PRINCIPAL LAW SCHOOLS
(Associates): Columbia (26),
Harvard (24), NYU (20), Yale
(8)

*NUMBER OF MINORITIES

	Partners	Associates
1990:	2	11
1989:	1	7
1988:	1	6
1987:	1	9
1986:	0	7

*SUMMER ASSOCIATES
1990: 43
1989: 39
1988: 37
1987: 40
1986: 35

Cleary Gottlieb is a rarity among New York's more successful law firms in that it is not a conglomeration of superstars. Instead, the firm has an excellence born of consistency and a purity of intellect through and through. "A very faceless firm," notes a senior litigator. "When I think of the words 'institutional law firm' Cleary best meets what I think of by that." Observers use unusual terms to describe Cleary's lawyers; "esoteric . . . pristine," muses a prominent litigator. Strangely enough, those same "pristine" lawyers have produced a powerful, transaction-driven corporate law firm that has ridden the M & A boom and created a boom of its own.

Financially, Cleary has had nothing but success in recent years. As a headhunter bluntly puts it, "They make a ton of money." Between 1986 and 1988, the firm's gross revenue grew from $100,500,000 to $155,000,000, thus moving Cleary up in *The American Lawyer* rankings of law firms from 20th to 17th. The firm's revenue per lawyer and profits per partner increased in absolute terms, but relative to other leading firms, remained virtually constant. Revenue per lawyer went from $400,000 to $490,000 but Cleary stayed put in eighth place; profits per partner jumped from $470,000 to $650,000, but the firm moved only one position, from 14th to 13th. In 1989 the firm continued its impressive growth: gross revenue rose to $181,000,000 (a 17% increase); revenue per lawyer, to $530,000 (9%); and profits per partner to $775,000 (19%).

Seven partners founded Cleary Gottlieb in 1946, simultaneously in New York and Washington. Four—George Cleary, Leo Gottlieb, Henry Friendly and Melvin Steen—were defectors from Root Clark (which would become Dewey Ballantine); two others, including Fowler Hamilton, who had been chief legal consultant to the U.S. Department of Justice (1944–1945), came from government service. All of the firm's founders were highly regarded in their specialties, particularly Cleary in tax and Gottlieb in corporate, which led some of Root Clark's biggest clients to follow him. Friendly, who had impressive intellectual credentials and was to become chief judge of the Court of Appeals of the Second Circuit, was general counsel to Pan American Airlines, which he brought to the new firm.

An eleven-member Executive Committee manages the firm. However, many critical firm decisions, such as partner elections and the setting of associate compensation rates, are made by a vote of the full partnership (one-lawyer, one-vote). The Executive Committee assigns partners to offices abroad for two- to five-year periods and determines partner compensation, but purely on the basis of seniority. Compensation of each partner and his billings are distributed to all partners. The partnership elects a managing partner—currently Ned Stiles—for a three-year term.

Cleary is not divided into any official departments or practice areas. Nevertheless, observers consistently laud the firm for being well-run and having an effective structure. The lack of segmentation has led to a top-to-bottom strength in ability and work product that is the firm's outstanding feature. "There are no stars there," notes a senior litigator. "They're all just very competent." Cleary "never does anything but good work," agrees a former house counsel. The firm does have specialties in M & A, litigation, securities, insolvency and debt structuring, taxation, banking, employee benefits, real estate, government regulation of business and other specialties involving individuals and charitable organizations. The only weak link in this list seems to be litigation. One prominent litigator says the firm has "no litigation capacity"; another litigator says Cleary "has not gotten behind their litigation." Although a corporate lawyer says Cleary's lawyers are "individually outstanding," he and most other sources do not proffer any names; the exceptions are litigators George Weiss and John Kerr ("eccentric but great") and Alan Applebaum and Jerome Hyman in corporate.

The firm maintains a large Washington branch office (57, 1946), and five smaller offices abroad: Paris (36, 1949), Brussels (29, 1960), London (10, 1971), Hong Kong (4, 1980) and Tokyo (4, 1987).

Cleary Gottlieb has recently expanded its commitment to *pro bono* work by establishing a full-time position with the Council of New York Law Associates. Three associates per year work for four months at a time at the council's Community Development Legal Assistance Center to help non-profit groups generate low-income housing. This program allows non-litigators to get involved with *pro bono* much in the way the firm's litigators have for over twenty years through the Community Action For Legal Services, representing indigents in Housing Court.

Associates gave the firm mixed reviews in 1986 and 1988 *American Lawyer* surveys. Cleary's strengths were also its weaknesses; associates appreciated the firm's flexible structure in that it gave them a maximum amount of choice, but also complained that this very flexibility translated to a lack of needed guidance. "You must have a strong sense of yourself to be happy here," wrote one associate. "If you don't, you can be overcome with work and feel directionless." On the positive side, associates agree that the firm has good internal relations and a pleasant ambience. The hours are long, but Cleary balances the scales with plenty of perks, including single offices, personal computers and free health club memberships. Observers consistently see the same type of associate excel at Cleary. In 1989 associates were even more impressed with the firm, placing it second among all New York firms. Cleary receives very high grades for client contact, compensation, office space, and its commitment to *pro bono* work. Associates were pleased with their treatment by partners. Said one associate, "We aren't bothered by petty rules, by petty conflicts between each other or between partners, or by unreasonable demands to bill ever more hours. The only 'rules' are that our work must be essentially flawless and that we must behave in a kind and civilized manner to every single employee of the firm." Said another associate, "Associates do generally feel that they are colleagues of the partners and, for the most part, are treated as such. This factor is by far . . . the one that contributes the most positively to my enjoying practicing law here." A legal consultant says that the firm reminds him of the CIA: "They get the smartest people who didn't want to be lawyers." Cleary's lawyers are "brilliant, eclectic, really smart," a headhunter adds. "The firm gets the top people. It's hard to get associates to leave. The partners are humanists . . . the firm has a loose structure, diverse opportunities."

THIS IS
CULTURE !

COUDERT BROTHERS

200 Park Avenue • New York, New York 10166 • (212) 880-4400

Rating:

Direction: **?**

*LAWYERS	PARTNERS	ASSOCIATES
1990: 160	61	94
1989: 146	58	81
1988: 150	NA	NA
1987: 122	53	64
1986: 106	NA	NA

	Paralegals	Support
1990:	33	260
1989:	61	221
1988:	45	NA
1987:	50	181
1986:	30	NA

*LATERAL HIRES

1989: 28
1988: 36
1987: NA
1986: 32

*CHAIRMAN: James B. Sitrick

*REPRESENTATIVE CLIENTS:

In the U.S.: Lanvin Parfums S.A., Fiat, Nippon Electric; Overseas: Bendix Corporation, Ford, Atlantic Richfield

*BRANCHES: a total of 184 lawyers in Washington, San Francisco, Los Angeles, San Jose, Paris, London, Tokyo, Brussels, Hong Kong, Beijing, Shanghai, Sydney, Singapore, Rio De Janeiro, Sao Paulo and Moscow

*AVERAGE ANNUAL BILLING HOURS:

Partners and associates combined average 1800+

*NUMBER OF WOMEN

	Partners	Associates
1990:	10	71
1989:	10	60
1988:	8	51
1987:	8	46
1986:	4	42

*PARTNERSHIP TRACK: 8 years

*NUMBER OF LAWYERS FROM ENTERING CLASS TO MAKE PARTNER:

1981: 4 of 16
1980: 11 of 17
1979: 2 of 13
1978: 7 of 12

*GROSS REVENUE

1989: $120,000,000
1988: $90,000,000
1987: $84,000,000
1986: $52,000,000

*REVENUE PER LAWYER

1989: $360,000
1988: $300,000
1987: $280,000
1986: $200,000

*PROFITS PER PARTNER

1989: $405,000
1988: $340,000
1987: $295,000
1986: $155,000

*STARTING ASSOCIATE SALARY

1990: $83,000
1989: $77,000
1988: $72,000
1987: $66,000
1986: $63,000

*PRO BONO: 1–3% of total time

*HOURLY RATES

Partners: $200–$325
Associates: $95–$225

*PRINCIPAL LAW SCHOOLS (Associates): Columbia (10), NYU (9), Harvard (8), Fordham (4), University of Virginia (4), University of Pennsylvania (4)

*NUMBER OF MINORITIES

	Partners	Associates
1990:	3	13
1989:	3	13
1988:	1	17
1987:	2	13
1986:	1	17

*SUMMER ASSOCIATES

1990: 36
1989: 47
1988: 38
1987: 20
1986: 21

Coudert Brothers once defined the term international law firm. Now however, the firm is, in the words of a legal consultant, "supported by its history and name." Other firms have overtaken Coudert internationally; "Coudert has not protected its turf," says a headhunter. High turnover of both partners and associates—as well as somewhat indiscriminate lateral hiring—has weakened the firm's departments and diminished the quality of its work product. Summarizes one legal consultant, Coudert "has made bad lateral moves, is arrogant and pompous and turnover is high."

Coudert's financial figures for 1986–1989 reflect a management philosophy, says a senior litigator, that "places money over work product." In this time period, gross revenue grew from $52,000,000 to $120,000,000, revenue per lawyer from a modest $200,000 to $360,000 and profits per partner from an extraordinarily low $155,000 to a respectable $405,000. In each category, there was a corresponding leap up *The American Lawyer* rankings, most remarkably from a 99th place finish in profits per partner in 1986 to 34th place in 1989.

Frederic Rene Coudert and his two brothers founded Coudert Brothers in New York in 1854 after emigrating to the United States. Leadership of the firm passed from Coudert to Coudert until 1980. Frederic Coudert, Jr. headed the firm until his death in 1972. Alexis Coudert, Frederic's brother, then took over and saw the firm through its greatest growth. Under Alexis' leadership, Coudert opened offices in Tokyo, Hong Kong and Singapore and was the first U.S. firm with an ongoing practice (though not an office) in Beijing. Alexis died in 1980. Aside from running the family business, both Frederic, Jr. and Alexis Coudert pursued other interests. The former served as an ultra-conservative congressman from New York's silk-stocking district in the 1950s. The latter was a chevalier of the French Legion of Honor and served stints as acting director of Columbia University's School of Foreign and Comparative Law and as a professor at Columbia Law School.

Divisiveness has plagued the firm since non-Couderts assumed its leadership. Allen Russell, Alexis Coudert's successor, almost immediately faced a challenge from within. Charles Stevens, the partner in charge of the Far Eastern offices, threatened to take up to thirty-five lawyers to another firm. Although, with the intervention of outside legal help, the matter was resolved, this episode presaged the management problems Coudert Brothers has faced in recent years.

Today, the Coudert firm is governed by two committees: a five-member Executive Committee chaired by James Sitrick and elected by the firm's New York partners for up to two two-year terms and the Inter-office Policy Committee (known as Interpol), which has a varying number of members selected by branch offices. The Executive Committee handles overall firm management, while Interpol recommends partnership shares, nominates candidates for the Executive Committee and supervises the election of new partners. The firm also has an Associates Committee and a Hiring Committee. Until 1972, when it merged with the New York partnership, the firm's Paris office acted under different partners and had a separate system for electing partners.

This management structure receives virtually universal criticism from observers. "The internal workings of the firm interfere with the final product," says a legal consultant, who labels Coudert "five years behind the times." Sources strongly criticize Sitrick, in particular, for his personality and pompous manner.

The New York office is divided into five departments: corporate, litigation, tax, banking and real estate. Generally, observers find Coudert lawyers "clever but not careful." Notes a legal consultant, "The work is not top-notch." Still, the firm can attract quality clients, top prospects and name laterals. In 1986 alone, Coudert took in thirty-two laterals, a total bolstered by the acquisition of anti-trust lawyer Gordon Litvack as well as his entire department from Lord Day & Lord. Coudert represents such foreign interests in the U.S. as Lanvin Parfums S.A., Fiat S.p.a. and the Japanese Nippon Electric Company Ltd. Overseas, Coudert represents the interests of such U.S. companies as Bendix Corporation, Ford Motor Company and Atlantic Richfield. Except for Tom Werther, a bankruptcy lawyer who came from Weil Gotshal, observers decline to single out any Coudert lawyers for special praise.

Coudert currently maintains offices in seventeen cities: three large offices in New York (1854), Paris (1880) and Hong Kong (1972); smaller offices in Washington (1943), San Francisco (1975), London (1960), Brussels (1965), Los Angeles (1986), San Jose (1986), Shanghai (1986), Beijing (1979), Sydney (1984) and Singapore (1972); and associated offices in Riyadh (1980), Tokyo (1987) and Rio De Janiero (1976).

Charles Torem headed the Paris office for more than thirty-five years. Sol Linowitz, the former chairman of the board of Xerox who served both presidents Johnson and Carter in various diplomatic capacities, leads the Washington office.

The New York office, with about 60% of the total lawyers in the firm, remains the center of Coudert's operations. All the firm's international offices are staffed mostly with U.S. lawyers who enter the firm's ranks in New York. Associates, except for those of the Paris office, ordinarily spend their first two years in New York, then are encouraged to spend two years in one of Coudert's offices outside the United States.

Associates love Coudert. In 1986 and 1984 *American Lawyer* surveys, they ranked the firm among the top three in New York. Coudert's laid-back atmosphere and smooth internal relations consistently draw praise. Associates do interesting work, get plenty of responsibility and receive top-notch training, but are not overworked. Nonetheless, the firm dropped to 11th place (out of 35) in 1989, with critical comments about compensation and commitment to *pro bono* work contributing to the decline. Observers comment that Coudert attracts an extremely diverse group of lawyers; one headhunter calls the firm's associates "eclectic," while another says the firm "gets a lot of flakes." Nevertheless, Coudert's associates appear to be a cohesive, happy bunch.

CRAVATH, SWAINE & MOORE

825 Eighth Avenue • New York, New York 10019 • (212) 474-1000

Rating: 💼💼💼💼💼 *Direction:* ↑

*LAWYERS	PARTNERS	ASSOCIATES
1990: 305	63	242
1989: 302	63	230
1988: 281	62	212
1987: 270	57	204
1986: 263	57	198

	Paralegals	Support
1990:	117	646
1989:	109	727
1988:	94	NA
1987:	63	NA
1986:	65	NA

*LATERAL HIRES

1989: 3
1988: 10
1987: NA
1986: 4

*PRESIDING PARTNER: Samuel C. Butler

*REPRESENTATIVE CLIENTS:

IBM, CBS, Time, Royal Dutch/Shell, Allied Chemical, Chemical Bank, Paine Webber, First Boston, Wasington Post

*BRANCHES: London (9)
Total: 9 lawyers (1p and 8a)

*AVERAGE ANNUAL BILLING HOURS:
Partners: NA
Associates: 2300

*NUMBER OF WOMEN

	Partners	Associates
1990:	2	66
1989:	2	52
1988:	2	55
1987:	NA	NA
1986:	NA	NA

*PARTNERSHIP TRACK: 6–7 years

*NUMBER OF LAWYERS FROM ENTERING CLASS TO MAKE PARTNER:

1981: 3 of 39
1980: 6 of 54
1979: 2 of 24
1978: 3 of 36

*GROSS REVENUE

1989: $213,000,000
1988: $200,000,000
1987: $151,000,000
1986: $119,000,000

*REVENUE PER LAWYER

1989: $740,000
1988: $720,000
1987: $560,000
1986: $510,000

*PROFITS PER PARTNER

1989: $1,765,000
1988: $1,595,000
1987: $1,220,000
1986: $970,000

*STARTING ASSOCIATE SALARY

1990: $83,000
1989: $80,000-$83,000
1988: $76,731
1987: $65,365
1986: $64,364

*PRO BONO: 4–5% of total time

*HOURLY RATES

Partners: NA
Associates: NA

*PRINCIPAL LAW SCHOOLS
(Associates): Harvard, Yale, Columia, NYU

*NUMBER OF MINORITIES

	Partners	Associates
1990:	0	7
1989:	0	12
1988:	0	10
1987:	NA	NA
1986:	NA	NA

*SUMMER ASSOCIATES

1990: 74
1989: 64
1988: 51
1987: NA
1986: NA

The name Cravath, Swaine & Moore is synonymous with the term institutional law firm. After all, Cravath virtually wrote the book on structuring large law firms.* The firm's greatest achievement, however, may be its inability to rest on its laurels. Cravath is an exceptional blend of prestige, performance and profits. It's "the best across-the-board firm in New York" according to one senior litigator. "A firm above all others," says a leading legal consultant. Surprisingly, however, the firm's methods are tough, hard-working and definitely un-white shoe. As one headhunter put it, "They always go for the jugular."

The Cravath legend—some say mystique—begins in 1819, but the firm's modern origin can be traced to Paul Cravath, who, in the early 1900s, was the senior partner of Cravath, Henderson & deGensdorff. The Cravath system, largely as we know it today, was the brainchild of Paul Cravath, who believed that a law firm's strength should rest not on the acumen or accomplishments of a few individuals, but on the performance of the firm as a whole.†

The Cravath system promoted able and hard-working—if not particularly imaginative—lawyers. Paul Cravath explained the firm philosophy in a 1920 speech at Harvard Law School: "Brilliant intellectual powers are not essential. Too much imagination, too much wit, too great cleverness, too facile fluency, if not leavened by a sound sense of proportion, are quite as likely

---

*Paul Cravath's formulations on the subject were collected in Robert Swaine's firm history published in 1948.

†An adumbrated version of the Cravath system follows: The firm is to be governed by one person, not by an executive committee or by the partners at large. A firm grows not on who it knows but what it knows; it must not become engaged in politics. Within the firm, merit is the only qualification; lawyers will be hired and promoted on the basis of legal acumen, not on business production. The firm will not employ lawyers because of nepotism. Lawyers should practice solely within the firm and not be engaged in sideline practices, engage in business or politics or public service. Possible conflicts of interest are to be prevented by barring lawyers from owning stock in client corporations or serving on their boards. Lawyers should not specialize until they have had several years of general experience. A young lawyer watches senior lawyers break a large problem into its component parts, is given one of the smaller parts and exhaustively does the part assigned to him under supervision. A young lawyer's responsibility will increase as is permitted by a growing competency. Those who evidence the capacity for delegation should expand their own activity by giving younger lawyers the same kind of training received by them. Members of the firm are to be promoted from within the firm, not from the outside. The cream of Ivy League law school graduates are to be paid salaries at least as high as that of any other firm in New York and indoctrinated into the firm's methods and groomed for leadership. If an associate cannot make partner, it is the responsibility of the firm to find an appropriate job for him.

to impede success as to promote it. The best clients are apt to be afraid of these qualities. They want as their counsel a man who is primarily honest, safe, sound and steady."

While Cravath largely continues to build on the specifications of this blueprint, there have been exceptions. Significantly, the firm has secured laterals to fill gaps in specialties. A middle step has been created for senior associates who did not make partner; they have become "permanent associates." And finally, the autocracy ruled first by Cravath and then Robert Swaine has become diluted over the years. While Samuel Butler has been the single presiding partner of Cravath since 1980, he does not, like Messrs. Cravath and Swaine, wield sole authority.

Otherwise, the formula has built Cravath into an across-the-board success, built on a bedrock of impressive clients and sustained by skill and hard work. In *American Lawyer* surveys the firm has steadily placed fifth or sixth among New York firms in gross revenue over the past several years; perhaps more remarkably, in 1988 and 1989 Cravath ranked first in profits per partner ($1,595,000 and $1,765,000).

The stellar client stable maintained by Cravath, many of which became identified with the firm only post–World War II, includes Royal Dutch/Shell, Ashland Oil, Chemical Bank, CBS, The Washington Post, Time-Warner, First Boston, Paine Webber, Salomon Bros., Allied Chemical, Bethlehem Steel and, of course, IBM.

The IBM anti-trust litigation instituted by the federal government lasted thirteen years, from January 17, 1969, until January 8, 1982, when, after trial, the case was settled and the government conceded that the suit had been "without merit." During this time there were six civil anti-trust claims in various parts of the country brought against IBM which either were dismissed or were settled to IBM's satisfaction. In order to conduct these large and complex cases, the firm occupied a large section of IBM's offices in White Plains, New York near the company's headquarters in Armonk. While the cases themselves were Kafkaesque in nature, so too were the surrounding circumstances. Thomas Barr, the partner in charge, superintended layers of junior partners who, in turn, superintended numerous associates (at times eighty lawyers were involved).

Cravath farmed out litigation to other firms due to a lack of lawyers. There was a devastating effect on the morale of associates who spent three or four years in White Plains working exclusively on minor (and not so minor) aspects of the litigation—cash and other bonuses were given to associates to induce them to continue on the matter. The loss of associates was far in excess of normal turnover because of dissatisfaction with the narrow experience. Partnerships were offered to lawyers who had shown their loyalty by spending time in White Plains. And for the first time in years Cravath needed to obtain lateral litigators, an implicit admission that the White Plains experience was not producing lawyers as well-rounded as they should be. While the revenues generated by the litigation were estimated to have run at about $20,000,000 a year—as Tom Barr put it, "There isn't a law firm in the country that wouldn't get down on its hands and knees and push a peanut down Main Street with its nose to get this case"—the long, arduous litigation placed a severe strain on Cravath and the institutional basis of its organization.

Out of the IBM saga emerged Cravath's two brightest litigating lights: Barr and David Boies. Boies' subsequent successful defense of CBS in a libel suit brought by General William Westmoreland gained him still greater recognition. "They are very formidable adversaries," affirms a senior litigator at one major firm. "It is probably the best firm in terms of professional skills."

One negative did surface about Cravath's litigators: observers often put the firm's failures in this department down to arrogance. "They seem to look down on judges, and judges notice that," comments a senior litigator at another New York firm. "Many would call it arrogant. I would call it over-aggressiveness," avers another litigator, adding that Cravath lawyers in his experience had frequently "overplayed their hand."

Nevertheless, observers praise several other Cravath litigators, including Allen Maulsby, Alan Hruska and John Hupper. Hupper gained renown as a financial litigator through his representation of Price Waterhouse and his successful 1979 antitrust defense of Royal Dutch/Shell Group.

Cravath's corporate department has also produced its share

of stars, particularly in the area of corporate finance. James Duffy is a standout, as was Richard Simmons, who supervised work for Chemical Bank until he became its vice chairman. Taken together, Cravath's forces are impressive. "It is the best firm in the country, having consistently the best work product," concludes a former house counsel.

Cravath has been able to assemble this array of talent at least in part because of a groundbreaking recruiting technique the firm pioneered in the mid-1960s. In 1968 Cravath dramatically raised salaries for law school graduates (to $15,000 from $10,000) and set the going rate for associates throughout the 1970s. (Other firms have since taken Cravath's impetus away.)

Today, however, Cravath is identified with more work, not more money. A 1988 *American Lawyer* survey of associates rated the firm among the most demanding in terms of billable hours and remarked upon its "sweatshop atmosphere." A senior corporate lawyer noted that "Cravath works its associates pretty hard and is very selective but it compensates very well." In 1989 Cravath's overall position increased to 7th from 9th. As one associate put it, "The firm basically keeps all its promises. They promised me lots of responsibility, long hours, at-or-above-market salaries, and no chance of partnership."

Ultimately, however, Cravath is Cravath. "Being a partner there is the pinnacle of an associate's ambition," concludes a legal consultant. Mystique and money combine to make the firm a place, one headhunter says, "associates rarely look to leave."

Cravath still stands for high professionalism at a time when this concept is under attack from all sides. While there can be no certainty that its standards can be maintained in these turbulent times, it would not be prudent to wager against Cravath's chances.

CURTIS, MALLET-PROVOST, COLT & MOSLE
....
101 Park Avenue • New York, New York 10178 • (212) 696-6000

Rating: 🗄🗄🗄🗄   Direction: ↔

*LAWYERS	PARTNERS	ASSOCIATES
1990: 104	35	64
1989: 114	40	66
1988: 101	36	57
1987: 112	NA	NA
1986: 95	NA	NA

	Paralegals	Support
1990:	19	147
1989:	27	140
1988:	31	NA
1987:	22	NA
1986:	18	NA

*LATERAL HIRES
1989: 8
1988: 8
1987: NA
1986: 3

*MANAGING PARTNER: Albert Francke, III

*REPRESENTATIVE CLIENTS:
Price Waterhouse, Rowe & Pitman,
Bethlehem Steel Corporation, Hitachi, Ltd.,
Drexel Burnham (before its reorganization)

*BRANCHES: Washington (7), London (4),
Paris (3), Mexico City (22)
Total: 36 lawyers (9p and 27a)

*AVERAGE ANNUAL BILLING HOURS:
Partners: NA
Associates: 2000

*NUMBER OF WOMEN

	Partners	Associates
1990:	0	23
1989:	1	22
1988:	0	20
1987:	NA	NA
1986:	NA	NA

*PARTNERSHIP TRACK: 8 years

*NUMBER OF LAWYERS FROM ENTERING CLASS TO MAKE PARTNER:
1981: NA of 8
1980: 2 of 11
1979: 1 of 11
1978: 1 of 7

*GROSS REVENUE
1989: NA
1988: NA
1987: NA
1986: NA

*REVENUE PER LAWYER
1989: NA
1988: NA
1987: NA
1986: NA

*PROFITS PER PARTNER
1990: NA
1988: NA
1987: NA
1986: NA

*STARTING ASSOCIATE SALARY
1990: $80,000
1989: $80,000
1988: $70,000
1987: $65,000
1986: $65,000

*PRO BONO: 4.7% of total time

*HOURLY RATES
Partners: $230–$400
Associates: $105–$210

*PRINCIPAL LAW SCHOOLS
(Associates): Fordham (11),
Brooklyn (4), NYU (4)

*NUMBER OF MINORITIES

	Partners	Associates
1990:	2	5
1989:	2	5
1988:	2	2
1987:	NA	NA
1986:	NA	NA

*SUMMER ASSOCIATES
1990: 21
1989: 12
1988: 11
1987: NA
1986: NA

Curtis, Mallet, several observers note, is really two firms co-habitating under a single roof. Peter Fleming's litigation group constitutes one separate entity, Albert Francke III's international group another. As one senior litigator observes, Curtis, Mallet is "not so much a firm as a loose association of people."

Although Fleming is perhaps the preeminent trial lawyer in New York and the firm's international practice appears to have explosive growth potential, Curtis, Mallet has not emerged as a comer. Growth also has not taken place financially. Between 1986 and 1988, the firm failed to rank among *The American Lawyer* list of top 100 firms nationally in gross revenue, revenue per lawyer or profits per partner.

The firm began as Graham & Graham (founded none too surprisingly, by the Graham brothers, John and James) in 1830. The name changed to Curtis, Mallet-Provost & Colt in 1897. William Edward Curtis, Jr. was assistant secretary of the Treasury Department in the Cleveland administration but is perhaps best remembered for his role in retaining the nation's gold standard in 1895. The Mexican-born Severo Mallet-Provost acted as special counsel to the United States in the early 1890s and successfully challenged documents which claimed that a Mexican citizen owned much of what is now Arizona. Mallet-Provost also originated the firm's international practice in the late 1800s. The firm established offices in Havana, Rio de Janeiro and Buenos Aires in the 1920s, all of which lasted only briefly. Reflecting the Latin roots of Mallet-Provost, the firm currently prepares the Martindale-Hubbell Law & Digest for all Latin American countries except Panama and Paraguay.

In an effort to centralize Curtis, Mallet, thus solving its vaunted "cohesion problem," one executive partner, elected for one-year terms by the full partnership, replaced an Executive Committee system in 1982. The executive partner, currently Francke, supervises the firm's daily operations and makes recommendations on broader policy matters. He also appoints the Compensation Committee, which suggests annual partnership draws, and the Recruitment Committee, which hires new associates, and approves associate compensation.

The firm has five departments: corporate/international, litigation, real estate, tax and trusts and estates. Corporate and litigation are equal in size and, in 1989, constituted roughly 80% of the firm's lawyers.

Without exception, observers identify Peter Fleming as the firm's star litigator. "That's Fleming's firm," says a judge of Curtis, Mallet. Fleming's reputation as a trial lawyer, particularly in the area of white collar crime, is national, if not international in scope. He has represented defendants in a number of highly visible cases, including former attorney general John Mitchell and former secretary of commerce Maurice Stans in the U.S. government prosecution for obstruction of justice, conspiracy and perjury (both were acquitted on all counts). He also defended three Arthur Anderson & Co. partners charged with fraud in preparing financial statements for Four Seasons Nursing Centers (two were acquitted and the third received a directed verdict of "not guilty"). His successes helped to persuade other leading firms to reconsider their disdain for white collar criminal defense work and to enter the field.

Fleming joined the firm in 1970 after nine years as an assistant U.S. attorney for the Southern District of New York under Robert Morgenthau. Once at Curtis, Mallet, Fleming teamed with John Sprizzo to form a legendary "odd couple." The balding, bespectacled, heavyset Sprizzo was the blunt law insider, while the tall, graceful, silver-haired Fleming—with his disarming manner and homespun eloquence—was the diplomat, the pair's public face. The partnership lasted until Sprizzo became a U.S. district court judge for the Southern District of New York in 1981.

Beyond Fleming, the firm has several highly respected litigators, including John Romans, Robert Lipton and Lawrence Kelly. Led by Fleming, the department has represented such clients as Price Waterhouse, Bethlehem Steel Corporation and Hitachi, Ltd. Romans specializes in aviation law and has represented TWA.

Francke is the firm's top international lawyer, and he has represented such interests as Robert Fleming & Co. Ltd, Fidelity Australian Fund N.V. and Rowe & Pitman. Observers also single out Jeremiah Mulligan, John Marden and John Campbell for their corporate work.

The firm currently has branch offices in Mexico City, Paris, Washington, D.C. and London.

Associates have become less enthusiastic about Curtis, Mallet in recent years. While mid-level associates ranked the firm 14th in a 1986 *American Lawyer* survey, by 1988 Curtis had slipped to 28th. Associates complained of less interesting work, less guidance and rockier partner-associate relations. Some of the partners, according to a headhunter, have developed reputations as "tyrants." Nevertheless, Curtis, Mallet remains a good place for the associate who is "there for particular practice areas" and, of course, who wants to travel.

DAVIS POLK & WARDWELL

· ·

One Chase Manhattan Plaza · New York, New York 10005 · (212) 530-4000

Rating: 💼💼💼💼💼   *Direction:* ↑

*LAWYERS	PARTNERS	ASSOCIATES
1990: 351	79	271
1989: 387	98	266
1988: 362	92	251
1987: 342	88	236
1986: 321	82	218

	Paralegals	Support
1990:	114	615
1989:	136	700
1988:	135	NA
1987:	136	698
1986:	124	NA

*LATERAL HIRES

1990: 1
1989: NA
1988: 2
1987: NA
1986: 2

*MANAGING PARTNER: Henry L. King

*REPRESENTATIVE CLIENTS:

Morgan Guaranty, Boeing, LTV,
International Paper, RJ Reynolds

*BRANCHES: Washington (34), Paris (12),
London (14), Tokyo (4)
Total: 64 lawyers (17p and 47a)

*AVERAGE ANNUAL BILLING
HOURS:

Partners: NA
Associates: NA

*NUMBER OF WOMEN

	Partners	Associates
1990:	8	117
1989:	8	104
1988:	5	101
1987:	4	93
1986:	3	90

*PARTNERSHIP TRACK: about 7 years

*NUMBER OF LAWYERS FROM ENTERING
CLASS TO MAKE PARTNER:

1982: 2 of 43
1981: 3 of 48
1980: 2 of 39
1979: 4 of 39

*GROSS REVENUE

1989: $240,500,000
1988: $218,500,000
1987: $180,000,000
1986: $155,000,000

*REVENUE PER LAWYER

1989: $630,000
1988: $580,000
1987: $535,000
1986: $505,000

*PROFITS PER PARTNER

1989: $1,125,000
1988: $1,050,000
1987: $830,000
1986: $730,000

*STARTING ASSOCIATE
SALARY

1990: $83,000
1989: $78,000
1988: $76,000
1987: $66,000
1986: $66,000

*PRO BONO: 4–7% of total
time

*HOURLY RATES

Partners: NA
Associates: NA

*PRINCIPAL LAW SCHOOLS
(Associates): Harvard,
Columbia, NYU

*NUMBER OF MINORITIES

	Partners	Associates
1990:	1	20
1989:	1	17
1988:	1	13
1987:	NA	NA
1986:	NA	NA

*SUMMER ASSOCIATES

1990: 69
1989: 76
1988: 60
1987: 53
1986: 49

To some, Davis Polk is "the Tiffany of law firms," the white shoe firm containing a higher proportion of *Social Register* names than any other. To those who have continuing dealings with Davis Polk, it is a top-of-the-line firm with consistently excellent departments, lawyers and clients. One legal consultant who rates Davis Polk one of New York's three best firms, states that, while "there are no key partners, it is just stacked down the line with excellent partners and marvelous associates."

Davis Polk has maintained its professional standards while matching the expansion rate, both in size and in profitability, of New York's leading law firms. According to *The American Lawyer,* between 1986 and 1988, the firm held steady at nineteenth in the national rankings while growing from 321 lawyers to 413. In the same period, the firm's financial results increased consistently; gross revenue went from $155,000,000 in 1986 to $218,000,000 in 1988 and revenue per lawyer rose from $505,000 to $580,000. The only real jump took place in profits per partner, which exploded from $730,000 in 1986 to $1,050,000 in 1988. Nevertheless, by all three financial barometers, Davis Polk achieved near-constancy relative to other firms. In three years, it slipped one rank in each category, from fifth to sixth in gross revenue, third to fourth in revenue per lawyer and from fifth to sixth in profits per partner. In 1989 revenue increased to $240,000,000, revenue per lawyer, to $630,000, and profits per partner, to $1,125,000. The evenness and the inexorability of each year's incremental advance make Davis Polk appear among the most invulnerable and least volatile of firms.

Although Davis Polk traces its roots to a firm founded in 1849 (with fourteen subsequent name changes before the current name was adopted in 1968) the modern era of the firm began in 1921 when John W. Davis became a partner. Davis, who ran for the presidency in 1924, was one of the nation's finest appellate litigators until his death in 1955. In 1925, the firm put Davis' name first (it had been fourth) where it has remained to this day. Frank Polk, counsel to the State Department during World War I, joined the firm just before Davis and was instrumental in bringing the latter to the firm. Alan Wardwell (son-in-law to Francis Stetson, a key partner at the firm in the early 1900s who did legal work relating to the organization of United States Steel) completed the firm name. Wardwell joined Red Cross missions in both the Russian Revolution and World War II.

The leaders of the firm since the 1960s—Leighton Coleman, Frederick A. O. Schwarz, C. Payson Coleman and Henry L. King—have guided and shaped the firm during its period of greatest growth. Control over the firm's affairs passed from four senior partners to a management committee elected by the whole partnership. The new leadership spearheaded expansion into new areas: banking, public finance and oil and gas. The firm was also among the first to formally change its rules concerning associates not elected to partnership. By creating an intermediate step between associate and partner—senior attorney—Davis Polk now retains lawyers whose training (and not insubstantial salaries) made them a firm investment who have become important to clients. For the associates in question (currently there are fifteen) the new system means more respect, more money—especially via performance bonuses—and more guidance. Some eventually even make partnership.

Davis Polk has four departments: corporate, litigation, tax and trusts and estates. Observers universally single out litigator Robert Fisk as the firm's leading light. "He is almost without peer as a trial lawyer," says a leading litigator. Don Bernstein and Steve Case, both in bankruptcy, an area of significant expansion for the firm, also receive plaudits. Davis Polk, however, does not rely on a star system; its excellence, top to bottom, is what has yielded such clients as Morgan Guaranty, Morgan Stanley Group, ITT, International Paper, Boeing, LTV and RJ Reynolds.

Davis Polk has offices in Paris (1963), London (1973), Washington (1980) and Tokyo (1987).

From its financial figures, particularly for revenue per lawyer and profits per partner, it is clear that Davis Polk uses its troops efficiently to achieve a steady increase. For the troops, however, the firm has definite ups and downs. The training, by all accounts, is stellar. One legal consultant calls it "excellent," another, "unparalleled." Nevertheless, a gap exists between the overall firm training and individual, on-going guidance. A senior corporate lawyer notes that though the firm is highly successful in recruiting and training new talent, it fails to provide enough personal supervision. Mid-level and summer associates have ranked the firm back in the pack in 1987, 1988, and 1989 *American Lawyer* surveys of New York firms because they often felt adrift in unstructured, impersonal surroundings. In 1988, long hours surfaced as a complaint. On a more positive note, associates praised Davis Polk's general class and high standards. One consultant called the firm "a particularly wonderful place for women . . . that has a strong concern for their social welfare." (In 1988, Davis Polk had five women partners out of a total of 92 and 101 women associates out of a total of 251). And in 1988 Davis Polk received the ultimate compliment from some of its corporate associates: they simply couldn't imagine practicing law anywhere else. Still, the overall score in the 1989 survey puts the firm somewhat below both the New York and national averages and raises questions concerning the actual environment of its associates.

DEBEVOISE & PLIMPTON
875 Third Avenue • New York, New York 10022 • (212) 909-6000

Rating: 💼💼💼💼   *Direction:* ↑

*LAWYERS	PARTNERS	ASSOCIATES
1990: 274	73	189
1989: 271	73	191
1988: 243	68	169
1987: 222	68	152
1986: 208	67	136

	Paralegals	Support
1990:	81	479
1989:	69	444
1988:	66	NA
1987:	42	368
1986:	37	NA

*LATERAL HIRES
1989: 12
1988: 11
1987: NA
1986: 12

*PRESIDING PARTNER: William B. Matteson

*REPRESENTATIVE CLIENTS:
American Airlines, Kelso and Company, Columbia University, Aetna, KLM Royal Dutch Airlines

*BRANCHES: Washington (36), Paris (11), Los Angeles (12), London (5)
Total: 64 lawyers (14p and 50a)

*AVERAGE ANNUAL BILLING HOURS:
Partners: NA
Associates: 1950

*NUMBER OF WOMEN

	Partners	Associates
1990:	4	79
1989:	4	74
1988:	4	62
1987:	4	56
1986:	3	51

*PARTNERSHIP TRACK: 7–9 years

*NUMBER OF LAWYERS FROM ENTERING CLASS TO MAKE PARTNER:
1982: NA of 37
1981: NA of 22
1980: 2 of 29
1979: 4 of 18

*GROSS REVENUE
1989: $147,000,000
1988: $119,000,000
1987: $93,000,000
1986: $77,000,000

*REVENUE PER LAWYER
1989: $485,000
1988: $435,000
1987: $365,000
1986: $350,000

*PROFITS PER PARTNER
1989: $655,000
1988: $610,000
1987: $550,000
1986: $435,000

*STARTING ASSOCIATE SALARY
1990: $83,000
1989: $81,000
1988: $77,000
1987: $71,000
1986: $66,000

*PRO BONO: 4–6% of total time

*HOURLY RATES
Partners: NA
Associates: NA

*PRINCIPAL LAW SCHOOLS
(Associates): Harvard (40), NYU (38), Columbia (33)

*NUMBER OF MINORITIES

	Partners	Associates
1990:	1	17
1989:	1	15
1988:	1	15
1987:	1	12
1986:	1	12

*SUMMER ASSOCIATES
1990: 66
1989: 67
1988: 50
1987: 41
1986: 41

Debevoise & Plimpton is that rare firm that has kept pace with New York's accelerated, increasingly bottom-line oriented practice without doing away with its genteel, Old World atmosphere. The people at Debevoise, as a headhunter puts it, "know how to be human beings as well as lawyers."

Nonetheless, the firm exhibits no evidence of financial sacrifice in balancing frequently conflicting demands. Between 1986 and 1988, Debevoise's gross revenue grew from $77,000,000 to $119,000,000, revenue per lawyer increased from $350,000 to $435,000 and profits per partner went up from $435,000 to $610,000. In *The American Lawyer* rankings, the firm remained virtually steady in gross revenue and profits per partner, going, respectively, from 30th place in 1986 to 31st place in 1988 and from 13th place to 16th place. Debevoise lost slightly more ground in revenue per lawyer (slipping from the 13th spot to 16th), but this can be attributed to the firm's growth in size, adding about forty-five lawyers between 1986 and 1988. In 1989 the firm continued its steady growth: gross revenue increased from $119,000,000 to $147,000,000; revenue per lawyer, from $435,000 to $485,000; and profits per partner, from $610,000 to $655,000.

The firm was started in 1931 as Debevoise, Plimpton, Lyons & Gates by Eli Whitney Debevoise (a direct descendant of the inventor of the cotton gin) and William Stevenson, both independently wealthy former Davis Polk associates. In 1933, Debevoise's Harvard classmate Francis T. P. Plimpton and Robert Page, who were associates at what is now Dewey, Ballantine, joined the firm.

Each of these men had illustrious careers in non-legal positions which gave the firm early prominence and prestige. Debevoise became counsel to the high commissioner for West Germany in 1951 and acting deputy high commissioner in 1952–53. Stevenson was ambassador to the Phillipines and then president of Oberlin College. Plimpton was the U.S. ambassador to the United Nations during the Kennedy and Johnson administrations and father of George Plimpton, Jr., the founder of *The Paris Review,* author and sports enthusiast. Page became president of Phillips Dodge Corporation, one of the firm's earliest and most important clients. In 1945 Marvin Lyons, one of the earlier name partners, came from Davis Polk to become the firm's leading tax lawyer. The other former name partner, Samuel Gates, a well-reputed litigator with a specialty in aviation law, joined in 1949 and went on to lead the litigation department. Upon its fiftieth anniversary in 1981, the firm dropped the last two names.

The watershed event in Debevoise's recent history occurred shortly before its fiftieth anniversary. The firm was selected as special counsel to Chrysler Corporation in its 1980 negotiations with the Federal Loan Guarantee Board and the roughly five hundred banks and other parties that enabled Chrysler to borrow $1.2 billion when the company was perilously close to bankruptcy. Although Kelley Drye & Warren, another leading New York firm, was Chrysler's traditional outside counsel, Chrysler chose Debevoise on perceived merit and because, unlike many other leading firms, the firm did not act as general counsel to a major bank (which probably would have created a conflict of interest by being a creditor of Chrysler). The six-month adventure—which entailed twenty-five lawyers working more than 30,000 hours on a series of extremely complicated and intricately interlocking negotiations and drafting sessions with the U.S. Treasury, American, Canadian, European and Japanese banks, insurance companies, a major foreign car manufacturer, common and preferred stockholders, note and debenture holders—ended successfully on June 24, 1980. The various elements in the overall financing took place at four preliminary closings in New York and a final simultaneous exchange of cross-receipts at the Debevoise firm. (The night before, during a dry run of the closing, a not-inconsequential fire broke out in Debevoise's building. The lawyers re-entered the building, packed up the closing papers and, using a number of carts, trundled the documents up Park Avenue to Shearman & Sterling.)

There were partners at Debevoise, particularly those not directly involved in the Chrysler project, who were appalled by the disruptions and dislocations caused by the case. The size and demands of the project superseded the firm's established procedures for assigning and managing associates and partners. There was concern both at the outset and thereafter that the firm would become enmeshed in a tedious, time-consuming bureaucratic project, as Cravath had been in the decade-long IBM anti-trust cases. Nevertheless, the project proved to be a success within a relatively short period and a bond between Chrysler and Debevoise was created that continues to this day.

Since 1988, the firm's presiding partner has been William Matteson. The presiding partner selects the eight members of the Operations Committee, which presents matters to the full partnership and implements their decisions. Usually the partnership will act by consensus on matters of importance. The departments submit lists of candidates for partner to the whole partnership, which then reaches a consensus on whom to admit.

Debevoise has five practice areas: corporate, litigation, tax, real estate and trusts and estates. All receive accolades from observers. Debevoise is "money-efficient," says a house counsel, "and assigns the right level of people, . . . provides great service and accessibility . . . they are very good at strategy."

The corporate department, headed by George Lindsay, is the largest and most significant in the firm. William Matteson, Michael Goff and Cecil Wray are key partners in the department. Meredith Brown heads an M & A subdivision which currently produces 30% of the firm's revenue. Mario Baeza, who in 1982 became one of the first blacks selected to partnership at a leading New York firm, also plays an important role in M & A, representing, among others, Kelso and Company.

The litigation department, though it does not have the same standing as corporate, has several distinguished litigators. Observers praise department head Robert Van Mehren, Judah Best—chairman of the American Bar Association's litigation section—Standish Medina and James Goodale, former general counsel and vice-chairman of *The New York Times*. Vincent Smith and Steven Alden are standouts in real estate.

Debevoise represents a number of large insurance companies including Prudential, Aetna, John Hancock, Equitable Mutual Life and Mass Mutual. The firm also represents American Airlines, KLM Royal Dutch Airlines, Continental Corporation, St. John Minerals, Tampax, Wheelabrator Frye, Cooper Laboratories and a number of non-profit organizations, including the Ford Foundation, Columbia and Princeton universities, Channel 13 and the Russell Sage and Hartford foundations. Debevoise emphasizes *pro bono* work and has a strong program, administered by its own six-lawyer committee within the firm.

The firm maintains branch offices in Paris (1964), Washington, D.C. (1982), London (1989) and Los Angeles (1989).

One unique feature of Debevoise is its formal program for partners' sabbaticals. After nine years of partnership, a partner is eligible for a paid six-month leave of absence.

Surprisingly, Debevoise's associates—described by a headhunter as "cerebral intellectual types"—give the firm mixed reviews. In 1986 and 1988 *American Lawyer* polls, associates complained that the firm has no systematic supervisory structure with the result that associates sometimes fall through the cracks. On the positive side, associates agreed that the firm encouraged *pro bono* and made reasonable time demands. Observers paint a rosier picture of associate life at Debevoise. According to a legal consultant, associates are treated "extraordinarily well . . . and love the firm." While associates in the 1989 survey continue to feel well treated by partners, the firm also continues to receive mixed reviews from associates on their attitudes toward the firm and its policies and environment.

DEWEY BALLANTINE

1301 Avenue of the Americas • New York, New York 10019 • (212) 259-8000

Rating: 💼💼💼💼   *Direction:* ↑

*LAWYERS	PARTNERS	ASSOCIATES
1990: 278	71	209
1989: 239	64	152
1988: 206	59	137
1987: 200	59	132
1986: 191	55	112

v.94

	Paralegals	Support
1990:	53	451
1989:	50	243
1988:	40	NA
1987:	42	243
1986:	37	NA

*LATERAL HIRES

1989: 15
1988: 8
1987: NA
1986: 15

*MANAGING PARTNER: Joseph Califano   *HARVEY KURZWEIL*

*REPRESENTATIVE CLIENTS:

Prudential Bache, the Louis Dreyfus Group, Martin Marietta Corporation, World Airways

*BRANCHES: Washington (64), Los Angeles (42), Boca Raton (2)

*AVERAGE ANNUAL BILLING HOURS (1989):

Partners: NA
Associates: 1877

*NUMBER OF WOMEN

	Partners	Associates
1990:	5	79
1989:	3	63
1988:	3	52
1987:	3	47
1986:	3	38

*PARTNERSHIP TRACK: 7–8 years

*NUMBER OF LAWYERS FROM ENTERING CLASS TO MAKE PARTNER:

1982: NA of 25
1981: 3 of 24
1980: 2 of 22
1979: 4 of 25

*GROSS REVENUE

1989: $139,000,000
1988: $115,000,000
1987: $91,000,000
1986: $71,500,000

*REVENUE PER LAWYER

1989: $410,000
1988: $400,000
1987: $355,000
1986: $280,000

*PROFITS PER PARTNER

1989: $465,000
1988: $455,000
1987: $405,000
1986: $345,000

*STARTING ASSOCIATE SALARY

1990: $83,000
1989: $80,000
1988: $77,000
1987: $66,000
1986: $66,000

*PRO BONO: 4–7% of total time

*HOURLY RATES

Partners: NA
Associates: NA

*PRINCIPAL LAW SCHOOLS (Associates): Fordham (27), NYU (25), Georgetown (12), Harvard (8)

*NUMBER OF MINORITIES

	Partners	Associates
1990:	0	13
1989:	1	11
1988:	2	5
1987:	1	7
1986:	1	4

*SUMMER ASSOCIATES

1990: 56
1989: 48
1988: 49
1987: 44
1986: 32

Since its founding in 1909, Dewey Ballantine has had an illustrious history, highlighted by such legendary lawyers as Elihu Root, Sr. and Jr., Grenville Clark, Emory Buckner, Arthur Ballantine, Wilkie Bushby, John Harlan and Thomas E. Dewey. After Dewey's death, however, the firm went into a decade-long decline in 1971 only to be revived shortly after Joseph Califano, an alumnus of the firm, rejoined the firm in 1983. The Califano program—moving older partners into early retirement, ridding the firm of unproductive partners, replacing lockstep seniority compensation for partners with a system emphasizing business origination and productivity, instituting numerous cost control measures and aggressive searches and acquisitions—once again has made Dewey Ballantine one of New York's most exciting and upwardly mobile firms.

In purely financial terms, Dewey's resurgence has been remarkable. In 1982, according to *The American Lawyer,* the firm had revenues of $42 million, which yielded revenues per lawyer of $216,000 and profits per partner of $190,000. In 1988, the firm's gross revenue was $115 million, which translated to revenues per lawyer of $400,000 and profits per partner of $455,000. In 1989 the firm's increase of gross revenue from $115,000,000 to $139,000,000 was not matched proportionately by revenue per lawyer which resulted in a modest increase from $400,000 to $410,000, or by profits per partner, which also rose modestly from $455,000 to $465,000. The only drawback to what several sources call the new Dewey "bottom-line consciousness" is the dissipation of the firm's once genteel, low-key image and atmosphere. As one judge says, now "Dewey is efficient and capable, but I miss the old firm."

Dewey Ballantine's reversal of fortune in the mid-1980s was not the firm's first. From the time of its founding as Root Clark Buckner & Harlan until the mid-1940s, the firm experienced steady growth and prosperity. In 1945, however, Clark retired. In 1946, partners George Cleary, Leo Gottlieb, Henry Friendly and Melvin Steen left the firm to form what is today Cleary, Gottlieb, Steen & Hamilton. In 1952, Root, Jr., retired and in 1954, John Harlan left, first to become a judge on the Court of Appeals for the Second Circuit and a few months later to become a justice on the Supreme Court. Within the same time span, the firm lost its largest client, Bank of Manhattan, when it was acquired by the Chase Bank.

At this low point, the firm reached out to Thomas Dewey, former special prosecutor (1935–1936), district attorney (1937–1941), governor of New York (1942–1954) and Republican presidential nominee (1944 and 1948). He also happened to be an excellent trial lawyer and appellate advocate, a major business originator and a tenacious administrator. From January 1, 1955 until his death in 1971, Dewey abjured politics and other extracurricular activities and devoted his full time and energies to rebuilding the firm. In his tenure at Dewey Ballantine, he missed but two working days. By the end of his reign, the firm had 174 lawyers—47 partners and 127 associates—and was the second largest in New York.

Under Dewey, the firm was basically a dictatorship. After Dewey's death, the firm strove for a democracy that soon devolved into near anarchy. Under Califano, governing power at Dewey Ballantine has once again become centralized and now rests largely in the hands of a seven-member Management Committee on which Califano sits. Formally, the Committee—which is chosen for staggered two-year terms by the entire partnership—provides recommendations for partnership shares and on other firm-wide issues on which the whole partnership votes. In reality, however, there are few formal votes and such matters as new partners and associate salary are decided on the basis of what is murkily defined as a consensus.

Califano has emerged as the firm's leader largely due to his forceful personality and powers of persuasion. Like Dewey himself, Califano has an extensive background in government service. He was special assistant to President Johnson and secretary of Health, Education and Welfare in the Carter administration. Initially, he was brought in to head the firm's Washington branch. As he remolded Dewey into a modern firm, Califano became a highly controversial figure. Critics have found him temperamental and exacting, an egomaniac and a slave driver. One prominent litigator calls him an "adventurer" while another accuses him of overnegotiating deals. Most observers acknowledge, however, that these traits might have been necessary to counteract the diffuse, unimaginative and overly conservative management previously in place.

The firm is divided into four departments: corporate, litigation, tax and trusts and estates. Corporate, the largest practice area, has four internal subdivisions: corporate representation, municipal bonds, private financing and real estate. Robert Fullem, one of Califano's closest advisors on the Management Committee, supervises the entire corporate department and is credited with significantly expanding its client base. Before he came on the scene, Dewey had represented American Can, AT&T, Conoco Inc., Chase Manhattan Bank, the Louis Dreyfus Group and Eli Lilly & Co. Under Fullem's guidance, the firm has attracted such corporate clients as the Martin Marietta Corporation, Prudential Bache, E.F. Hutton, and World Airways. Leonard Larrabee and Kenneth LaVoy (a former department head) are corporate standouts. Sanford Morhouse leads the real estate division, which represents the Chase Manhattan Bank in its real estate activities and placement of mortgage-backed securities. Dewey's real estate department also does work for the General Electric Pension Trust, a large equity investor in real estate. The firm recently brought in, by lateral acquistion, Stanley Hirschfeld to head its bankruptcy practice.

Harvey Kurzweil leads a litigation department significantly augmented by laterals. Sanford Litvack, formerly the star attraction at Donovan Leisure, came to Dewey in 1986. The department as a whole has been on an upswing since it bottomed out in 1982, when its largest client AT&T settled the monumental anti-trust suit brought against it by the federal government. Kurzweil himself has made great contributions toward replacing this business by being instrumental in landing such clients as Prudential Bache and the Federal Savings and Loan Insurance Corporation. Observers also single out litigator J. Paul McGrath for praise.

The tax department is led by Everett Jassy, another highly influential member of the Management Committee. Paul Nash receives plaudits from several sources for his work as the firm's administrative partner, a role he assumed in 1984.

For many years the firm was known as Dewey, Ballantine,

Bushby, Palmer & Wood. When the firm moved from 140 Broadway to its present offices in September, 1990, it adopted its current name—Dewey Ballantine—which was the name it most frequently was referred to by everyone.

After closing the twenty-year-old Paris office in 1985 as part of its cost reduction program, Dewey opened a Los Angeles branch in 1986 by acquiring the commercial litigation group of Lillick McHose & Charles. The firm also maintains a relatively large Washington office.

Associates surveyed by *The American Lawyer* in 1986 and 1988 ranked Dewey in the middle of the pack. In 1986, associate perceptions of the firm varied wildly. Many found that the firm provided interesting work and excellent training, put little pressure on associates vis-à-vis billable hours and had a pleasant atmosphere; conversely, one associate opined that "the partners are obsessed with improving their take-home share and cost cutting has assumed ridiculous proportions." Associate opinions of the firm in 1988 tended to be more benign, although two women expressed the view that Dewey treated its women lawyers badly, especially those who were pregnant. In 1989, while the firm actually rose in ranking to ninth position in New York, associates expressed concern over "an informal bottom-line attitude" and a confusion over billing policy (should one bill just more hours or more efficient hours). There is also a recurring perception of sexism.

DONOVAN LEISURE NEWTON & IRVINE

30 Rockefeller Plaza • New York, New York 10112 • (212) 632-3300

Rating:    *Direction:* ?

*LAWYERS	PARTNERS	ASSOCIATES
1990: 103	37	60
1989: 105	38	62
1988: 97	34	57
1987: 103	NA	NA
1986: 102	NA	NA

	Paralegals	Support
1990:	18	149
1989:	18	157
1988:	25	NA
1987:	20	NA
1986:	16	NA

*LATERAL HIRES

1989: 9
1988: 11
1987: NA
1986: 23

*CHAIRMAN: J. Peter Coll, Jr.

*REPRESENTATIVE CLIENTS: NA

*BRANCHES: Washington (27), Los Angeles (21), Paris (7)
Total: 57 lawyers (18p and 29a)

*AVERAGE ANNUAL BILLING HOURS:
Partners: NA
Associates: NA

*NUMBER OF WOMEN

	Partners	Associates
1990:	2	29
1989:	1	25
1988:	1	19
1987:	NA	NA
1986:	NA	NA

*PARTNERSHIP TRACK: 8 years

*NUMBER OF LAWYERS FROM ENTERING CLASS TO MAKE PARTNER:

1981: 20 of 20
1980: 1 of 25
1979: 3 of 22
1978: 5 of 16

*GROSS REVENUE

1989: NA
1988: NA
1987: NA
1986: NA

*REVENUE PER LAWYER

1989: NA
1988: NA
1987: NA
1986: NA

*PROFITS PER PARTNER

1989: NA
1988: NA
1987: NA
1986: NA

*STARTING ASSOCIATE SALARY

1990: $79,000
1989: $76,000
1988: $71,000
1987: $65,000
1986: $65,000

*PRO BONO: 1–3% of total time

*HOURLY RATES
Partners: NA
Associates: NA

*PRINCIPAL LAW SCHOOLS (Associates): Fordham (12), Harvard (4), Virginia (4), Georgetown (4), NYU (3)

*NUMBER OF MINORITIES

	Partners	Associates
1990:	0	4
1989:	0	4
1988:	0	2
1987:	NA	NA
1986:	NA	NA

*SUMMER ASSOCIATES

1990: 16
1989: 18
1988: 15
1987: NA
1986: NA

Prior to 1978, Donovan Leisure was one of New York's preeminent law firms. Venerable, prestigious and highly profitable, Donovan seemed invulnerable, featuring a litigation department which many considered New York's best and which routinely handled huge, high-profile anti-trust cases.

This all-important reputation was shattered by the firm's disastrous representation of Eastman Kodak in the 1978 anti-trust case instituted by Berkey Photo. During the trial, a Donovan partner confessed to lying to the court about the destruction of evidence sought by Berkey. The Kodak debacle has become a modern-day parable, as Donovan Leisure quaked and nearly crumbled in the aftermath of the scandal. Under the leadership of Sanford Litvack and more recently Kenneth Hart, Donovan has undergone an overhaul. The firm is "no longer plummeting," as one legal consultant observes, but it is also no longer the top-tier powerhouse it once was.

The origins and history of Donovan Leisure are almost romantic in nature. The firm was founded in 1929 by George Leisure, Sr. and General William Donovan. The latter won fame as commander of the "Fighting 69th" in World War I and later, while head of the Office of Strategic Services—which he founded during World War II—became widely known as "Wild Bill" Donovan. In the 1920s, Donovan led the anti-trust division of the Justice Department. Donovan's high profile proved magnetic to prospective clients; prophetically, as he was well known to the Kodak executives based in his hometown of Rochester, New York, Kodak retained his young firm to advise on anti-trust matters almost from its inception. Ralston Irvine, who had worked in the Justice Department with Donovan, also joined the firm in 1929 but was not yet a name partner. Carl Newton and J. Edward Lumbard, Jr. joined the firm in 1934 after a stint in the U.S. Attorney's office for the Southern District of New York and for the decade from 1943 to 1953 the firm was known as Donovan Leisure Newton Lumbard & Irvine. The firm adopted its present name in 1953, when Lumbard departed and assumed the office of U. S. attorney.

Donovan Leisure quickly developed the capacity—unusual for the time—to handle massive, industry-wide cases for major corporate clients. Frequently, this work led to broader representation; in this way Donovan came to represent Mobil, American Standard, Ford, Walt Disney Productions, MCA, Capitol Records, Westinghouse, Allegheny, Genesco and Kidde.

The firm's representation of Socony Vacuum and Hanover Shoe Corp. (against United Shoe Machinery in 1968), among others, established Donovan as a leader in anti-trust litigation. To some extent, this reputation has survived the Kodak disaster. Donovan has also represented coal and cement industry clients in large-scale anti-trust suits.

To meet the extraordinary demands of these matters, over the years Donovan assembled a first-rate team of litigators including George Leisure, Sr. (and his son George Leisure, Jr.), Edward Lumbard, Jr. (who would later be the U.S. attorney for the Southern District of New York and then chief judge of the Court of Appeals for the Second Circuit), Ralston Irvine, Carl Luton, James Withrow, Jr., Vernon Conahan and Samuel Murphy.

Litigation, however, would nearly bring about Donovan's downfall. With the benefit of hindsight, the Berkey case has been discussed and analyzed *ad nauseam.* The facts were most peculiar: the then-unusual decision to go outside the firm and admit John Doar of Watergate acclaim as a partner in 1978 to spearhead the case; Doar's failure in pre-trial activity initially to question fellow partner Mahlon Perkins, Jr. about Perkins' alleged destruction of the requested documents and to determine that they were still extant; Doar's further failure to rectify the problem when the court ordered the firm to submit an affidavit explaining the details surrounding the destruction of the evidence; the subsequent order by the court at trial of an additional affidavit on the subject; the confession at that time by Perkins to Doar that the documents had not been destroyed; the conflict between Doar and the firm, as he strove to protect his own innocence in the matter before the court and the firm struggled to protect its interests; the continuing tension between Doar and other partners on how to handle the trial, including the Perkins problem; the jury verdict of $113 million against Kodak; the replacement by Kodak of Donovan Leisure with Sullivan & Cromwell to finish the case; the reversal of the judgment by the Court of Appeals in the Second Circuit; and finally, the setttlement of the case for $4.75 million cash and $2 million in credits.

Well before the case's resolution, both Doar and Perkins resigned from the firm. Perkins was convicted of criminal contempt and sentenced to a month in jail. It was small comfort to Donovan that the academically inclined, highly respected Perkins—a behind-the-scenes litigator—was an unlikely perpetrator, or that the incident was neither a reflection nor a result of the firm's overall integrity or credibility. The good will that had taken almost three generations to build was deeply tarnished in the legal and business communities; no one was interested in particulars or explanations.

The effect of the case on Donovan was immediate: a serious attrition of clients and lawyers. Sanford Litvack, former head of the Justice Department anti-trust division, was brought into the firm to salvage what was left of the old institution and to create a new Donovan as well. During the months before Litvack's reorganization, nine key partners, including litigation star and Executive Committee chairman Murphy, tax department head John Baity and corporate lawyer John Tobin, as well as thirty-three associates, left the firm. Notwithstanding, in the next three years under Litvack's plan—trimming nonproductive lawyers, placing certain partners on salary and subletting a portion of the firm's Rockefeller Center premises for substantial profit—Donovan increased its profits per partner to the $225,000–$235,000 range in 1987. (Gross revenue and revenue per lawyer remained relatively constant.) Word of mouth on the firm became increasingly optimistic. "Donovan Leisure was better than its sullied reputation," recalls a former house counsel. Finally, the firm seemed to be emerging from the Kodak cloud.

Donovan's momentum, however, came screeching to a halt when Litvack, to the dismay of his partners, announced in October 1986 that he was joining Dewey Ballantine (and taking with him a number of the firm's traditional, older clients such as Mobil, Genesco and Kidde). While greater compensation undoubtedly played a role in his decision, it is not clear what other factors influenced Litvack.

Kenneth Hart, a litigator, took over the reins with the proposed aim of shifting the mix of business from litigation (which accounted for approximately 65% of Donovan's practice in 1987) to corporate finance and securities (22%), the balance being contributed by its tax, real estate, and trusts and estates departments. To this end, the firm acquired a number of lateral partners and associates, and has (unsuccessfully) sought out merger partners. During the last decade Stuart Pierce, a corporate partner, has been a key person, especially in strategic planning.

These moves garner positive reviews from most observers. A senior litigator believes that "Donovan has rebuilt nicely from Berkey and has diversified well." "It was comatose a few years ago," a headhunter adds. "It's gotten a lot of lateral partners in the last two years and is no longer run by the litigation department. Internationally, it is picking up." The firm now maintains offices in Los Angeles, Washington, Paris and London.

Hart, however, expressed a more pessimistic point of view. As he stated in a 1987 *American Lawyer* interview, "When somebody's thinking about a financing or an acquisition, they don't think of us as a major player in those fields." The numbers bear Hart out; while Donovan declined to furnish any information about itself for this purpose, according to surveys done by *The American Lawyer,* Donovan failed to place among the top 100 firms in the country in gross revenue, revenue per lawyer or profits per partner between 1986 and 88.

While Donovan has attempted to make dramatic changes to achieve greater balance in its practice, the firm's governance has been stable in recent times. The internal system used under Litvack largely remains in place. A seven-member Executive Committee—voted in for staggered five-year terms by all active partners—determines partnership shares and associate salaries. A three-member Administration Committee, appointed by the Executive Committee, handles the firm's day-to-day administration and recommends associate salary levels to the Executive Committee. The entire partnership votes on the admission of new partners (it is necessary to receive an approval rate of 90%) and on issues of firm policy.

Perhaps the most pressing dilemma facing Donovan Leisure is the firm's paucity of business originators. Donovan has not been able to replace those lost in the Berkey case shuffle with lawyers of equal quality and prominence. "The problem," says a legal consultant, "is that there are no super-lawyers." Echoes a senior partner, "They don't have any stars." And, because of the turmoil surrounding Donovan, they are not likely to get any. The firm's recruiting has slipped dramatically. The class of 1986 included no law school graduates from Harvard, Yale or Columbia. In a 1987 *American Lawyer* survey of summer associates, Donovan ranked 18th—down from second in 1985— largely due to summer associates' reluctance to accept permanent offers from the firm. One associate attributed this reluctance to "the storm of dust and bad press" kicked up when Litvack left. Without bright stars guiding it in the future, Donovan may remain on the periphery instead of regaining its position atop the New York legal firmament.

EPSTEIN BECKER & GREEN, P.C.
. . . .
250 Park Avenue • New York, New York 10177 • (212) 351-4500

Rating: 💼💼💼

Direction: ↓

*LAWYERS

	PARTNERS	ASSOCIATES
1990: 80	27	40
1989: 81	30	44
1988: 79	29	45
1987: 82	27	53
1986: 64	20	NA

	Paralegals	Support
1990:	11	90
1989:	8	89
1988:	7	NA
1987:	6	105
1986:	10	NA

*LATERAL HIRES
1989: 2
1988: 7
1987: NA
1986: 5

*MANAGING PARTNER: George Sape

*REPRESENTATIVE CLIENTS:
Federal Express, Hertz, Ryder Systems, Prudential Bache, Sutter Health Systems

*BRANCHES: Washington (53), Los Angeles (11), San Francisco (19), Stamford (6), Dallas (8), Princeton (5)
Total: 83 lawyers (43p and 40a)

*AVERAGE ANNUAL BILLING HOURS:
Partners: NA
Associates: 1950

*NUMBER OF WOMEN

	Partners	Associates
1989:	5	26
1988:	3	18
1987:	2	22
1986:	1	18

*PARTNERSHIP TRACK: 7–10 years

*NUMBER OF LAWYERS FROM ENTERING CLASS TO MAKE PARTNER:
Firm formed in 1978; does not maintain these statistics

*GROSS REVENUE
1989: $48,000,000
1988: $43,000,000
1987: NA
1986: NA

*REVENUE PER LAWYER
1989: NA
1988: NA
1987: NA
1986: NA

*PROFITS PER PARTNER
1989: $230,000 (equity partners)
1988: NA
1987: NA
1986: NA

*STARTING ASSOCIATE SALARY
1990: $69,000
1989: $65,000
1988: $65,000
1987: NA
1986: $50,000

*PRO BONO: 5% of total time

*HOURLY RATES
Partners: $200-$280
Associates: $85-$200

*PRINCIPAL LAW SCHOOLS
(Associates): St. John's (5), Columbia (3), Hofstra (3)

*NUMBER OF MINORITIES

	Partners	Associates
1990:	0	1
1989:	0	1
1988:	0	4
1987:	0	3
1986:	0	2

*SUMMER ASSOCIATES
1990: 5
1989: 12
1988: 9
1987: 12
1986: 7

Epstein Becker & Green, P.C., while holding itself out as a full service law firm, is predominantly engaged in the practice of labor and equal employment law (thirty-three partners) and health law (twenty-four partners) which, with litigation support, occupies approximately 70% of the firm's partners. Observers are rather harsh with Epstein Becker; a senior corporate lawyer flatly says that the firm "is not in the same class as many other leading firms."

Although the firm did not respond to the questionnaire or subsequent oral inquiries, information furnished by headhunters and legal consultants confirm that the firm's results of operation are appreciably below those of most leading New York firms, that its charges to clients are frequently discounted and that it has unsuccessfully tried to merge into a number of other New York firms within the last several years. A headhunter confirms that the firm has "financial problems." Epstein Becker did not make *The American Lawyer* list of top 100 firms nationally in gross revenues, revenue per lawyer or profits per partner between 1986 and 1988. (The 1989 financial information included in the data sheet is derived from an interview of name partner Ronald Green contained in *The American Lawyer*.) Since February 1989 15 partners have left the firm. In mid-1990 the firm had seventy partners and eighty associates— a 1/1.1 partner/associate ratio, which is unusually low and gives very little leverage with which to generate profit. Also, atypically, a substantial majority of Epstein Becker's partners are non-equity partners and paid on a flat contractual basis. Although the firm advertises that in 1988, first-year associates were paid $65,000 per annum, the records of one legal consultant reflect annual compensation of $50,000 for first-year associates and $75,000 for one fifth-year associate.

The predecessor firm to Epstein Becker was founded in New York and Washington in 1973 by Stephen Epstein and Jeffrey Becker. According to one legal consultant, however, the firm was saved from extinction by joining forces in 1978 with Ronald Green, today the firm's key business originator and dominant partner. A senior litigator, criticizing the progress of the firm, says that Epstein Becker was "thrown together by a couple of wheeler-dealers . . . It has no particular quality." In 1978, the firm's name changed to Epstein Becker Borsody & Green. Epstein Becker has since continued to expand through lateral acquisitions, many of which observers judge to be questionable. "The firm takes lateral partners with relatively small portable business," says a headhunter. By the mid-1980s, as the firm expanded nationally, the firm became Epstein Becker Borsody, Stromberg & Green and then, finally, Epstein Becker & Green (Epstein Becker Mulkeen Stromberg & Green in California).

While it was impossible to confirm with the firm itself, a legal consultant describes the firm's internal governance, while theoretically managed by a six-person board, as an oligarchy ruled by Messrs. Epstein, Becker and Green, Green having the most significant voice by far.

The firm identified two "primary practice areas" in its National Association for Law Placement questionnaire: "labor/employment/litigation" and "corporate/health, including tax, ERISA, real estate, bankruptcy and trusts and estates." Observers judge the firm's work to be of dubious quality in most of these areas. Epstein Becker's work product is "well below the top firms," says a legal consultant. Nonetheless, one headhunter lauds the firm's "phenomenal health care practice" while house counsel to a major corporation uses the firm nation-wide in discrimination cases and finds its work "very good." While Epstein Becker does produce voluminous professional writings in its two specialties and takes pains to keep its clients apprised of current developments in these fields, the firm's efforts are frequently viewed with a jaundiced eye by many in the legal community.

Starting in 1978, Epstein Becker opened branch offices in Los Angeles, San Francisco and Dallas. Between 1986 and 1989, the firm created branches in Miami, Boston, Detroit, Stamford, Princeton, Tallahassee, and Alexandria, Virginia. Detroit was subsequently closed. Boston and Miami were established only as affiliations. The Tallahassee office is no longer staffed by firm lawyers. Of the firm's 163 lawyers in 1989, 80 were in New York, 53 in Washington and the remaining 30 in the five other offices.

FRIED, FRANK, HARRIS, SHRIVER & JACOBSON

One New York Plaza • New York, New York 10004 • (212) 820-8000

Rating: 💼💼💼💼💼   *Direction:* ↑

*LAWYERS	PARTNERS	ASSOCIATES
1990: 256	72	177
1989: 254	69	179
1988: 242	69	167
1987: 206	65	135
1986: 180	54	120

	Paralegals	Support
1990:	75	503
1989:	73	493
1988:	60	NA
1987:	55	355
1986:	54	NA

*LATERAL HIRES

1989: 9
1988: 23
1987: NA
1986: 20

*MANAGING PARTNERS: Arthur Fleisher, Jr. and Robert Mundheim

*REPRESENTATIVE CLIENTS:

General Electric, GTE Corporations, Tri-Star Pictures, Goldman, Sachs & Co.

*BRANCHES: Washington (118), Los Angeles (19), London (4)
Total: 141 lawyers (NAp and NAa)

*AVERAGE ANNUAL BILLING HOURS:

Partners: NA
Associates: 2000

*NUMBER OF WOMEN

	Partners	Associates
1990:	11	76
1989:	11	69
1988:	10	71
1987:	10	51
1986:	7	44

*PARTNERSHIP TRACK: 7–8 years

*NUMBER OF LAWYERS FROM ENTERING CLASS TO MAKE PARTNER:

1982: 6 of 24
1981: 2 of 15
1980: 3 of 16
1979: 6 of 24

*GROSS REVENUE

1989: $213,000,000
1988: $194,000,000
1987: $136,000,000
1986: $107,000,000

*REVENUE PER LAWYER

1989: $580,000
1988: $530,000
1987: $445,000
1986: $420,000

*PROFITS PER PARTNER

1989: $815,000
1988: $775,000
1987: $560,000
1986: $520,000

*STARTING ASSOCIATE SALARY

1990: $82,000
1989: $80,000
1988: $77,000
1987: $73,000
1986: $65,000

*PRO BONO: 3–5% of total time

*HOURLY RATES

Partners: NA
Associates: NA

PRINCIPAL LAW SCHOOLS (Associates): NYU (35), Columbia (18), Yeshiva (10), Harvard (9)

*NUMBER OF MINORITIES

	Partners	Associates
1990:	1	6
1989:	1	11
1988:	0	17
1987:	0	11
1986:	0	10

*SUMMER ASSOCIATES

1990: 52
1989: 46
1988: 43
1987: 40
1986: 56

Until the mid-1960s, Fried Frank was just another small financial district firm. With the emergence of corporate supernova Arthur Fleischer, however, the firm has, in the words of a legal consultant, "gone from good to super." "Fried Frank always had first-class people but didn't reach its current size and eminence until Arthur Fleischer came along," says a prominent litigator. Fried Frank epitomizes the modern legal success story by becoming institutionalized, but largely on the basis of a transaction-driven, crisis-oriented practice.

The firm's financial statistics reflect its large-scale success. Between 1986 and 1988, Fried Frank's gross revenues grew from $107,000,000 to $194,000,000; the firm also jumped from 16th to 9th on *The American Lawyer* list of the top 100 firms nationally in this category. Revenue per lawyer increased from $420,000 to $530,000 from 1986 to 1988 and profits per partner rose from $520,000 to $775,000, while the firm held steady in the rankings (slipping one place from fifth to sixth in revenue per lawyer and placing tenth for both years in profits per partner).

Today's Fried Frank can be traced back to the early 1900s with the firm of Riegelman and Bach which became known for representing many "Our Crowd" families and also for being a revolving door for name partners. As Baron Ireland wrote in *The New Yorker*:

> Leventritt, Riegelman, Cranes & Schwarz
> Argue no longer in New York courts.
> But their loss will be recompensed more or less
> by Limburg, Riegelman, Hirsch & Hess.

The firm became Strasser, Spiegelberg, Fried & Frank in the 1950s and 1960s; Sam Harris, formerly with the SEC and assistant to Justice Robert Jackson at the Nuremberg trials, was then the principal corporate partner, while George Spiegelberg was the chief litigator. Spiegelberg also brought in litigation powerhouse Leon Silverman, who, with Fleischer, currently heads Fried Frank.

The firm hired Fleischer as an associate right out of law school in the late 1950s. In 1961, he left the firm to become executive assistant to SEC Chairman William Cary. When he returned to

Fried Frank in 1964, Fleischer concentrated on corporate work and was taken under Sam Harris' wing. Fleischer, who became a partner in 1967, is now generally considered just behind Joseph Flom of Skadden Arps and Martin Lipton of Wachtell Lipton in M & A work. Observers respect Fleischer for his low-key manner and integrity as much as for his legal ability. "Fleischer is very good—a first-rate guy and a first-rate mind," says a prominent trial lawyer. "Fleischer is a fine lawyer and a true gentleman," agrees a senior litigator.

A Steering Committee, chaired by Silverman and Robert Preiskel, governs the firm. The full partnership, however, on recommendations from the Compensation Committee, sets partnership shares. Beyond the Steering Committee, Fried Frank has thirteen other permanent committees, including the Associate Committee, the Finance Committee, the Management Committee and the Governance Committee. In addition, the firm recently appointed an Executive Director, Dennis Binder, to handle the firm's administrative work. Individual departments review associates and bring the names of prospective new partners to the Steering Committee. If approved by the Steering Committee, the nominees are put before the whole partnership.

The firm is divided into seven departments: corporate, litigation, real estate, tax, estates and trusts, pension and creditors' rights. Observers give Fried Frank high marks for its quality of lawyers and work in all areas. The firm functions like "a beautiful machine," says a litigator, and calls the experience of working with Fried Frank lawyers "bloodless," impersonal yet perfectly smooth. Beyond Fleischer, observers single out such corporate department standouts as Herbert Galant, Leonard Chazan, Stephen Fraidin, Jean Hanson and Sanford Krieger. In litigation, Silverman is both the most admired and the most controversial figure. "Leon Silverman is one of the best litigators in New York," says one senior litigator; another, however, offers up the more biting "able, but a man almost defined by his affectations." Observers also praise Sheldon Raab in litigation. Franklin Bass heads an outstanding real estate department, while Robert Preiskel leads a tax department called "generally topnotch" by a senior tax lawyer at another leading New York firm. Martin Ginsberg, a brilliant tax mind, is a star in Fried Frank's Washington branch. Herbert Minkel wins kudos in creditors' rights.

Fried Frank has represented investment banking concerns including Goldman, Sachs & Company, Merrill Lynch and Bear, Stearns and Co.; major corporations such as General Electric, GTE Corporation, Philip Morris Companies Inc., Ivan Boesky, Tri-Star Pictures, Procter & Gamble, Burlington Resources and Credit Suisse.

The firm maintains branch offices in Washington (115, 1949), Los Angeles (17, 1986) and London (4, 1970). The Washington branch—under the name Fried, Frank, Harris, Shriver & Kampelman—functions largely independently; it has its own managing partner and committees.

Associates have found Fried Frank a mixed bag. They ranked the firm 12th, 17th and 22nd in, respectively, 1986, 1988 and 1989 *American Lawyer* mid-level associate surveys in New York. On the positive side, Fried Frank has very good offices and support services, offers interesting work—particularly in corporate, less so in litigation—puts little billing pressure on associates and is working to improve its once strained internal relations. Still, "it is a *very* aggressive place," says a headhunter. "There is room and money enough for people to be upwardly mobile. An eclectic group—people think they live there." A legal consultant sums up the firm's negatives for associates: "Fried Frank finds it hard to keep associates because it is downtown, works people very hard and is usually understaffed."

HAWKINS, DELAFIELD & WOOD

67 Wall Street • New York, New York 10005 • (212) 820-9300

Rating: 💼💼💼

Direction: ↓

*LAWYERS

	LAWYERS	PARTNERS	ASSOCIATES
1990:	70	33	34
1989:	108	26	78
1988:	108	26	78
1987:	113	26	84
1986:	112	25	84

	Paralegals	Support
1989:	NA	NA
1988:	NA	NA
1987:	19	103
1986:	25	NA

*LATERAL HIRES
1989: NA
1988: NA
1987: NA
1986: 6

*CHAIRMAN: None

*REPRESENTATIVE CLIENTS:
Municipal Assistance Corporation, Port Authority of New York and New Jersey, PASNY

*BRANCHES: Woodland Hills, California (2), Hartford (1), Newark (1)

*AVERAGE ANNUAL BILLING HOURS:
Partners: NA
Associates: NA

*NUMBER OF WOMEN

	Partners	Associates
1989:	NA	NA
1988:	NA	NA
1987:	1	29
1986:	1	32

*PARTNERSHIP TRACK: NA

*NUMBER OF LAWYERS FROM ENTERING CLASS TO MAKE PARTNER:
1981: NA
1980: NA
1979: NA of 9
1978: 2 of 8

*GROSS REVENUE
1989: NA
1988: NA
1987: NA
1986: NA

*REVENUE PER LAWYER
1989: NA
1988: NA
1987: NA
1986: NA

*PROFITS PER PARTNER
1989: NA
1988: NA
1987: NA
1986: NA

*STARTING ASSOCIATE SALARY
1990: NA
1989: NA
1988: NA
1987: $65,000
1986: $62,000

*PRO BONO: 1–3% of total time

*HOURLY RATES
Partners: NA
Associates: NA

*PRINCIPAL LAW SCHOOLS
(Associates): NA

*NUMBER OF MINORITIES

	Partners	Associates
1989:	NA	NA
1988:	NA	NA
1987:	1	6
1986:	1	6

*SUMMER ASSOCIATES
1989: NA
1988: NA
1987: 12
1986: 20

Hawkins Delafield, as a legal consultant puts it succinctly, "lives and dies with bonds." Seven years ago, when the bond market was solid, Hawkins Delafield was one of New York's most profitable firms. When the bond market went into a downturn in the second half of the 1980s, however, the firm struggled. Financial difficulties brought other latent problems to the surface; the firm was "full of fiefdoms," says a headhunter. "In good times it makes so much money that the inner divisiveness isn't important." The firm lost partners and brought in laterals but made no significant gains. Hawkins Delafield also considered a number of mergers and, although they did not materialize, the firm has partially recovered—"substantively but not substantially," according to a legal consultant. Still, the deals are not there the way they were and pay rates for the firm have not returned to their pre-slump level. The firm has not made *The American Lawyer* list of the top 100 firms nationally in gross revenue, revenue per lawyer or profits per partner between 1986 and 1989.

The firm was founded in 1892 by Eugene Hawkins and Lewis L. Delafield. Louis Auchincloss, who until January 1989 headed the firm's trusts and estates practice and is a prominent figure in American letters (having written twenty-one novels on the Eastern establishment and their law firms), is currently of counsel. His presence continues to attract new business and associates to the firm.

A five- or six-member Executive Committee and co-managing partners Robert Rosenberg and Richard Segal govern the firm. Segal has a strong personality and is therefore a somewhat controversial figure but is also highly respected for his managerial skills.

The firm is divided into six departments: public finance, litigation, banking/real estate, tax, corporate and general securities. Public finance is by far the largest and strongest, while the other practice areas, corporate in particular, service the firm's bond work and offerings. Observers agree that the quality of lawyers and work is skewed toward public finance. The firm's practice is "70-90% in municipal finance and it is extraordinary at that, but not at anything else," says a headhunter. Overall, observers stress the limited, formatted nature of Hawkins Delafield's work. "Not high law, not geniuses," judges a legal consultant.

Hawkins Delafield serves as head counsel to Big MAC—the Municipal Assistance Corporation—the Port Authority of New York and New Jersey and PASNY, the Power Authority of the State of New York. In 1975 and 1976, the firm's involvement (along with other New York firms) in drafting the legislation establishing Big MAC and the related public offering documents, including the trust indenture, bonds, etc. and in fending off lawsuits seeking to invalidate the legislation were critical in keeping New York City out of bankruptcy. In particular, its issuance of an unqualified "no merit" opinion relating to a pending case seeking to declare the Big MAC legislation illegal and unconstitutional was as unusual as it was necessary; without an opinion upon which other lawyers and the business community could rely, no bonds could have been sold, and according to the authorities in the field, there would have been no Big MAC.

The firm maintains branch offices in Hartford, Newark and Woodland Hills, California.

HUGHES HUBBARD & REED

Battery Park Plaza • New York, New York 10004 • (212) 837-6000

Rating: 🗂🗂🗂🗂

Direction: ?

*LAWYERS	PARTNERS	ASSOCIATES
1990: 131	48	105
1989: 178	48	117
1988: 170	49	110
1987: 154	48	98
1986: 120	38	77

	Paralegals	Support
1990:	27	270
1989:	47	327
1988:	49	NA
1987:	31	240
1986:	29	NA

*LATERAL HIRES

1989: 3
1988: 8
1987: NA
1986: 10

*EXECUTIVE DIRECTOR: Charles Scherer

*REPRESENTATIVE CLIENTS:

Bendix Corporation, Merck & Co., Bristol-Myers, Kraft, Hallmark Cards, Inc.

*BRANCHES: Washington (5), Los Angeles (28), Miami (14), Paris (13)
Total: 60 lawyers (23p and 27a)

*AVERAGE ANNUAL BILLING HOURS (1989):

Partners: NA
Associates: 1950

*NUMBER OF WOMEN

	Partners	Associates
1990:	5	34
1989:	5	43
1988:	6	39
1987:	6	32
1986:	5	28

*PARTNERSHIP TRACK: 7–9 years

*NUMBER OF LAWYERS FROM ENTERING CLASS TO MAKE PARTNER:

1981: NA of 20
1980: 1 of 13
1979: 2 of 19
1978: 2 of 19

*GROSS REVENUE

1989: $76,000,000
1988: $71,000,000
1987: $62,000,000
1986: $45,000,000

*REVENUE PER LAWYER

1989: $325,000
1988: $325,000
1987: $295,000
1986: $255,000

*PROFITS PER PARTNER

1989: $330,000
1988: $260,000
1987: $300,000
1986: $275,000

*STARTING ASSOCIATE SALARY

1990: $80,000
1989: $78,000
1988: $76,000
1987: $65,000
1986: $65,000

*PRO BONO: 4% of total time

*HOURLY RATES

Partners: $225–$370
Associates: $115–$225

*PRINCIPAL LAW SCHOOLS (Associates): NYU (12), Harvard (11), Columbia (9), Fordham (8), University of Michigan (7)

*NUMBER OF MINORITIES

	Partners	Associates
1990:	1	8
1989:	1	7
1988:	1	8
1987:	1	5
1986:	0	7

*SUMMER ASSOCIATES

1990: 35
1989: 21
1988: 35
1987: 27
1986: 25

The venerable and distinguished Hughes Hubbard, observers agree, is not the powerful firm it used to be. It has not adapted to profession-wide changes and, as a result, has lost important partners and clients. "People are running out the door," says a senior corporate lawyer. As a headhunter explains, "Hughes Hubbard cares less than enough about money." What is left is a firm with "great" ambience," but says the same headhunter, "too nice for its own good."

The firm's financial results confirm the assessment that Hughes Hubbard had been experiencing a decline. Although in absolute terms the firm's gross revenues and revenue per lawyer had increased, relative to the growth of comparable firms, Hughes Hubbard had actually fallen behind. Between 1987 and 1988, the firm's gross revenues grew from $62,000,000 to $71,000,000, but the firm's ranking within *The American Lawyer* list of top 100 firms fell from 58th to 61st; similarly, revenue per lawyer increased from $295,000 to $325,000, but the firm slipped from 37th to 38th position. The most dramatic evidence of its fiscal woes is its plummeting profits per partner. While profits per partner were $300,000 in 1987, placing the firm 42nd, the numbers nosedived in 1988 to $260,000 and a 73rd place finish. These figures point to high overhead and inadequate management as the root of the firm's problems. It should be noted however, that profits per partner increased from $260,000 in 1988 to $330,000 in 1989 on a $5,000,000 increase in revenue (revenue per lawyer remained steady), suggesting that the firm has begun to operate more efficiently.

Hughes Hubbard was founded in 1872 by Walter Carter as Carter & Russell. Charles Evans Hughes—who went on to serve as governor of New York (1906–1910), associate justice of the Supreme Court (1910–1916), secretary of state (1921–1925) and chief justice of the Supreme Court (1930–1941)—became the firm's lead name partner in 1904. His son, Charles Evans Hughes, Jr., joined the firm in 1916; in 1929, he was named solicitor general of the United States by President Hoover. In 1930, however, he stepped down to allow his father to be appointed to the Supreme Court. Hughes, Jr., and a group of his colleagues left the original firm in 1937 and started Hughes

Hubbard Blair & Reed. The name was shortened to Hughes Hubbard & Reed in 1969. Other distinguished alumni of the firm include Orville Schell, Jr., who served as president of the Association of the Bar of the City of New York, and Amalya Kearse, who in 1969 became the first black partner at a leading New York firm. Currently, Kearse is a judge on the Court of Appeals for the Second Circuit.

A two-partner Management Committee and a seven-partner Firm Committee govern Hughes Hubbard. Prior to 1975, the firm had been managed by an Executive Committee which perpetuated itself. The Management Committee handles the firm's daily operations and, with the Firm Committee, elects members to other firm committees and fixes partner compensation. Jerome Shapiro, the firm's chairman and senior partner since 1975, and managing partner John Fontaine composed the Management Committee until Charles Scherer was selected managing partner commencing June 1, 1989. The entire firm elects new partners from those recommended by each department.

Hughes Hubbard has three major practice areas: litigation, corporate and tax. The firm also has a smaller personal affairs department. Litigators Shapiro, Philip Lacovara (until he left the Washington branch in May 1989) and particularly Robert Sisk receive plaudits from outside sources. In corporate, the standouts are Thomas Schueller, Thomas Gilroy, Edward Davis and Charles Scherer. Observers also single out tax lawyer David Tillingast. The firm has represented such major corporations as Bendix, Merck & Co., Bristol-Myers, Atlantic Richfield, Ford, Hallmark Cards, Inc., Coopers & Lybrand and Kraft. In 1989, Hughes Hubbard lost business from Coopers & Lybrand and Kraft because key partners left the firm and took in-house positions at those corporations.

The firm has offices in Washington, Paris and Miami in addition to the larger, troubled Los Angeles branch. Hughes Hubbard got a head start on most other leading New York firms when it opened its Los Angeles office sixteen years ago. With poor management decisions, bad timing and a lack of focus, however, the firm squandered an opportunity to carve out a leading position; today Hughes Hubbard is on the outside of the Los Angeles–branch boom, looking in.

In 1986 and 1988 *American Lawyer* surveys, Hughes Hubbard associates voiced myriad displeasures with the firm. In 1988, the biggest concern was a paucity of work caused by lost clients. Boredom was a frequent complaint. On the other hand, Hughes Hubbard associates reported working humane hours. Litigators generally had better experiences and received more responsibility than corporate associates. In 1986, when the firm ranked a dismal 38th of 41, associates also complained of inadequate training and murky partnership chances. The 1989 survey, which ranked the firm 28th out of 35, found the firm last in client contact and second to last in compensation (based on hours worked).

JACKSON, LEWIS, SCHNITZLER & KRUPMAN
. . . .
261 Madison Avenue • New York, New York 10016 • (212) 697-8200

Rating: 💼💼💼💼   *Direction:* ↑

*LAWYERS	PARTNERS	ASSOCIATES
1990: 31	14	17
1989: 35	12	23
1988: NA	NA	NA
1987: 27	NA	NA
1986: NA	NA	NA

	Paralegals	Support
1989:	NA	NA
1988:	NA	NA
1987:	NA	NA
1986:	NA	NA

*LATERAL HIRES
1989: 2
1988: 20
1987: NA
1986: NA

*MANAGING PARTNER: William A. Krupman

*REPRESENTATIVE CLIENTS:
Holiday Inns

*BRANCHES: White Plains (21), Atlanta (16), Los Angeles (10), San Francisco (14), Boston (6), Washington (3), Morristown, N.J. (9), Pittsburgh (2), Greenville, S.C. (1), Jericho, N.Y. (2)
Total: 90 lawyers (34p and 56a)

*AVERAGE ANNUAL BILLING HOURS:
Partners: NA
Associates: NA

*NUMBER OF WOMEN
	Partners	Associates
1990:	2	7
1989:	NA	NA
1988:	NA	NA
1987:	NA	NA
1986:	NA	NA

*PARTNERSHIP TRACK: 7 years

*NUMBER OF LAWYERS FROM ENTERING CLASS TO MAKE PARTNER:
1981: NA
1980: NA
1979: NA
1978: NA

*GROSS REVENUE
1989: NA
1988: NA
1987: NA
1986: NA

*REVENUE PER LAWYER
1989: NA
1988: NA
1987: NA
1986: NA

*PROFITS PER PARTNER
1989: NA
1988: NA
1987: NA
1986: NA

*STARTING ASSOCIATE SALARY
1990: $65,000
1989: $60,000
1988: $55,000
1987: NA
1986: NA

*PRO BONO: NA

*HOURLY RATES
Partners: NA
Associates: NA

*PRINCIPAL LAW SCHOOLS
(Associates): Boston University (3), Emory (3), Fordham (3), Albany (3)

*NUMBER OF MINORITIES
	Partners	Associates
1989:	NA	NA
1988:	NA	NA
1987:	NA	NA
1986:	NA	NA

*SUMMER ASSOCIATES
1989: NA
1988: NA
1987: NA
1986: NA

Jackson Lewis can be considered not so much a leading New York law firm as a national firm headquartered in New York. Only 31 of its 121 lawyers are based in New York City. In 1990, the firm had 11 branch offices: White Plains (21, 1981), Atlanta (16, 1978), Los Angeles (10, 1977), San Francisco (14, 1978), Boston (6, 1986), Washington (3, 1981), Morristown, N.J. (9, 1988), Greenville, S.C. (1, 1983) and Chicago (4, 1989). In 1990 Jackson Lewis opened a Pittsburgh office (2) and relocated the Woodbury, Long Island branch to Jericho, Long Island (2).

The firm's practice is limited to labor and employment law and litigation on behalf of management. Observers think highly of the firm's work in these areas, although some are put off by its reputation as union-busters. A headhunter calls the firm "the best of its ilk." "With Proskauer it has the best labor practice in the business," seconds a senior corporate lawyer. "Nakedly aggressive in the labor field," says a litigator with a hint of admiration. "The Pancho Villa of the field."

There are observers who believe the firm is highly lucrative, particularly for its size, although Jackson Lewis was not on *The American Lawyer* list of top 100 firms nationally for gross revenue, revenue per lawyer or profits per partner; one legal consultant places its profits per partner in the $215,000 range.

Louis Jackson and Robert Lewis founded the firm in New York in 1958. William Krupman is the firm's managing partner. The partnership has three tiers. The Compensation Committee sets partnership draws.

Top to bottom, observers describe Jackson Lewis' lawyers as hard-nosed and knowledgable. "They know what they're doing," says a litigator. Other sources use more picturesque language. "They're killers," says a senior corporate lawyer. "If you want to play dirty, you go there," notes a headhunter. While it is difficult to obtain information on individual stars, it appears that Elise Bloom is one of the firm's up-and-coming young partners.

Jackson Lewis handles labor disputes for such clients as Holiday Inns.

For associates, the firm demands geographic flexibility. "Jackson Lewis needs independent aggressive people who are willing to change cities," says a headhunter.

KAYE, SCHOLER, FIERMAN, HAYS & HANDLER

• •

425 Park Avenue • New York, New York 10022 • (212) 836-8000

Rating: 💼💼💼💼💼 2.16

Direction: ↑

*LAWYERS	PARTNERS	ASSOCIATES
	93	201
1990: 287	89	192
1989: 281	86	176
1988: 278	79	181
1987: 272	74	180
1986: 275	75	175

	Paralegals	Support
1990:	65	433
1989:	65	447
1988:	NA	NA
1987:	42	525
1986:	50	NA

*LATERAL HIRES

1989: 11
1988: 19
1987: NA
1986: 17

*MANAGING PARTNER: ~~Peter M. Fishbein~~ FREDRIC W. YERMAN

*REPRESENTATIVE CLIENTS:

GTE Corporation, Pfizer Inc., Xerox Corporation, General Foods, Drummond Company, Chemical Bank, Marine Midland

*BRANCHES: Washington (29), Los Angeles (33), Hong Kong (4)
Total: 66 lawyers (15p and 51a)

*AVERAGE ANNUAL BILLING HOURS (1989):

Partners: NA
Associates: 1910

*NUMBER OF WOMEN

	Partners	Associates
1990:	14	67
1989:	13	51
1988:	10	54
1987:	7	60
1986:	6	43

*PARTNERSHIP TRACK: 8 years

*NUMBER OF LAWYERS FROM ENTERING CLASS TO MAKE PARTNER:

1981: 2 of 31
1980: 7 of 28
1979: 4 of 35
1978: 1 of 22

*GROSS REVENUE

1989: $188,000,000
1988: $147,000,000
1987: $109,000,000
1986: $100,000,000

*REVENUE PER LAWYER
1990 660 ???
1989: $550,000
1988: $450,000
1987: $370,000
1986: $340,000

*PROFITS PER PARTNER

1989: $685,000
1988: $640,000
1987: $480,000
1986: $395,000

*STARTING ASSOCIATE SALARY

1990: $83,000
1989: $82,000
1988: $77,000
1987: $65,000
1986: $65,000

*PRO BONO: 2% of total time

*HOURLY RATES

Partners: NA
Associates: NA

*PRINCIPAL LAW SCHOOLS (Associates): NYU (27), Fordham (13), Yeshiva (12), University of Pennsylvania (10), Columbia (9), Georgetown (9)

*NUMBER OF MINORITIES

	Partners	Associates
1990:	0	9
1989:	0	7
1988:	0	9
1987:	1	5
1986:	1	13

*SUMMER ASSOCIATES
1990: 47
1989: 36
1988: 35
1987: 37
1986: 36

Kaye Scholer was built on the foundation of its towering litigation department. To this day, despite largely successful efforts at diversification, the firm's identity remains strongly linked to that one practice area. Though "one of the great Jewish firms," as a senior litigator phrases it, over the years Kay Scholer has broadened its client and lawyer base while concurrently cultivating the growing and prosperous Orthodox Jewish community. A period of high turnover and rocky internal relations seem to be the firm's only significant problems. As a former house counsel summarizes, Kaye Scholer is "well-managed, aggressive, growing and growing well."

The firm's financial picture reflects this assessment. Between 1986 and 1989, Kay Scholer's gross revenue, revenue per lawyer and profits per partner all grew steadily, and the firm moved up within *The American Lawyer* list of top 100 firms nationally in all three categories. In 1989 its gross revenue of $188,000,000 placed it 17th in the nation; its revenue per lawyer of $555,000, 8th; and its profits per partner of $685,000, 15th.

The firm was founded in 1917 by banking lawyers Benjamin Kaye and Jacob Scholer. Litigator Harold Fierman joined the firm in 1919 and James Hays joined in 1925. Milton Handler, a professor at Columbia Law School, joined the firm in 1951. The present name of the firm was adopted in 1956.

A nine-member Executive Committee, elected by a two-thirds vote of the full partnership for staggered three-year terms, manages Kaye Scholer. The Executive Committee offers recommendations for the selection of additional partners which are then voted on by the entire partnership on a one-partner, one-vote basis. The Committee also decides partner and associate compensation, the latter on the basis of suggestions made by the Personnel Committee. The Committee chooses a chairman annually; from 1983 until the end of 1990 it had been Peter Fishbein, who observers believe did a particularly outstanding job. No member of the Executive Committee can be over 65 years of age.

The firm is divided into seven departments: corporate/finance, litigation/anti-trust, real estate, tax, bankruptcy, labor and trusts and estates.

When Milton Handler, perhaps the nation's preeminent antitrust practitioner, substantially reduced his workload in the early 1980s, Kay Scholer's litigation department lost, in the words of a prominent trial lawyer, "a monument." Nevertheless, Kaye Scholer remains best known and regarded for its litigation and is not short on litigators of substantial talent and standing. Observers single out Fishbein, Stanley Robinson, Michael Malina, Sheldon Oliensis and Paul Curran, former U.S. attorney for the Southern District of New York. In recent years, the department has represented GTE Corporation, Pfizer Inc. and Equitable Life Assurance Society of the United States in important matters. Robinson, also and most notably, led the firm's successful representation of Xerox Corporation in a $1.5 billion law suit brought by SCM Corporation in 1981. The only major blot on Kaye Scholer's litigation record is the firm's disastrous representation of Texaco in its dispute with Pennzoil.

The corporate department, headed by Sidney Silberman, has roughly forty fewer lawyers than the litigation department and is not viewed as being on quite the same level. "The leaders of the corporate departments are a little too old," comments a legal consultant. Clients include General Foods, U.S. Home Corporation and Drummond Company. Stanley Waxberg leads the banking and finance branch of the corporate department, which does work for such clients as Chemical Bank, Bankers' Trust, Marine Midland, National Westminister Bank USA, CIT, Security Pacific, Rosenthal & Rosenthal and Congress Financial Corp. The firm first gained entry into the institutional lending and bank business when it acquired Dodge Salzberg & Waxberg in 1962. Observers single out Stuart Marks, Fred Fishman and Bernard Nimkin as the firm's corporate standouts.

Martin Saiman's real estate department represents, among others, the Canadian Olympia & York Developments, Ltd., a major commercial developer in the United States. This department has been hurt by the recent defections of several key partners, particularly that of Martin Baron.

In 1980 the firm lost almost its entire tax and bankruptcy departments because of disputes concerning conflicting policy considerations. The firm attempted to fill the void through lateral acquisitions of "dubious quality" say sources. "It brought in people by reputation, not ability," says a tax lawyer. Although observers laud individuals such as the outstanding Harvey Strickson in bankruptcy, most agree that neither department as a whole fully recouped. However, in July 1990 the firm acquired Michael Crames and four other lawyers from a small but prominent bankruptcy firm and thereby solved one of its problems. In the mid-1980s William Borchard, who had headed the trademark, copyright and intellectual property department left the firm, thus damaging a small but prestigious practice.

Two well-known lawyers, Stanley Fuld and Abraham Ribicoff, are of counsel to the firm. Fuld had been chief judge of the Court of Appeals until his retirement in 1974. Ribicoff was a senator from Connecticut for eighteen years until 1981. Wilfred Feinberg, chief judge of the United States Court of Appeals for the Second Circuit, and Barbara Thomas, a former SEC commissioner, are notable alumni of the firm.

The firm recently has expanded its relatively small Washington and Palm Beach offices by opening offices in Los Angeles and Hong Kong, both of which appear to be successful and successfully managed. Kenneth Fierman, a specialist in Agent Orange product liability litigation, was a founding partner of the D.C. office and is its star.

Kaye Scholer's associates placed the firm in the middle of the pack in 1986 and 1988 *American Lawyer* surveys of New York firms but dropped it to near the bottom in the 1989 survey. Interrelations are continually a sore spot. The firm is "less personal" than many leading firms, says a former house counsel, and "harsh at times, even acidic." "Neurotic," adds a headhunter, "a little nasty." The same headhunter characterizes the typical Kaye Scholer associate as a "smart loser." More positively, observers note that Kaye Scholer associates are not particularly overworked and receive good training and high levels of responsibility and autonomy. "People leave because of numbers, not because of poor treatment," summarizes another headhunter.

KELLEY DRYE & WARREN

101 Park Avenue • New York, New York 10178 • (212) 808-7800

Rating: 💼💼💼💼

Direction: ?

*LAWYERS

	LAWYERS	PARTNERS	ASSOCIATES
1990:	223	NA	NA
1989:	225	69	151
1988:	204	67	133
1987:	190	NA	NA
1986:	174	NA	NA

	Paralegals	Support
1990:	NA	NA
1989:	23	280
1988:	57	NA
1987:	41	NA
1986:	37	NA

*LATERAL HIRES

1989: 5
1988: 4
1987: NA
1986: 25

*MANAGING PARTNER: H. Thomas Davis, Jr.

*REPRESENTATIVE CLIENTS:

L.A. Gear, Manufacturers Hanover Trust, Bacardi Corporation, Greyhound Financial Corporation, Union Carbide Corporation, Exxon Corporation

*BRANCHES: Washington (38), Los Angeles (35), Miami (54), Chicago (10), Stamford (27), Parsippany, N.J. (2) Total: 165 lawyers (NAp and NAa)

*AVERAGE ANNUAL BILLING HOURS (1988):

Partners: NA
Associates: 2000

*NUMBER OF WOMEN

	Partners	Associates
1990:	8	94
1989:	6	67
1988:	6	62
1987:	NA	NA
1986:	NA	NA

*PARTNERSHIP TRACK: 8 years

*NUMBER OF LAWYERS FROM ENTERING CLASS TO MAKE PARTNER:

1981: 6 of 20
1980: 3 of 18
1979: 4 of 15
1978: 3 of 12

*GROSS REVENUE

1989: $112,500,000
1988: $92,000,000
1987: $79,000,000
1986: $58,000,000

*REVENUE PER LAWYER

1989: $300,000
1988: $285,000
1987: $260,000
1986: $280,000

*PROFITS PER PARTNER

1989: $365,000
1988: $375,000
1987: $250,000
1986: $360,000

*STARTING ASSOCIATE SALARY

1990: $83,000
1989: $76,000
1988: $71,000
1987: $65,000
1986: $64,000

*PRO BONO: 1–3% of total time

*HOURLY RATES

Partners: $178–$325
Associates: $85–$200

*PRINCIPAL LAW SCHOOLS (Associates): Fordham (27), Boston University (12), New York Law School (11), St. John's (11)

*NUMBER OF MINORITIES

	Partners	Associates
1990:	11	20
1989:	3	7
1988:	3	5
1987:	NA	NA
1986:	NA	NA

*SUMMER ASSOCIATES

1990: 45
1989: 34
1988: 52
1987: NA
1986: NA

Kelley Drye, through lateral acquisitions and geographic expansion, became the tenth largest firm in New York in 1988. The quality of the firm, however, has not kept pace with its quantity: the expansion has seemingly passed the point of diminishing returns. "Kelley Drye is acquiring for the sake getting larger," says a legal consultant. "It is not a quality firm." Some observers believe that, in expanding, the firm has become indiscriminate and amoral. "They're adventurers, opportunists," says a prominent litigator. Others think Kelley Drye merely suffers from a lack of respect in the legal community, a natural phenomenom for a new kid on the block. "It's a mystery," says a former house counsel. "Everybody there is nice, they do excellent work, but they never pop up when I think of outstanding firms."

Financially, the increase in lawyers has yielded a proportionate increase in gross revenue, which grew from $58,000,000 to $92,000,000 between 1986 and 1988, causing Kelley Drye to move up in *The American Lawyer* rankings in this category, from 53rd place to 44th. More importantly, however, the firm has seen minimal advances in revenue per lawyer (from $280,000 to $285,000) and profits per partner (from $360,000 to $375,000)—and this only after a disastrous 1987 in which the firm actually lost ground—and slipped in the rankings in both categories. Kelley Drye placed 32nd in revenue per lawyer in 1986; the firm placed 65th in 1988. Similarly, the firm ranked 24th in profits per partner in 1986; by 1988, Kelley Drye had dropped to 33rd. In 1989 revenue increased to $112,500,000 from $92,000,000 in 1988, while profits per partner dropped from $375,000 to $365,000. Thus, while Kelley Drye has a lot more lawyers, it is getting a lot less out of them.

Hiram Barney, a personal friend of President Lincoln, and litigator William Minott Mitchell founded the firm in 1841. Mitchell died soon after and was replaced by William Allen Butler, who later brought in the account of the Central Trust Company, which evolved into the Hanover Bank. Since the merger of Hanover Bank with Manufacturers Trust Company in 1961, the firm has represented the trust division of Manufacturers Hanover Trust Company. Nicholas Kelley, a former Cravath associate who had been the assistant secretary of the treasury (1920–1921), joined the firm in 1921. Kelley initiated the firm's association with Chrysler Corporation which continued until the company's refinancing in the early 1980s, at which time Chrysler moved much of its business to Debevoise & Plimpton. Tax lawyer John Drye, Jr. started at Kelley at the associate level in 1920, was made a partner in 1930 and a name partner in 1943. The final name partner, Louis Warren, came to the firm in 1930, made partner in 1940 and became a name partner in 1962. Warren also enjoyed the unusual distinction of being an honorary fellow at Trinity College, Oxford, and was awarded both the French Legion of Honor (1971) and Commander of the British Empire (1972).

A five-member Executive Committee, elected annually on a one-partner, one-vote principle, governs the firm. Chaired by administrative partner H. Thomas Davis, Jr., this committee handles the firm's daily operations and staffs the firm's other committees. The three-member Partner Profit Distribution Percentage Committee, appointed annually by the Executive Committee, makes up a profit schedule which can be vetoed by fifty or more votes weighted according to draws of the preceding year. The ten-member Attorneys Committee nominates associates for partnership; those who receive more than seventy weighted votes become partners. These decisions, however, are usually made by consensus.

The firm is divided into seven departments: litigation, corporate, real estate, tax, employee benefits, labor and personal services. Observers did not single out any individuals but readily offered generalizations on Kelley Drye's work product. Litigators are the most critical; one calls Kelley Drye's litigation work "very pedestrian," another, "mediocre at best." Nonetheless, a legal consultant views its defense of Union Carbide in the Bhopal incident, and other corporate defense work to be outstanding. The firm's most significant litigators are Bud Holman and Robert Ehrenbard. In the corporate department— called "heavy-handed" by a corporate lawyer at another leading New York firm—the key figures are Terrance Schwab and Leland Markley. Nonetheless, a legal consultant believes it has a strong international capacity.

Kelley Drye represents such diverse interests as L.A. Gear,

Manufacturers Hanover Trust, Bacardi Corporation, Greyhound Financial Corporation, Sterling Drug Inc., New York Hospital and Union Carbide Corporation—which the firm represented in an infamous product liability case—as well as the embattled Exxon Corporation.

The firm maintains branch offices in Miami (54, 1982), Washington (38, 1981), Los Angeles (35, 1984), Stamford (27, 1979), Chicago (10, 1988), and Parsippany, N.J. (1, 1989).

Mid-level associates have ranked Kelley Drye second to last in two consecutive *American Lawyer* polls of New York firms. In 1986, the firm placed 40th among 41 firms. Associates complained about being left in the dark about their partnership chances and few expected to be with the firm for the long term. By 1988, when the firm placed 36th of 37, associates' problems had become more diverse and specific. The firm offered plenty of responsibility but too little guidance and structure. The office space and support services were inadequate. The lone positive point was Kelley Drye's relaxed yet active atmosphere. However, in 1989, with perceived improvement in training and guidance and a modest increase in the interest level of associates' work and better treatment by partners, the firm moved from 36th to 6th place. Nonetheless, associates unfavorably view the firm's lack of support for *pro bono* work, including their receiving no credit for that work toward compliance with a firm policy instituted in 1988 which requires a minimum of 2,000 annual billable hours and provides a $2,000 bonus for every 100 hours of billable time beyond the minimum.

KRAMER, LEVIN, NESSEN, KAMIN & FRANKEL
· ·
919 Third Avenue · New York, New York 10022 · (212) 715-9100

Rating: 🖤🖤🖤🖤

Direction:?

*LAWYERS

	LAWYERS	PARTNERS	ASSOCIATES
1990:	140	45	91
1989:	129	43	81
1988:	126	43	77
1987:	114	43	66
1986:	111	40	67

	Paralegals	Support
1990:	33	217
1989:	40	218
1988:	34	NA
1987:	33	189
1986:	28	NA

*LATERAL HIRES
1989: 23
1988: 14
1987: NA
1986: 15

*MANAGING PARTNER: Geoffrey M. Kalmus

*REPRESENTATIVE CLIENTS:
MCI, Liz Claiborne, Gibbons Green, Maxxam

*BRANCHES: None

*AVERAGE ANNUAL BILLING HOURS (1989):
Partners: NA
Associates: 1750

*NUMBER OF WOMEN

	Partners	Associates
1990:	3	34
1989:	2	36
1988:	2	36
1987:	2	32
1986:	2	29

*PARTNERSHIP TRACK: 8.5 years

*NUMBER OF LAWYERS FROM ENTERING CLASS TO MAKE PARTNER:
1981: 1 of 12
1980: 1 of 11
1979: 3 of 3
1978: 4 of 10

*GROSS REVENUE
1989: NA
1988: NA
1987: NA
1986: NA

*REVENUE PER LAWYER
1989: NA
1988: NA
1987: NA
1986: NA

*PROFITS PER PARTNER
1989: NA
1988: NA
1987: NA
1986: NA

*STARTING ASSOCIATE SALARY
1990: $83,000
1989: $80,000
1988: $77,000
1987: $65,000
1986: $65,000

*PRO BONO: 2–4% of total time

*HOURLY RATES (1989)
Partners: $235–$400
Associates: $115–$230

*PRINCIPAL LAW SCHOOLS
(Associates): NYU (23), Harvard (15), Columbia (11), Fordham (5)

*NUMBER OF MINORITIES

	Partners	Associates
1990:	0	0
1989:	0	2
1988:	0	3
1987:	0	1
1986:	0	1

*SUMMER ASSOCIATES
1990: 14
1989: 13
1988: 16
1987: 12
1986: 12

Kramer Levin, founded in 1968, is a relative newcomer to the ranks of leading New York firms. Observers seem to be struggling to define it. One leading litigator calls Kramer Levin "good but strange"; a legal consultant generalizes that it is "a mid-size firm trying to decide its direction." Kramer Levin is indisputably a child of its generation, perceived predominantly on cultural and psychological (rather than professional) terms. It is, as a headhunter puts it, the "touch me–feel me firm," complete with in-house psychologist ever at the ready to mediate internal disputes.

These distinctions aside, however, institutional clients have eluded the firm, and therefore, predictably, Kramer Levin's financial picture remains cloudy. The firm was not among the top 100 firms nationally, according to *The American Lawyer*, in gross revenues, revenue per lawyer or profits per partner from 1986 to 1989.

Since its founding in 1968 by Arthur Kramer, Sherwin Kamin, Maurice Nessen and Louis Lowenstein, the firm has had five name changes before adopting its current one in 1984. From 1971 to 1977, when former Nassau County executive Eugene Nickerson was a partner, his was the lead name in the firm. Nickerson was appointed as a federal judge of the Eastern District of New York in 1977. Ezra Levin, a former partner at the now dissolved firm of Marshall Bratter, joined the firm in 1980; Marvin Frankel, a former federal judge of the U.S. District Court for the Southern District of New York, joined the firm in 1983. Messrs. Kramer and Nessen are former U.S. attorneys for the Southern District of New York as is litigator Gary Naftalis.

The firm's governance is unusually democratic. There is no executive committee and, with the exception of partner compensation, all major issues, including the selection of new partners, are voted on by the whole partnership on a one-lawyer, one-vote principle. There are no formally designated committee or department heads. The full partnership elects the Committee on Committees, which recommends members to other firm committees, and the Compensation Committee, which decides partner compensation. The Compensation Committee bases its decisions on each partner's seniority, reputation, business generation, and participation in management and training. The firm circulates information about each partner's billings and hours billed to all partners and then interviews them individually about the proposed compensation schedule. All partners are provided with copies of the final schedule. Kramer Levin's governance specifically protects against outdated and unbalanced management. Both committees must include a partner less than fifteen years out of law school and each year the two members of each committee who have served the longest must step down. Geoffrey Kalmus acts as the firm's managing partner, in effect its chief operating officer.

Kramer Levin also delegates an unsually large amount of administrative power and responsiblity to associates. Two associates and four partners comprise the Operations Committee, which oversees day-to-day matters. Associates also choose their own representatives for other firm committees—only the Recruiting Committee excludes associates. Typically, Kramer Levin's partners evaluate its associates; untypically, associates, in turn, evaluate partners on the basis of assignments, feedback and overall treatment. The partners review these evaluations at their annual fall retreat.

The firm is divided into nine practice areas: litigation, corporate, real estate, creditors' rights, tax, employee benefits, labor and employment, trusts and estates and public finance. In the litigation department, Kramer and Frankel, says a former house counsel, "are the players." Beyond them, Naftalis—who joined the firm in 1981 and has significantly expanded its white-collar practice—Charlotte Fishman and Ellen Nadler garner plaudits. Levin and Paul Schreiber, a lateral hire in 1982, are the standouts in corporate. The corporate department represents such clients as MCI, Gibbons, Green and Liz Claiborne. Observers praise creditors' rights head Joel Zweibel and his department, which was established in 1981 when Zweibel came to Kramer Levin. (In 1990 he left to join a larger firm.) "They do very good work there," says a bankruptcy lawyer. Real estate and tax appear to be the firm's sore spots. According to a key real estate lawyer at another leading New York firm, Kramer Levin is consistently losing its real estate people and those who remain "don't know how to close deals properly." Observers also say that since Kamin retired, the tax department has not been as strong.

Kramer Levin has no branch offices as such. The firm did, however, create an international precedent by joining forces with a Parisian firm in 1982. The hybrid firm, called Kramer, Levin, Cohn & Klein, was the first domestic French firm to gain permission to enter such a venture with a foreign affiliate.

Associates at Kramer Levin, say several sources, either "love it or hate it." The associates themselves ranked the firm 29th of 41 in a 1986 *American Lawyer* survey of New York firms. One associate summarized the firm's deficiencies by saying, "Kramer Levin is living off a reputation that is no longer accurate. As each year passes, the firm becomes more like all the other large firms except that it has trouble attracting large firm clients and thus offering associates quality work.'" In the 1988 survey, the firm placed 35th out of 37 firms, rising to 24th out of 35 firms in the 1989 survey. The problem is not overwork, however; as a senior corporate lawyer says with some hyperbole, Kramer Levin lawyers "don't work that hard because they have no clients." On the other hand, Kramer Levin is "a place where you make partner on merit," according to a headhunter and, as associates are involved in administering the firm's operations, they have a larger impact on the firm.

LeBoeuf, Lamb, Leiby & MacRae

520 Madison Avenue • New York, New York 10022 • (212) 715-8000

Rating: 🧳🧳🧳🧳

Direction: ↔

*LAWYERS	PARTNERS	ASSOCIATES	
1990: 211	73	126	1.13
1989: 230	74	144	
1988: 226	72	144	
1987: 207	68	127	
1986: 207	64	109	

	Paralegals	Support
1990:	80	314
1989:	76	332
1988:	NA	NA
1987:	86	261
1986:	85	NA

*LATERAL HIRES
1989: 8
1988: 5
1987: NA
1986: 12

*MANAGING PARTNER: Donald J. Greene

*REPRESENTATIVE CLIENTS:
Lloyd's of London, ITT, Aetna, Bradford National, Bay State Gas, Niagara Mohawk Power

*BRANCHES: Washington (45), Los Angeles (20), Raleigh (20), Salt Lake City (17), San Francisco (18), Newark (18), Brussels (6), Others (29)—Albany, Harrisburg, Hartford, Jacksonville, London
Total: 173 lawyers (NAp and NAa)

*AVERAGE ANNUAL BILLING HOURS:
Partners: NA
Associates: NA

*NUMBER OF WOMEN

	Partners	Associates
1990:	8	53
1989:	5	65
1988:	6	56
1987:	7	45
1986:	6	38

*PARTNERSHIP TRACK: 8 years

*NUMBER OF LAWYERS FROM ENTERING CLASS TO MAKE PARTNER:
1981: 5 of 11
1980: 2 of 10
1979: 7 of 13
1978: 7 of 10

*GROSS REVENUE
1989: $117,000,000
1988: $109,500,000
1987: $93,000,000
1986: $71,500,000

*REVENUE PER LAWYER
1989: $330,000
1988: $300,000
1987: $270,000
1986: $255,000

*PROFITS PER PARTNER
1989: $305,000
1988: $285,000
1987: $250,000
1986: $255,000

*STARTING ASSOCIATE SALARY
1990: $83,000
1989: $76,000
1988: $71,000
1987: $65,000
1986: $65,000

*PRO BONO: 4–7% of total time

*HOURLY RATES (1989)
Partners: $210–$300
Associates: $95–$200

*PRINCIPAL LAW SCHOOLS (Associates): NYU (18), Brooklyn (8), Yale (7)

*NUMBER OF MINORITIES

	Partners	Associates
1990:	0	17
1989:	0	17
1988:	0	15
1987:	0	9
1986:	0	8

*SUMMER ASSOCIATES
1990: 25
1989: 23
1988: 25
1987: 33
1986: 34

LeBoeuf Lamb began with a bang. It was founded by Randall J. LeBoeuf, Jr., on October 9, 1929—the day of the Wall Street stock crash. Although the firm initially depended on an extensive utilities and energy practice, in recent times LeBoeuf's bread and butter has come from its insurance work. Indeed, one headhunter describes the firm as "driven by its insurance practice." LeBoeuf's lopsided growth has disappointed many observers and created stark divisions within the firm. "LeBoeuf is actually four firms under one name," observes a legal consultant. "Each could split off, there is no crossover."

After its somewhat dubious start, it took LeBoeuf another three decades to take off. In 1959, Randall LeBoeuf was named special assistant attorney general representing New York in the Great Lake diversion dispute, which pitted the lake states against the Mississippi River states in a battle over how much water could be diverted through the Chicago Drainage Canal. LeBoeuf was a logical choice as he previously had served as assistant attorney general in the 1920s under Lake States special counsel Newton Baker, Woodrow Wilson's secretary of war. This tangle took over a decade to resolve and throughout LeBoeuf, retained by New York, enjoyed a period of high profitability.

In the late 1970s, despite the deaths of LeBoeuf and other name partners Horace Lamb and Adrian Leiby (as well as the virtual retirement of Cameron MacRae), the firm experienced another boom. This time, LeBoeuf Lamb rode a wave of government regulation in each of its three major specialties—utilities, energy and insurance. The firm cemented its growth by acquiring Reed, McCarthy and Giordano, thus creating a practice in municipal bond underwriting. During this period and shortly thereafter LeBoeuf also opened a host of small branch offices, being the first leading New York firm to do so under the innovative leadership of Taylor Briggs. Currently, the firm maintains a relatively large office in Washington, D.C. (1952) and smaller ones in London (1978), Boston (1981), Salt Lake City (1981), Southport, Connecticut (1982), Raleigh (1982), San Francisco (1983) and Jacksonville (1987).

The firm's expansion, however, may have gone awry. According to *The American Lawyer*, while the number of lawyers has ballooned from 281 in 1986 to 362 in 1988—a leap of approximately 29%—profits per partner in the same period have grown only from $255,000 to $285,000, an increase of 12%. One legal consultant says flatly that LeBoeuf is "not well-managed . . . and takes in marginal people. It is not picking off good laterals." Certainly, the financial data suggests that Le-Boeuf fails to get as much mileage from its lawyers as do firms comparable in size. Although the firm was the 7th largest in size in New York in 1988, its gross revenues of $109,500,000 ranked 18th in the country. In 1989, when the firm was 12th in size, its gross revenue of $117,000,000 placed it 40th in the country. These ratios prompt another consultant to label LeBoeuf "not a healthy law firm."

LeBoeuf is formally divided into six departments: corporate, utilities/energy, insurance, litigation, tax and trusts and estates. In large measure, litigation and corporate service the utility/ energy and insurance departments.

The firm received its first insurance work from Lloyd's of London in 1965 when a lateral partner (who left LeBoeuf in 1968) brought the business with him from Mendes & Mount. Recently, under Donald Greene's leadership, the firm has expanded into many related areas: finance transactions for insurance company clients and for investment bankers dealing with insurance company clients; M & A transactions involving different types of insurance companies; insolvencies; reinsurance arbitration; coverage and policy disputes; and defense of medical malpractice.

Greene pioneered the firm's insurance boom as the head of that department and is LeBoeuf's premier business originator. In 1986, it is believed that he contributed $12.6 million in billings, more than triple that of the partner with the next highest total. Beyond Greene, observers did not spotlight any individual LeBoeuf lawyer. One headhunter called them, as a group, "benign," then opted for a harsher generalization, "mediocre."

While Lloyd's appears to be the firm's largest client, LeBoeuf represents a number of other significant companies: Aetna, Bradford National, Bay State Gas, Delmarva Power & Light, ITT, Medical Liability Mutual Insurance Company, Niagara

Mohawk Power Corp., Panhandle Eastern Pipeline Company and Teachers Insurance and Annuity Association of America.

The firm is managed by a triumvirate of the Administrative Committee, the Council and the full partnership. The Administrative Committee is made up of five partners who oversee day-to-day operations. The Council recommends candidates for partner; its recommendations customarily have been adopted by the entire partnership. The Council also suggests partnership shares.

Associates at LeBoeuf praise its relaxed, pleasant atmosphere and pace, yet note that this can be a double-edged sword. The firm's lack of structure left 1987 summer associates looking for challenges and 1988 mid-level associates bemoaning a scarcity of guidance. Associates in 1988 also noted a dearth of non-insurance-related litigation, which again points out the firm's division into specialty factions. LeBoeuf remains what one head-hunter calls a "lovely, decent firm" but, despite an increasing concern for billable hours, not the place for hard-nosed ambition.

LORD DAY & LORD, BARRETT SMITH

1675 Broadway • New York, New York 10019 • (212) 969-6000

Rating: 💼💼💼💼   *Direction:* ?

*LAWYERS	PARTNERS	ASSOCIATES
1990: 184	60	118
1989: 166	56	102
1988: 167	NA	NA
1987: 123	NA	NA
1986: 121	NA	NA

	Paralegals	Support
1990:	45	270
1989:	42	268
1988:	44	NA
1987:	NA	NA
1986:	20	NA

*LATERAL HIRES

1989: 7
1988: 14
1987: NA
1986: 6

CHAIRMAN: Henry deForest Baldwin

*REPRESENTATIVE CLIENTS:

American Stock Exchange, New York
Times Company, Lloyd's of London, Morgan
Guaranty, U.S. Air, Chemical Bank, City of
New York

*BRANCHES: Washington (10), London (2)
Total: 12 lawyers (5p and 7a)

*AVERAGE ANNUAL BILLING
HOURS (1989):
Partners: NA
Associates: 1850

*NUMBER OF WOMEN

	Partners	Associates
1990:	6	48
1989:	7	40
1988:	NA	NA
1987:	NA	NA
1986:	NA	NA

*PARTNERSHIP TRACK: 8 years

*NUMBER OF LAWYERS FROM ENTERING
CLASS TO MAKE PARTNER:

1981: 1 of 21
1980: 4 of 27
1979: 3 of 23
1978: 4 of 34

*GROSS REVENUE
1989: NA
1988: NA
1987: NA
1986: NA

*REVENUE PER LAWYER
1989: NA
1988: NA
1987: NA
1986: NA

*PROFITS PER PARTNER
1989: NA
1988: NA
1987: NA
1986: NA

*STARTING ASSOCIATE
SALARY
1990: $82,000
1989: $77,000
1988: $76,000
1987: NA
1986: $65,000

*PRO BONO: 4% of total time

*HOURLY RATES
Partners: NA
Associates: NA

PRINCIPAL LAW SCHOOLS
(Associates): Columbia,
Fordham, Georgetown, Hofstra,
NYU

*NUMBER OF MINORITIES

	Partners	Associates
1990:	3	7
1989:	3	5
1988:	NA	NA
1987:	NA	NA
1986:	NA	NA

*SUMMER ASSOCIATES
1990: 32
1989: 25
1988: 33
1987: NA
1986: NA

Lord Day & Lord, Barrett Smith is an old-line white shoe firm that has attempted to thicken the blood and spur financial growth through lateral acquisitions and mergers. "Lord Day brought in people with real specialties," says a headhunter. "They bring in outsiders for business." The fact that Lord Day failed to make *The American Lawyer* list of top 100 firms nationally in gross revenues, revenue per lawyer or profits per partner between 1986 and 1989 reflects the need for this policy. Opinions differ as to its success. For example, a legal consultant calls Lord Day's 1988 acquisition of 60 lawyers from the dividing Barrett, Smith, Shapiro, Simon & Armstrong firm "a merger of two weak firms" while a senior corporate lawyer calls it "a good marriage."

Daniel Lord founded the firm in 1817. Its name was institutionalized in 1848, when the senior Lord's son Daniel Lord, Jr. and son-in-law Henry Day joined. Early on, the firm established a strong trusts and estates practice. The corporate practice did not take off until the 1950s, when Lord Day represented Robert Young against the Vanderbilts in his fight for control of the New York Central Railroad. After World War II, Herbert Brownell—though his tenure with the firm was interrupted by his stint as U.S. attorney general in the Eisenhower administration—was the firm's best-known lawyer. The New York Times Company was the firm's most significant client; that relationship largely ended in 1971 when the firm refused to defend the paper in the Pentagon Papers case. By the 1970s, Lord Day had sunk into a gentlemanly lethargy; senior and near-senior partners averaged between 1,500 and 1,600 billable hours per year. The firm relied almost exclusively on inherited institutional business.

A four-member Executive Committee elected annually governs Lord Day. Its members can serve unlimited numbers of consecutive terms but cannot serve over age 65. The committee's chairman is typically chosen according to seniority. The Executive Committee sets partnership shares based on performance and business generation; all partners receive information about the schedule chosen. The Executive Committee also staffs the firm's other committees, which include the Hiring Committee, Management Committee, Personnel Committee and

Planning Committee. New partners are admitted by the full partnership upon the recommendations of the Executive and Personnel Committees. The full partnership also decides associate salaries.

The firm is divided into eight departments: corporate, litigation, real estate, tax, labor, executive compensation, trusts and estates and environmental, the strongest of which is litigation. John Castles, Michael Armstrong and John Gordan are among Lord Day's outstanding litigators. The firm has acquired many of its stronger lawyers laterally but has also sustained serious losses by this route. "The tax department fell apart," says a tax partner at another leading New York firm. "People left." The most important loss for Lord Day, however, occurred when anti-trust star Gordon Spivak and "his" associates left for Coudert Brothers in late 1986 because the firm could not find an acceptable way to integrate his highly profitable specialty within the firm or to promote senior associates. Before Spivak departed, his spirited dispute with Lord Day undermined the firm's chance to merge with the real estate firm of Tufo & Zuccoti, which subsequently was acquired by Brown & Wood. Sam Friedman is considered a key player in creating and implementing strategic planning.

The firm maintains branch offices in Washington (10, 1980) and London (2, 1980).

Until 1989 Lord Day was none too popular among associates. The firm ranked 31st in a 1986 *American Lawyer* survey of New York firms, associates complaining that the firm provided uninteresting work and not much of it, especially for litigation associates. With all the lateral hiring, associates believed there was little chance for them to make partner. A headhunter then described the firm as "pretty creepy" for associates, although conditions have improved after the firm's late-1989 move to 1675 Broadway. In the 1989 survey the firm shot up to seventh place in the rankings, primarily as a result of its exceptional training program and *pro bono* commitment. Associates, however, did not view favorably opportunities for client contacts or drafting court documents.

M

but its decisi
a weighted v
ship). The par
ommendation
individual de
mendations o
utive Commit

Mudge Ros
igation, public
The strongest
ticularly publi
Donald Zoell
gained acclaim
vestigation. M
twenty years.
Zoeller and la
in which a To
summate illeg
investigation,
Japanese com
export sanctic
company in th
on the investi
future violatic
include Judah
In 1983 Eva
York law firm
real legal wor
others, the pro
schools in Ne
It has become
not only about
learning in ge
partment. Ob
Walker for pra
clients as Gene
El Paso Comp
Through its
and Nicholas (

of that department has come to underli
Still, Forger represents a break with th
his central position, in part, because of
the firm's traditional business sources
such as the Rockefellers and Chase. Ins
attracting a new flow of prominent clie
queline Onassis and Mrs. Paul Mellon
matic and a dedicated humanitarian, h
Milbank that one former house counse
half-facetiously) as "the world of Forge
shaker . . . the glue of the firm," secon

Under Forger, Milbank has become
tocracy. Milbank is governed by a Firr
of ten partners elected for staggered
mandatory one-year hiatus between ter
partners and sets partnership shares. H
ship vote is necessary to approve all
mation concerning partner compensatic
Firm Committee also appoints lawyers
mittees, including the Legal Personne
responsible for setting associate salaries
Firm Committee and partners in each

Milbank Tweed has nine departmer
bankruptcy, litigation, real estate, empl
and estates and general. Francis D. Lc
for his work involving Chase, is a sup
side of the firm's banking practice. Mi
foreign banking and handles clients su

The litigation department, as one le
"has made enormous strides." Co-head
ard Tufaro and Andrew Connick each
servers. Adlai Hardin, who handles litig
and who defended it in a critical anti-
as a star.

In recent years, a Forger-regime foc
tion. The tax and bankruptcy departm
flourished. Marty Cowen (whom one t
but too technical") and Robert Jacobs

MILBANK, TWEED, HADLEY & McCLOY

One Chase Manhattan Plaza • New York, New York 10005 • (212) 530-5000

Rating: 💼💼💼💼💼   *Direction:* ↑?

*LAWYERS	PARTNERS	ASSOCIATES
1990: 369	101	250
1989: 334	96	224
1988: 285	86	189
1987: 249	74	166
1986: 243	NA	NA

	Paralegals	Support
1990:	91	663
1989:	75	556
1988:	62	NA
1987:	47	513
1986:	53	NA

*LATERAL HIRES

1989: 33
1988: 57
1987: NA
1986: 11

*CHAIRMAN: Alexander D. Forger

*REPRESENTATIVE CLIENTS:

Chase Manhattan Bank, Rockefeller family,
Credit Suisse, Jacqueline Onassis

*BRANCHES: Washington (30), Los Angeles
(64), Tokyo (6), London (4), Hong Kong
(3), Singapore (1)
Total: 107 lawyers (30p and 77a)

*AVERAGE ANNUAL BILLING
HOURS (1989):

Partners: NA
Associates: 2057

*NUMBER OF WOMEN

	Partners	Associates
1990:	7	88
1989:	7	74
1988:	7	61
1987:	NA	NA
1986:	NA	NA

*PARTNERSHIP TRACK: 8 years

*NUMBER OF LAWYERS FROM ENTERING
CLASS TO MAKE PARTNER:

1982: 1 of 32
1981: 8 of 28
1980: 6 of 26
1979: 7 of 27
1978: 4 of 31

*GROSS REVENUE

1989: $187,500,000
1988: $144,000,000
1987: $108,000,000
1986: $96,000,000

*REVENUE PER LAWYER

1989: $450,000
1988: $440,000
1987: $385,000
1986: $370,000

*PROFITS PER PARTNER

1989: $665,000
1988: $605,000
1987: $445,000
1986: $410,000

*STARTING ASSOCIATE
SALARY

1990: $83,000
1989: $83,000
1988: $77,000
1987: $65,000
1986: $65,000

*PRO BONO: 4–7% of total
time

*HOURLY RATES (1989)

Partners: $260–$375
Associates: $95–$245

*PRINCIPAL LAW SCHOOLS
(Associates): Harvard (64),
Columbia (51), NYU (33),
Georgetown (29), Yale (23)

*NUMBER OF MINORITIES

	Partners	Associates
1990:	2	30
1989:	2	30
1988:	2	22
1987:	NA	NA
1986:	NA	NA

*SUMMER ASSOCIATES

1990: NA
1989: 57
1988: 54
1987: NA
1986: NA

Since 1931, Milbank Tweed's fo[...]
linked to those of the Rockefeller [...]
Bank. Although the firm has dive[...]
trusts and estates, a somewhat ou[...]
terizes Milbank's lawyers and pr[...]
quently used to describe the firm[...]
their work, Milbank's lawyers are, [...]
put it, like "Boy Scouts—honest, tr[...]
itage," adds a legal consultant, "co[...]

While Milbank Tweed's roots l[...]
contemporary history began in 193[...]
Jr. persuaded Albert Milbank to [...]
Winthrop Aldridge as counsel to [...]
ing his firm, Masten & Nichols, w[...]
Aldridge & Webb. For many years[...]
Masten and Murray firms remaine[...]
of the combined firm continued [...]
clients. Milbank, the firm's senio[...]
1949, was a practical lawyer who[...]
negotiating business transactions[...]
Tweed, the firm's second name par[...]
partner from the Murray branch a[...]
death in 1969. He also was a fo[...]
Association of the City of New Y[...]
poused a strongly liberal agenda. [...]
name partner, came from the firm'[...]
excellent business originator. The f[...]
John J. McCloy, came to the firm [...]
which he was the assistant secreta[...]
sioner of West Germany. McClo[...]
World Bank and chairman of the (

Current chairman Alexander For[...]
of evolution at Milbank. Like H[...]
Forger heads both the firm and th[...]
ment; thus, the unusual, longstand[...]

*This characterization came under visible attack
from a matter as a result of a conflict of interest
official investigation.

Charles [...]
early nan[...]
and beca[...]
Stern, W[...]
Rose & [...]
Todd.

The fi[...]
1963 to [...]
Hand & [...]
Richard [...]
Rose Gu[...]
governor[...]
bond fir[...]
name wa[...]
field of p[...]
Capozzol[...]
name was[...]
States in[...]
(1969–1[...]
in June 1[...]
only to b[...]
to defen[...]
Watergat[...]

The fi[...]
Mitchell'[...]
both Nix[...]
left and t[...]
lured aw[...]
gation jo[...]
sociates [...]
positive [...]
clients ir[...]
Stone & [...]
barked o[...]
which yie[...]
Bove and[...]

Mudge[...]
sisting of[...]
ecutive (

[handwritten marginal note] Changed: Now located in NY

---

bond underwriters and a geographically diverse clientele of state and local governments and authorities. The department also has been involved in numerous public power financings either as counsel to the issuer or the underwriter. It also has represented rural electric cooperatives such as the Municipal Electric Authority of Georgia in their public and private financings as well as financings by health care and educational facilities. Mudge Rose represents the Triboro Bridge and Tunnel Authority and the Metropolitan Transportation Authority of New York and it participates in the financing of transit systems, ports, airports, bridges and toll roads.

The firm maintains branch offices in Washington (15, 1963), Los Angeles (5, 1982), West Palm Beach, Fla. (8, 1985) and Paris (6, 1962).

Although a headhunter refers to Mudge Rose as "nice and scrappy," associates have not found the firm so nice. In its 1988 *American Lawyer* survey, associates ranked the firm 34th of 37 firms, and the worst for partners' treatment of associates. Other complaints included the firm's alleged stinginess, boring work and little responsibility. One associate wrote that Mudge Rose associates are "obedient drones . . . subject to arbitrary justice." In the 1989 survey the firm remained in about the same position and ranked 30th out of 35, obtaining better scores in training, *pro bono,* and associate relations but worse scores in client contact, participation in client matters, court appearances and deal-making involvement.

MILBANK, TWEED, HADLEY & MCCLOY

One Chase Manhattan Plaza • New York, New York 10005 • (212) 530-5000

Rating: 💼💼💼💼💼

Direction: ↑?

*LAWYERS	PARTNERS	ASSOCIATES
1990: 369	101	250
1989: 334	96	224
1988: 285	86	189
1987: 249	74	166
1986: 243	NA	NA

	Paralegals	Support
1990:	91	663
1989:	75	556
1988:	62	NA
1987:	47	513
1986:	53	NA

*LATERAL HIRES

1989: 33
1988: 57
1987: NA
1986: 11

*CHAIRMAN: Alexander D. Forger

*REPRESENTATIVE CLIENTS:

Chase Manhattan Bank, Rockefeller family, Credit Suisse, Jacqueline Onassis

*BRANCHES: Washington (30), Los Angeles (64), Tokyo (6), London (4), Hong Kong (3), Singapore (1) Total: 107 lawyers (30p and 77a)

*AVERAGE ANNUAL BILLING HOURS (1989):

Partners: NA
Associates: 2057

*NUMBER OF WOMEN

	Partners	Associates
1990:	7	88
1989:	7	74
1988:	7	61
1987:	NA	NA
1986:	NA	NA

*PARTNERSHIP TRACK: 8 years

*NUMBER OF LAWYERS FROM ENTERING CLASS TO MAKE PARTNER:

1982: 1 of 32
1981: 8 of 28
1980: 6 of 26
1979: 7 of 27
1978: 4 of 31

*GROSS REVENUE

1989: $187,500,000
1988: $144,000,000
1987: $108,000,000
1986: $96,000,000

*REVENUE PER LAWYER

1989: $450,000
1988: $440,000
1987: $385,000
1986: $370,000

*PROFITS PER PARTNER

1989: $665,000
1988: $605,000
1987: $445,000
1986: $410,000

*STARTING ASSOCIATE SALARY

1990: $83,000
1989: $83,000
1988: $77,000
1987: $65,000
1986: $65,000

*PRO BONO: 4–7% of total time

*HOURLY RATES (1989)

Partners: $260–$375
Associates: $95–$245

*PRINCIPAL LAW SCHOOLS (Associates): Harvard (64), Columbia (51), NYU (33), Georgetown (29), Yale (23)

*NUMBER OF MINORITIES

	Partners	Associates
1990:	2	30
1989:	2	30
1988:	2	22
1987:	NA	NA
1986:	NA	NA

*SUMMER ASSOCIATES

1990: NA
1989: 57
1988: 54
1987: NA
1986: NA

Since 1931, Milbank Tweed's fortunes have been inextricably linked to those of the Rockefeller family and Chase Manhattan Bank. Although the firm has diversified beyond banking and trusts and estates, a somewhat outdated gentility still characterizes Milbank's lawyers and practice. The word most frequently used to describe the firm is "decent." Consistent in their work, Milbank's lawyers are, as one former house counsel put it, like "Boy Scouts—honest, trustworthy and loyal."* "Heritage," adds a legal consultant, "counts a little more."

While Milbank Tweed's roots lead as far back as 1860, its contemporary history began in 1931 when John D. Rockefeller, Jr. persuaded Albert Milbank to replace his brother-in-law Winthrop Aldridge as counsel to Chase Manhattan by merging his firm, Masten & Nichols, with Aldridge's firm, Murray, Aldridge & Webb. For many years, however, the merger of the Masten and Murray firms remained incomplete as each branch of the combined firm continued to serve its former base of clients. Milbank, the firm's senior partner until his death in 1949, was a practical lawyer who excelled in arranging and negotiating business transactions. The legendary Harrison Tweed, the firm's second name partner, was a trusts and estates partner from the Murray branch and head of the firm until his death in 1969. He also was a former president of the Bar Association of the City of New York, where he fervently espoused a strongly liberal agenda. Maurice Hadley, the third name partner, came from the firm's Murray branch and was an excellent business originator. The fourth and final name partner, John J. McCloy, came to the firm after World War II, during which he was the assistant secretary of war and high commissioner of West Germany. McCloy also was president of the World Bank and chairman of the Chase Manhattan Bank.

Current chairman Alexander Forger represents a subtle form of evolution at Milbank. Like Harrison Tweed before him, Forger heads both the firm and the trusts and estates department; thus, the unusual, longstanding and ongoing significance

*This characterization came under visible attack in 1989 when a partner was disqualified from a matter as a result of a conflict of interest which was determined to exist after an official investigation.

of that department has come to underline the firm's continuity. Still, Forger represents a break with the past, too. He rose to his central position, in part, because of his independence from the firm's traditional business sources, "old money families" such as the Rockefellers and Chase. Instead, Forger focused on attracting a new flow of prominent clients, which included Jacqueline Onassis and Mrs. Paul Mellon. Today, Forger, charismatic and a dedicated humanitarian, has become so critical to Milbank that one former house counsel refers to the firm (only half-facetiously) as "the world of Forger." He is "a mover and shaker . . . the glue of the firm," seconds a legal consultant.

Under Forger, Milbank has become known as a true meritocracy. Milbank is governed by a Firm Committee consisting of ten partners elected for staggered three-year terms with a mandatory one-year hiatus between terms; it recommends new partners and sets partnership shares. However, a full-partnership vote is necessary to approve all new partners and information concerning partner compensation is available to all. The Firm Committee also appoints lawyers to the firm's other committees, including the Legal Personnel Committee, which is responsible for setting associate salaries in conjunction with the Firm Committee and partners in each department.

Milbank Tweed has nine departments: banking, corporate, bankruptcy, litigation, real estate, employee benefits, tax, trusts and estates and general. Francis D. Logan, known principally for his work involving Chase, is a supernova on the national side of the firm's banking practice. Michael Orr specializes in foreign banking and handles clients such as Credit Suisse.

The litigation department, as one leading trial lawyer says, "has made enormous strides." Co-heads Thomas Puccio, Richard Tufaro and Andrew Connick each receive praise from observers. Adlai Hardin, who handles litigation for Amerada Hess and who defended it in a critical anti-trust case, has emerged as a star.

In recent years, a Forger-regime focus has been diversification. The tax and bankruptcy departments, in particular, have flourished. Marty Cowen (whom one tax lawyer calls "brilliant but too technical") and Robert Jacobs have become tax standouts, while John Jerome's entire bankruptcy department receives praise. "A very fine practice," says a bankruptcy partner at another leading New York firm.

Several observers laud Jacob Worenklein, who helped found and now leads Milbank's leasing and project finance practice. This division closed more project financings than any in the country in 1988 and has become an enormous revenue producer for Milbank.

There has also been expansion in Milbank's international practice. The firm opened offices in 1977 in Hong Kong and Taiwan, and in 1979 in London. In 1989, the firm reestablished a branch in Tokyo and opened a new office in Singapore.

Generally, Milbank has been on a steady financial incline. According to *The American Lawyer*, gross revenue has gone from $96,000,000 in 1986 to $108,000,000 and then to $144,000,000 in 1988, keeping the firm ranking nationally between twentieth and twenty-fifth. Revenue per lawyer and profits per partner follow the same pattern; a modest increase in 1986–1987, and then a larger push forward in 1988, particularly in profits per partner, which jumped from $445,000 in 1987 to $605,000 in 1988. The firm ranks highest in revenue per lawyer, ranging from 11th to 13th, which indicates that the firm makes the most of its human resources. However, in 1989, while revenues rose $43,500,000 to $187,500,000 (a 30% increase), revenue per lawyer rose a modest $10,000 to $450,000 (4%) and profits per partner, $60,000 (10%).

Associates at Milbank have borne the brunt of the firm's efforts to modernize. Mid-level associates surveyed by *The American Lawyer* in 1986 reported that increased pressure to bill more hours had dissipated the firm's commitment to *pro bono* work and lowered the quality of life. The summer associates surveyed in 1987 gave Milbank the second-lowest acceptance rate for permanent positions in New York. A legal consultant observes that perhaps the firm cannot hold associates because there is "no room at the top." She also points out that there are gaps in the three-to-five year associate level. A headhunter notes that, for many associates, Milbank would be a bad fit. "Uptight people," she says, thrive there. While in 1986 and 1987 associates were lukewarm about the firm's program, by

1988 their response was positive. Observers outside the firm uniformly praise its training. One legal consultant calls it nothing short of "great." In 1989 the firm finished 12th in overall ranking in New York compared to 13th in 1988. Training and guidance, client contact and responsibility continued high, but the work was considered only of average interest and dissatisfaction was expressed with the lack of hands-on experience.

MUDGE ROSE GUTHRIE ALEXANDER & FERDON

180 Maiden Lane • New York, New York 10038 • (212) 510-7000

Rating: 💼💼💼✒️   *Direction:* ↔

*LAWYERS

	PARTNERS	ASSOCIATES
1990: 251	75	170 _γ.∜_
1989: 227	76	141
1988: 229	71	146
1987: 207	64	132
1986: 199	59	116

	Paralegals	Support
1990:	52	329
1989:	55	352
1988:	59	NA
1987:	55	359
1986:	60	NA

*LATERAL HIRES

1989: NA
1988: 14
1987: NA
1986: 19

*CHAIRMAN: ~~Robert E.~~ _Don Zoeller_ Ferdon (term expires 1991)

*REPRESENTATIVE CLIENTS:

General Foods Corporation, Culbro Corporation, Metropolitan Transportation Authority of New York _Nintendo_

*BRANCHES: Washington (15), Los Angeles (15), Paris (7), West Palm Beach (8)
Total: 45 lawyers (NAp and NAa)

*AVERAGE ANNUAL BILLING HOURS (1989):
Partners: NA
Associates: NA

*NUMBER OF WOMEN

	Partners	Associates
1990:	4	57
1989:	4	56
1988:	5	51
1987:	5	42
1986:	3	41

*PARTNERSHIP TRACK: 8 years

*NUMBER OF LAWYERS FROM ENTERING CLASS TO MAKE PARTNER:
1981: NA
1980: 6 of 18
1979: 10 of 16
1978: 6 of 24

*GROSS REVENUE
_1990 98_
1989: $91,000,000
1988: $89,000,000
1987: $79,000,000
1986: $64,000,000

*REVENUE PER LAWYER
_90   355_
1989: $340,000
1988: $345,000
1987: $325,000
1986: $305,000

*PROFITS PER PARTNER
_90   465_
1989: $355,000
1988: $335,000
1987: $335,000
1986: $300,000

*STARTING ASSOCIATE SALARY
1990: $82,000
1989: $82,000
1988: $77,000
1987: $65,000
1986: $65,000

*PRO BONO: 2–3% of total time

*HOURLY RATES
Partners: NA
Associates: NA

*PRINCIPAL LAW SCHOOLS (Associates): Fordham (14), Columbia (12), NYU (10)

*NUMBER OF MINORITIES

	Partners	Associates
1990:	2	8
1989:	2	5
1988:	2	10
1987:	2	11
1986:	1	13

*SUMMER ASSOCIATES
1990: 28
1989: 30
1988: 22
1987: 27
1986: 25

Mudge Rose's history could well be divided into pre-Nixon, post-Mitchell and the interval in between. This interval, from 1964 to 1973, has defined Mudge Rose in a way that is neither accurate nor in keeping with the firm's current objectives. Though perhaps predestined to be perceived to this day as "Nixon's old firm" or "Mitchell's old firm," since the late 1970s Mudge Rose, while no longer politically connected, has expanded and diversified largely through the acquisition of lateral partners. Today's Mudge Rose, which was guided by its universally acclaimed managing partner Judah Gribetz until the summer of 1990, is still searching for definition. A senior litigator speaks for many observers when he says that the firm "mystifies" him. Some sources, however, have already reached a positive verdict on the new, improved Mudge Rose. The firm is "progressive, expansive and good," says a senior corporate lawyer.

Financially, however, the firm has backtracked in recent years, supporting a legal consultant's conclusion that "it is not going anywhere . . . the money isn't good either." Although Mudge Rose has edged forward in absolute terms, relative to other firms it has fallen behind. According to *The American Lawyer* rankings, Mudge Rose's gross revenue grew from $64,000,000 to $89,000,000 between 1986 and 1988, but the firm slipped from 44th place to 48th. Similarly, revenue per lawyer increased from $305,000 to $345,000 and profits per partner increased from $300,000 to $335,000, but the firm dropped, respectively, from 23rd to 33rd and from 33rd to 46th in these categories. In 1989 there were modest increases and decreases in its financial operations, revenues increasing from $89,000,000 to $91,000,000, revenues per lawyer decreasing from $345,000 to $340,000 and profits per partner increasing from $335,000 to $355,000.

Mudge Rose's roots extend back to 1869 and a single practitioner Simon Hunt Stern. Three years later, Stern joined forces with Henry Root. The firm grew swiftly and represented such clients as the Manhattan Company (which had been started by Aaron Burr to compete with Alexander Hamilton's New York Company, which later became the Bank of Manhattan), and General Cigar Corporation, presently Culbro Corporation.

Charles Rushmore, for whom Mt. Rushmore is named, was an early name partner. Alfred Mudge joined the firm in the 1920s and became a name partner in 1934. In 1955, what was Mudge, Stern, Williams & Tucker merged with Baldwin Todd Herold Rose & Cooper and was renamed Mudge Stern Baldwin & Todd.

The firm's greatest growth took place in the decade from 1963 to 1973. The spurt started when Mudge acquired Dorr Hand & Whitaker, a railroad specialty firm. Then, also in 1963, Richard Nixon joined the firm (which became Nixon Mudge Rose Guthrie & Alexander) after his unsuccessful campaign for governor of California. In 1967, the firm acquired the municipal bond firm Caldwell Trimble & Mitchell and John Mitchell's name was added to the firm's. The firm gained expertise in the field of public power finance law with the addition of Nicholas Capozzoli, Jr., and Robert Ferdon in the late 1960s. Nixon's name was removed when he was elected President of the United States in 1968. When John Mitchell was attorney general (1969–1972) his name was also dropped. When he returned in June 1973, the firm name was changed again to include his, only to be dropped four months later when Mitchell resigned to defend himself against various charges arising out of the Watergate scandal.

The firm fell on hard times with Nixon's resignation and Mitchell's conviction for his part in the Watergate cover-up; both Nixon and Mitchell were subsequently disbarred. Clients left and the firm's municipal bond business soured as other firms lured away some of its specialists. Mudge Rose's head of litigation joined another firm, taking business with him. Old associates left and new ones were harder to recruit. On the positive side, the firm retained many of its most important clients including Warner-Lambert, Studebaker-Worthington, Stone & Webster and Consolidated Cigar. The firm then embarked on an ambitious campaign to acquire lateral partners, which yielded Judah Gribetz, Jed Rakoff, Joel Davidow, John Bove and Robert Peduzzi.

Mudge Rose is governed by an Executive Committee consisting of five members elected for two-year terms. The Executive Committee handles all matters concerning firm policy,

PARKER CHAPIN FLATTAU & KLIMPL

1211 Avenue of the Americas • New York, New York 10036 • (212) 704-6000

Rating: 💼💼💼

Direction: ↔

199√ *31* *70*

*LAWYERS	PARTNERS	ASSOCIATES
1990: 130	~~43~~ *38*	76 *1.76*
1989: 119	44	66
1988: 126	46	71
1987: 104	39	57
1986: 103	40	55

	Paralegals	Support
1990:	21	146
1989:	26	165
1988:	25	NA
1987:	19	144
1986:	19	NA

*LATERAL HIRES

1989: 6
1988: 15
1987: NA
1986: 13

MARK ABRAMOWITZ

*MANAGING PARTNER: Alvin Stein

*REPRESENTATIVE CLIENTS:

Leslie Fay Company, Hebrew National Kosher Food, the Shubert Organization, Morgan Stanley & Co., Tishman Construction Corporation

*BRANCHES: Jericho, N.Y. (4)
Total: 4 lawyers (1p and 3a)

*AVERAGE ANNUAL BILLING HOURS (1989):
Partners: NA
Associates: 1900–2000

*NUMBER OF WOMEN

	Partners	Associates
1990:	5	34
1989:	4	30
1988:	4	29
1987:	3	25
1986:	3	21

*PARTNERSHIP TRACK: 9 years

*NUMBER OF LAWYERS FROM ENTERING CLASS TO MAKE PARTNER:

1981: 2 of 6
1980: 1 of 7
1979: 3 of 8
1978: 3 of 7

*GROSS REVENUE
1989: NA
1988: NA
1987: NA
1986: NA

*REVENUE PER LAWYER
1989: NA
1988: NA
1987: NA
1986: NA

*PROFITS PER PARTNER
1989: NA
1988: NA
1987: NA
1986: NA

*STARTING ASSOCIATE SALARY
1990: $75,000
1989: $70,000
1988: $70,000
1987: NA
1986: $52,000

*PRO BONO: NA

*HOURLY RATES
Partners: NA
Associates: NA

*PRINCIPAL LAW SCHOOLS
(Associates): NYU (14), Columbia (6), Brooklyn (5), New York Law School (5)

*NUMBER OF MINORITIES

	Partners	Associates
1990:	0	3
1989:	0	3
1988:	0	3
1987:	0	1
1986:	0	0

*SUMMER ASSOCIATES
1990: 11
1989: 11
1988: 13
1987: 8
1986: 9

Parker Chapin is a mature Jewish-oriented firm that primarily represents medium-sized companies in corporate and litigation matters. Observers characterize the firm as ethical, pleasantly seedy and old-fashioned but atmospheric. One headhunter genially calls Parker Chapin her "favorite polyester law firm. You wouldn't mistake them for investment bankers."

Financial problems have impeded the firm in recent years. According to *The American Lawyer*, Parker Chapin did not rank among the top 100 firms nationally in gross revenues, revenue per lawyer or profits per partner between 1986 and 1988. One result of the firm's fiscal shortfalls is a higher departure rate; "People leave because they want to make more money," says a headhunter. Alvin Stein, the firm's lone star litigator and managing partner, "is carrying Parker Chapin during a time of financial troubles," asserts a senior litigator.

Albert Parker, Samuel Chapin and Henry Flattau started the firm in 1934. Major clients—such as Interstate Department Stores, Karl L. Norden, Inc. (builder of the Norden bombsight), and the Bank of the Manhattan Company—gave the firm an early focus in banking and corporate work. A substantial practice in government contracts developed during the Second World War and, soon thereafter, the firm forayed into the fields of labor law, trusts and estates, tax and securities litigation.

A seven-member Executive Committee manages Parker Chapin's operations. Albert Parker, Manuel Klimpl and Alvin Stein are members for life. The four other partners on the Executive Committee are elected by the entire partnership. Partners' votes are weighted according to partnership shares. Committee members can serve terms of up to five years. The Executive Committee finalizes the recommendations made by department heads on the admission of new partners and appoints members to the firm's other committees: Finance, Administrative and Personnel. The Executive Committee also determines associate compensation after reviewing proposals from the Personnel Committee.

The firm has six departments: litigation/bankruptcy, corporate, real estate, labor and employment, tax and trusts and estates. Lloyd Frank, a 1977 lateral hire whom a senior corporate lawyer labels "superb," leads a corporate department that represents such diverse interests as the Leslie Fay Company, Hebrew National Kosher Foods, Inc. and the Shubert Organization.

Stein heads the litigation department. Trained by Milton Gould, Stein gained prominence with his representation of Berkey Photo in its anti-trust action against Kodak. Mark Abramowitz, though somewhat in Stein's shadow, is another outstanding Parker Chapin litigator.

When Parker Chapin merged with the nine-lawyer Estroff, Waldman & Poretsky firm in 1982, Stephen Estroff took charge of the firm's real estate practice. Parker Chapin also inherited name partners Hannah Waldman and Joel Poretsky as well as such clients as Morgan Stanley & Co., Tishman Construction Corporation and Lazard Freres & Co. Currently, John Gutheil heads the real estate department.

The firm maintains a small branch office in Jericho, Long Island (4, 1987).

Parker Chapin is a mixed bag for associates. The firm has a relaxed atmosphere, collegiality to spare and demands fewer hours than most other leading New York firms. "Associates like it," says a legal consultant. "It's a nice, nice place." The down side is that the firm does not pay top dollar, and more importantly, seems to be shrinking.

PATTERSON, BELKNAP, WEBB & TYLER

30 Rockefeller Plaza • New York, New York 10112 • (212) 698-2500

Rating: 💼💼💼💼

Direction: ↓?

*LAWYERS

	PARTNERS	ASSOCIATES
1990: 154	46	94
1989: 136	43	83
1988: 127	38	82
1987: 122	37	77
1986: 120	35	79

	Paralegals	Support
1990:	NA	NA
1989:	37	200
1988:	33	NA
1987:	37	180
1986:	28	NA

*LATERAL HIRES

1989: 19
1988: 15
1987: 21
1986: 15

*CHAIRMAN OF THE MANAGEMENT COMMITTEE: Antonia M. Grumbach

*REPRESENTATIVE CLIENTS:

Johnson & Johnson, Amerace Corporation, Estee Lauder, Inc., ESPN, Dime Savings Bank of New York, Bill Cosby, Zeckendorf Company

*BRANCHES: Washington (9) (NAp and NAa)

*AVERAGE ANNUAL BILLING HOURS:
Partners: 1695
Associates: 1711

*NUMBER OF WOMEN

	Partners	Associates
1990:	5	44
1989:	5	31
1988:	4	31
1987:	4	34
1986:	3	34

*PARTNERSHIP TRACK: 8 years

*NUMBER OF LAWYERS FROM ENTERING CLASS TO MAKE PARTNER:

1981: 3 of 5
1980: 2 of 6
1979: 1 of 7
1978: 3 of 4

*GROSS REVENUE

1989: NA
1988: NA
1987: $38,900,000
1986: $32,800,000

*REVENUE PER LAWYER

1989: NA
1988: NA
1987: NA
1986: NA

*PROFITS PER PARTNER

1989: NA
1988: NA
1987: NA
1986: NA

*STARTING ASSOCIATE SALARY

1990: $83,000
1989: $77,000
1988: $71,000
1987: $65,000
1986: $65,000

*PRO BONO: 8–10% of total time

*HOURLY RATES (1989)
Partners: $225–$350
Associates: $100–$215

*PRINCIPAL LAW SCHOOLS (Associates): NYU (18), Columbia (12), Fordham (11)

*NUMBER OF MINORITIES

	Partners	Associates
1990:	1	7
1989:	1	5
1988:	1	3
1987:	2	1
1986:	2	0

*SUMMER ASSOCIATES

1990: 13
1989: 15
1988: 15
1987: 12
1986: 9

Patterson Belknap is a conscientious, highly respected mid-size firm that, in the words of a legal consultant, is "struggling to survive in New York City." In terms of quality of work and lawyers the firm has undergone a renaissance since Harold "Ace" Tyler joined the firm in 1977. Nevertheless, for financial reasons the firm is looking to merge. In 1987, Patterson had gross revenue of $38.9 million; in 1986, $32.8 million. Neither total was enough for the firm to graduate into the top 100 nationally according to *The American Lawyer*. "Patterson Belknap is the best of the little firms" summarizes a senior corporate lawyer. "It has collegiality, decency, is ethnically mixed but is not that profitable."

Ace Tyler is indisputably the key figure at the firm. When he came to Patterson Belknap as a name partner, he already had an impressive resume. He had been the Assistant Attorney General in charge of the Justice Department's Civil Rights Division in the Eisenhower and Kennedy administrations. He was a U.S. District Court judge, Southern District of New York, from 1962 to 1975. In the Ford administration, he became the deputy attorney general of the U.S. In 1987, New York mayor Ed Koch appointed Tyler to conduct the investigation of Bess Myerson. The gutsy, highly visible Tyler receives near-universal praise from observers, both for his legal and organizational ability. "Patterson Belknap is a one-man show—Ace Tyler," says a prominent trial lawyer. "Ace Tyler is a first-rate person, terrific lawyer and practical jurist," says a house counsel. Tyler consistently has drawn bright young talents to Patterson Belknap, originated substantial business for the firm and erased its previously stodgy reputation. However, with Tyler fast approaching retirement age, the firm faces a serious, if not critical, leadership problem.

Winfred Denison, former assistant U.S. attorney general and partner at a predecessor firm to Davis Polk, and James Curtis, former assistant secretary of the treasury and general counsel of the Federal Reserve Bank of New York, founded the firm in 1919. Chauncey Belknap was one of the firm's original two associates and became a name partner in 1921. Belknap, the firm's managing partner for over forty years, represented the Rockefeller Foundation and was general counsel to the Metropolitan Opera. Vanderbilt Webb joined the firm—which became Curtis, Belknap & Webb—in 1938 after resigning from what would ultimately be Milbank Tweed. When Curtis retired in 1947, Robert Patterson took his place. Patterson was a former undersecretary of war (1942–1946), the last U.S. secretary of war (1946–1947) and a former District and Circuit Court judge. Robert Morgenthau and Rudolph Giuliani, a Tyler protégé, are both former Patterson Belknap partners.

A Management Committee chaired by Antonia Grumbach oversees the firm's operations in concert with newly hired executive director Marvin Brittman. The Management Committee also appoints other firm committees as needed for administrative purposes. Patterson has two additional permanent committees besides the Management Committee: the Cut Committee, headed by Tyler, which sets partnership shares, and the Planning Committee, also headed by Tyler, which handles long-term strategic planning, including mergers and lateral acquisitions.

The firm is divided into six practice areas: litigation, corporate, real estate, trusts and estates, labor and tax. Tyler has built the litigation department into the firm's strongest and observers praise such litigation partners as David Dobbins, Gregory Diskant, Frederick Davis and Philip Forlenza. Antonia Grumbach is a standout in corporate. Stephen Lefkowitz, the real estate department head, also receives kudos. In recent years, however, the firm has lost some of its young talent—tax partner Yale Tauber to LeBoeuf Lamb, corporate partner Peter Skinner to Dow Jones, litigator Michael Mukasey to the Southern District bench and litigator Robert Sack, who took the Dow Jones account with him, to Gibson, Dunn & Crutcher. In the fall of 1990 Arthur Kroll, a multi-million dollar ERISA rainmaker, amidst much publicity, withdrew at the firm's request over a dispute concerning his disbursement vouchers.

The firm represents such interests as Johnson & Johnson, Amerace Corporation, Estee Lauder, Inc., ESPN, The Dime Savings Bank of New York, the Zeckendorf Company and Bill Cosby.

Patterson maintains a branch office in Washington (7, 1981). Its Los Angeles office (1986) was closed in January 1990.

Associates go to Patterson Belknap for specific reasons and are usually satisfied with it. The firm ranked ninth and eleventh in 1988 and 1986 in respectively, in *American Lawyer* surveys of New York firms, and garnered positive marks for giving associates a good deal of responsibility without deluging them with work. "The firm encourages its lawyers to have an outside life," says a corporate lawyer. Patterson considers 1,850 total annual billable hours to be the target for associates; between 1986 and 1988, however, the firm fell below this average. Internal relations too are a strong point; until 1989 all agreed that the firm had a pleasant, relaxed atmosphere. The tradeoff for the firm's benefits is less money. "Many partners and associates here are refugees from more driven firms and have made deliberate decisions to sacrifice some money in order to not let work overwhelm their lives," wrote an associate polled in 1988. Notwithstanding, the 1989 survey revealed a dramatic drop in associate perceptions of the firm, which placed it last in the nation in overall rankings. Patterson Belknap is now seen as having very uninteresting work, poor training, guidance and feedback and little client and deal-making involvement. While it is unusual for there to be such an about-face in one year, the change in associate views may parallel the changing fortunes of the firm or perhaps its questionable growth potential.

PAUL, WEISS, RIFKIND, WHARTON & GARRISON

•••

1285 Avenue of the Americas • New York, New York 10019 • (212) 373-3000

Rating: 💼💼💼💼💼   *Direction:* ↑

*LAWYERS

	PARTNERS	ASSOCIATES
1990: 377	77	291
1989: 340	74	233
1988: 323	76	221
1987: 302	75	219
1986: 288	NA	NA

	Paralegals	Support
1990:	116	647
1989:	110	565
1988:	94	NA
1987:	83	559
1986:	72	NA

*LATERAL HIRES

1989: 23
1988: 27
1987: NA
1986: 22

*MANAGING PARTNER: [Burton J. Cohen] › LEWIS KAPLAN EYEC DIR

*REPRESENTATIVE CLIENTS:

Warner Communications, Inc., Coca-Cola Company, Mitsubishi Corporation, Aetna, ASCAP

*BRANCHES: Washington (18), Paris (9), Shanghai (1), Tokyo (2) [Hong Kong and Beijing offices closed—summer of 1990] Total: 33 lawyers (NAp and NAa)

*AVERAGE ANNUAL BILLING HOURS (1988):

Partners: NA
Associates: 1871

*NUMBER OF WOMEN

	Partners	Associates
1990:	5	94
1989:	5	76
1988:	5	71
1987:	NA	NA
1986:	NA	NA

*PARTNERSHIP TRACK: 8 years

*NUMBER OF LAWYERS FROM ENTERING CLASS TO MAKE PARTNER:

1981: 3 of 23
1980: 3 of 14
1979: 1 of 25
1978: 6 of 15

*GROSS REVENUE

1989: $195,000,000
1988: $163,500,000
1987: $114,000,000
1986: $102,000,000

*REVENUE PER LAWYER

1989: $535,000
1988: $490,000
1987: $360,000
1986: $340,000

*PROFITS PER PARTNER

1989: $915,000
1988: $795,000
1987: $435,000
1986: $450,000

*STARTING ASSOCIATE SALARY

1990: $83,000
1989: $81,000
1988: $76,000
1987: $71,000
1986: $66,000

*PRO BONO: 7% of total time

*HOURLY RATES

Partners: NA
Associates: NA

*PRINCIPAL LAW SCHOOLS (Associates): NYU (39), Harvard (29), Columbia (26), Yale (11)

*NUMBER OF MINORITIES

	Partners	Associates
1990:	2	18
1989:	1	24
1988:	0	19
1987:	0	NA
1986:	0	NA

*SUMMER ASSOCIATES

1990: 61
1989: 60
1988: 94
1987: NA
1986: NA

Paul Weiss is the quintessential liberal democratic firm. Its alumni include Adlai Stevenson, Arthur Goldberg, Ramsey Clark and Newton Minow. Current partners Theodore Sorenson, Matthew Nimetz, Jerome Kurtz, Ed Costikyan and Morris Abram have all held various governmental positions. The firm is also quite successful at the practice of law, having one of New York's top litigation departments, a rising corporate department and a highly regarded tax department. "They are hard-driving, hard-working and effective," summarizes a former house counsel.

The firm is also highly profitable. According to *The American Lawyer,* Paul Weiss hovered among the top twenty firms nationwide in gross revenue, revenue per lawyer and profits per partner in 1986 and 1987. In 1988, however, the firm burst into the top 10 in the latter two categories, with a revenue per lawyer of $490,000 and profits per partner of $795,000 (an increase of $350,000 over the previous year). In 1989 the firm maintained its lofty position by posting substantial increases over 1988 in all categories: from $163,500,000 to $195,000,000 in revenue; from $490,000 to $535,000 in revenue per lawyer; and from $795,000 to $915,000 in profits per partner.

Antecedents of Paul Weiss date back to 1875 but the present-day firm took shape in 1946 when tax specialist Randolph Paul and labor lawyer Lloyd Garrison joined forces with partners Cohen, Cole, Weiss and Wharton. In 1950, federal judge Simon Rifkind left the bench to join the firm and soon became its driving force. Judge Rifkind, both an outstanding litigator and leader of the bar, is most responsible for putting together the various pieces of the firm, particularly the litigation department, and setting its tone and direction. "The firm," says a senior litigator, "is the creation of Si Rifkind, who is universally respected."

The firm's centerpiece remains its litigation department, which, in turn, is dominated by the forceful and seemingly ubiquitous Arthur Liman. Liman enjoys a national reputation for both his trial work (he has represented Chris Craft, Gulf & Western, the Manhattan Transportation Authority, Drexel Burnham Lambert and Michael Milken) and his role in various governmental activities (he has been counsel to the New York commission investigating the Attica prison riots and was involved with the House impeachment hearings on Nixon as well as the House Iran-Contra investigation). He is "both a litigator and corporate dealmaker and does everything well," notes another leading litigator. "Minus him, Paul Weiss drops a level."

Not all observers find Liman that impressive. Various house counsel describe him as "irritating and lucky" and attack him for "taking on too much . . . he can't go into enough depth." "Egocentric beyond ordinary proportions," adds a legal consultant, "arrogant and very difficult." No one, however, argues Liman's worth to Paul Weiss or questions his membership in that select group of true trial—as opposed to pre-trial—litigators in New York's leading law firms.

The firm's other key litigators—Jay Tompkins, Jay Greenfield, Ed Costikyan, Martin London and Liman's protégé, Martin Flumenbaum—are, as one senior litigator puts it, "first-rate and form a very formidable group." Like Liman, the litigation department evokes praise for its skills and complaints about its idiosyncrasies. The same litigator adds that while they have "many good trial lawyers, they have an amazing aversion to trying cases. Their response to every case is to throw people and paper at it and to make it as complicated and expensive as it can be." This may be no more than sour grapes.

Whatever their methods, Paul Weiss' top-quality lawyers have attracted an equally impressive client roster, including Warner Communications Inc. (now Time-Warner Inc.), The Coca-Cola Company, Mitsubishi Corporation, Aetna and the American Society of Composers, Authors and Publishers. This last entry reflects a long-standing source of business for the firm; the entertainment department over the years has been involved in numerous Broadway and movie financings and contractual matters, and represents many other organizations in the arts.

Beyond its powerful one-two punch of litigation and corporate, Paul Weiss has a highly regarded tax department and a new-born environmental practice. One lawyer describes the tax department, led by Arthur Kalish, as "good overall . . . with a lot of depth." In June 1989, the firm established an environmental practice by acquiring Gaines Gwathmey III, chief of the Environmental Protection Unit in the U.S. attorney's office between 1979 and 1983.

Paul Weiss has no formal, titled department heads; instead, each legal department is administered by one partner chosen from within. The firm does not have a managing partner. The Deciding Group determines partnership shares and the Committee on Committees appoints members to the firm's various committees and develops long-term policy. Both the Deciding Group and the Committee on Committees have a varying number of members.

As one senior litigator noted, "Paul Weiss is probably the most democratic possible law firm of its size; it probably is the most tolerant of idiosyncrasies of any firm its size—very happily a collection of individuals." For some observers, however, this laissez-faire system has led to a leadership vacuum. As one legal consultant queried, "Who's in charge here?"

Associates play critical roles in this free-floating environment and are given unusual amounts of responsibility. The firm is known for "taking the best academic performers among law school graduates," submits a legal consultant, and offers a flexible, highly interesting program firmly committed to *pro bono.* According to *American Lawyer* associate surveys in 1986 and 1987, however, the longer associates were at Paul Weiss, the more disillusioned they became with the firm. Despite placing first in 1986 on a list of most sought-after firms during Columbia Law School's early-bird interview period, Paul Weiss' 1986 mid-level associates criticized the firm for poor morale ascribed to arduously long hours and aloof, uncaring partners. Associates were more likely to leave Paul Weiss within three years than any other firm. By 1988, Paul Weiss had turned this trend around; mid-level associates ranked the firm 12th, up from 26th in New York, and rated work interesting, the long hours worthwhile. 1989 saw Paul Weiss continue upward in associates' eyes and climb to 5th position. The firm's *pro bono* commitment, which is ranked highest in the nation, is a very strong factor in keeping associates from leaving for other pastures. Now, as a legal consultant notes, there is "low associate turnover" even though a headhunter observes, "they work their people pretty hard."

Today's Paul Weiss not only has expanded its areas of practice, but, during the last two decades, it also has substantially diversified its ethnic mix. Nonetheless, Paul Weiss still retains its old identity for some lawyers. "It is the top Jewish law firm in New York," observes one senior corporate lawyer, with "a higher quality of lawyers than most others among the powerful group of almost purely Jewish firms." It has accomplished this by keeping a Jewish orientation while attracting a well-balanced mix of lawyers.

PHILLIPS, NIZER, BENJAMIN, KRIM & BALLON
• •
31 West 52nd Street • New York, New York 10019 • (212) 977-9700

Rating: 💼💼💼

Direction: ?

*LAWYERS	PARTNERS	ASSOCIATES
1990: 109	46	56
1989: 110	45	56
1988: 112	42	63
1987: 103	43	54
1986: 88	44	38

	Paralegals	Support
1990:	22	153
1989:	25	145
1988:	25	148
1987:	15	129
1986:	17	121

*LATERAL HIRES
1989: 10
1988: 0
1987: 5
1986: 0

*CHAIRMAN: None

*REPRESENTATIVE CLIENTS:
Occidental Petroleum, Orion Pictures, The Bic Corp., Mutual Benefit Life, Prudential Bache

*BRANCHES: Garden City, N.Y. (1p, 2a)

*AVERAGE ANNUAL BILLING HOURS (1989):
Partners: NA
Associates: NA

*NUMBER OF WOMEN

	Partners	Associates
1989:	7	19
1988:	6	22
1987:	6	18
1986:	5	13

*PARTNERSHIP TRACK: NA

*NUMBER OF LAWYERS FROM ENTERING CLASS TO MAKE PARTNER:
1981: NA
1980: NA
1979: NA
1978: NA

*GROSS REVENUE
1989: $32,000,000
1988: NA
1987: NA
1986: NA

*REVENUE PER LAWYER
1989: $285,000
1988: NA
1987: NA
1986: NA

*PROFITS PER PARTNER
1989: $240,000
1988: NA
1987: NA
1986: NA

*STARTING ASSOCIATE SALARY
1990: $75,000
1989: $70,000
1988: $65,000
1987: $60,000
1986: $50,000

*PRO BONO: 1–3% of total time

*HOURLY RATES (1989)
Partners: $210–$385
Associates: $120–$185

*PRINCIPAL LAW SCHOOLS
(Associates): NYU (10), Hofstra (6), Cornell (3), Fordham (3), St. John's (3)

*NUMBER OF MINORITIES

	Partners	Associates
1989:	NA	NA
1988:	NA	NA
1987:	1	2
1986:	1	1

*SUMMER ASSOCIATES
1989: 6
1988: 6
1987: 6
1986: 6

To many, Phillips Nizer *is* Louis Nizer. The legendary litigator is still litigating at age 88, while virtually all his contem-
poraries either have passed the Great Divide, retired or
substantially reduced their workload. While Nizer's prodigious
talent and ego have given the firm visibility, clients, fees and
influence, they also for many years had prevented a younger
generation from taking control. Voicing the doubts of many
about Phillips Nizer's future, one headhunter asked rhetori-
cally, "What happens when Nizer dies?"

The Nizer firm—for that is what it is frequently called—has
not kept pace with many comparable firms in the last decade.
Indeed, Phillips Nizer has been outdistanced by a number of
smaller, less profitable and less distinguished firms. Although
the firm has declined to reveal its results of operation (except
for disclosures concerning 1989 financial results in a *Manhattan
Lawyer* articles in the fall of 1990), two telling statistics are
indicative of its problems: in the decade from 1979 to 1989
the firm grew from 85 to just 110 lawyers (or less than 3% per
year); and the firm's most recent partner/associate ratio was
1:1.2—extraordinarily low.

Nonetheless, within the last several years the young Turks,
who for more than a decade had tried and failed to lessen Nizer's
domination and to further institutionalize the firm's operations,
have taken at least formal control. Under its new leadership,
the firm has increased and diversified its client base and practice
somewhat. Moreover, it also has had newfound success in attracting lateral partners with significant portable business. While
no single leader has emerged, now four partners each apparently
generate annual billings of $1 million and fourteen others, more
than $500,000.

The firm was founded in 1925 when John Phillips, counsel
to the New York Film Board of Trade, invited his assistant to
become an equal partner in Phillips & Nizer. From the outset,
the firm was involved in various aspects of the motion picture
business. Phillips became head of litigation for Paramount Pictures in 1928. In 1932, name partners Robert Benjamin and
Arthur Krim were added. Between 1939 and 1949, the firm
name was Phillips, Nizer, Benjamin and Krim. Finally, Charles
Ballon, Krim's fellow student at Columbia Law School, was

added as a name partner and at the age of 78, he is still active. The firm's representation of the film production and distribution industries blossomed into a global practice, thanks in part to Benjamin's affiliation with the Rank Organization. In the early 1950s, three Phillips Nizer partners simultaneously held office at United Artists—Krim was president, Benjamin was chairman of the board and Seymour Peyser was vice-president and general counsel. In 1978, after policy disagreements with Transamerica (United Artists' parent), Krim and Benjamin broke away from United Artists to form Orion Pictures Corporation and, in 1985, opened a Los Angeles office, which closed in 1988 due to policy disagreements with the New York branch. An attempt to maintain a Washington, D.C., office had already failed in 1978.

During this entire stretch, Nizer became involved in numerous high-visibility cases (a number of which found their way into his best-selling books), including representing John Henry Faulk in his libel action against blacklisters; Loew's in the proxy contest instituted by shareholders seeking control of the company; Eleanor Holm in her divorce action against Billy Rose; Quentin Reynolds in his libel action against Westbrook Pegler; Maurice Baron in his plagiarism action against Leo Feist, Inc. concerning "Rum and Coca Cola"; Jack Bronston in his criminal trial involving the New York City bus shelter scandal; and the owners of La Costa in their libel action against *Penthouse* magazine. Nizer also has brought into the firm such clients as Occidental Petroleum and its subsidiary Hooker Chemical.

The firm is governed by a five-person Executive Committee which is currently composed of David Jacoby, Neil Kleinhandler, Eugene Kline, Alan Mansfield, and Michael Silverberg. Louis Nizer is the honorary chairman (with no vote); there is no acting chairman. Members are elected to one-year terms on a one-partner, one-vote basis. There is no limitation on successive terms. Among other matters, the Executive Committee determines each partner's annual profit allocation (subject to partnership approval) and handles the admission of new partners (subject to the approval of two-thirds of the partnership interests). The Executive Committee also appoints members of other committees, which currently total fifteen, including Associate Evaluation, Audit and Opinion, Automation, Banking and Accounting, Business Acceptance, Business Development, Ethics, Equal Opportunity, Finance, Lateral Acquisitions, Loans, Partner/Associate Liaison, Recruiting, Public Relations and Charter Reform.

The firm's largest department by far is litigation (forty-nine lawyers), which also includes a four-lawyer subdivision that handles product liability matters. The second largest is the corporate and securities department (twenty-eight lawyers), including banking, franchising and not-for-profit matters. The remaining six departments are real estate, family law, trusts and estates, tax and ERISA, environmental and entertainment. A number of lawyers practice in more than one area.

Recently the firm has expanded its environmental law practice both in size and scope; it not only represents clients who negotiate and litigate with governmental agencies concerning compliance with applicable law, it also is involved with counselling and transactional work. The department even publishes a newsletter. This aspect of the practice dovetails with the firm's related insurance litigation and counselling practice. The firm also has become affiliated with a prominent EEC counsel with offices in Brussels and Rome with whom it is co-editing a newsletter on Europe 1992. In the entertainment field, the firm's oldest and best-known practice area, Phillips Nizer counsels and documents investments in motion pictures for financial institutions. The firm continues to be active in copyright counselling and litigation. In addition, the firm has carved out niches in several areas, including work for banks and other corporate trustees, franchising and licensing work for *haute couture* firms, telecommunications companies and the defense of professionals in various disciplinary proceedings. Angelo Cometa, a litigating partner, is currently president of the New York State Bar Association.

While, as noted, no lawyer has emerged to replace Nizer, a number of lawyers generate substantial business, including George Berger (litigation), Neil Pollio (product liability), Jack Rabin (corporate and real estate), Monte Engler (corporate and telecommunications), Andrew Tunick, Neil Kleinhandler and Stanley Halperin. The firm is confident that, after the retirement of Messrs. Nizer and Ballon, it will retain the lion's share of their business. Its confidence in the future also was demonstrated when it decided to relocate its West 57th Street offices in the spring of 1991 to 31 West 52nd Street pursuant to a sublease of 115,000 square feet of space. While the returns are by no means in, the firm's management exudes energy, excitement and commitment—characteristics that had not been evident in the early and mid-1980s.

PROSKAUER ROSE GOETZ & MENDELSOHN

1585 Broadway • New York, New York 10036 • (212) 769-3000

Rating: 💼💼💼💼   *Direction:* ↑

*LAWYERS	PARTNERS	ASSOCIATES
1990: 325	96	199 ⟩ ⁰⁷
1989: 276	98	165
1988: 246	86	150
1987: 217	75	136
1986: 186	NA	NA

	Paralegals	Support
1990:	84	585
1989:	78	684
1988:	73	NA
1987:	56	468
1986:	50	NA

*LATERAL HIRES

1989: 30
1988: 26
1987: NA
1986: 35

STANLEY KOMAROFF

*CHAIRMAN: Edward Silver

*REPRESENTATIVE CLIENTS:

United Parcel Service, Home Box Office, Rhone-Poulenc, Republic National Bank, Club Med, Pirelli Cable, National Basketball Association, New York Philharmonic

*BRANCHES: Los Angeles (33), Washington (10), San Francisco (10), Boca Raton (2), Palm Beach (2), Clifton, N.J. (5), London (3)
Total: 67 lawyers (25p and 42a)

*AVERAGE ANNUAL BILLING HOURS:

Partners: NA
Associates: 1820

*NUMBER OF WOMEN

	Partners	Associates
1990:	8	79
1989:	8	53
1988:	7	44
1987:	NA	NA
1986:	NA	NA

*PARTNERSHIP TRACK: 8 years

*NUMBER OF LAWYERS FROM ENTERING CLASS TO MAKE PARTNER:

1981: 3 of 21
1980: 1 of 20
1979: 4 of 16
1978: 3 of 15

*GROSS REVENUE

1989: $120,000,000
1988: $97,500,000
1987: $80,000,000
1986: $65,000,000

*REVENUE PER LAWYER

1989: $355,000
1988: $335,000
1987: $300,000
1986: $285,000

*PROFITS PER PARTNER

1989: $360,000
1988: $340,000
1987: $315,000
1986: $285,000

*STARTING ASSOCIATE SALARY

1990: $82,000
1989: $82,000
1988: $77,000
1987: $66,000
1986: $65,000

*PRO BONO: NA

*HOURLY RATES (1989)

Partners: $205–$365
Associates: $100–$245

*PRINCIPAL LAW SCHOOLS (Associates): NYU (31), Columbia (24), Brooklyn (24), Fordham (23)

*NUMBER OF MINORITIES

	Partners	Associates
1990:	0	9
1989:	0	3
1988:	0	5
1987:	NA	NA
1986:	NA	NA

*SUMMER ASSOCIATES

1990: 45
1989: 41
1988: 47
1987: 23
1986: 30

For many years, Proskauer* was a haven for top Jewish law school graduates and lawyers systematically denied opportunities at white shoe firms. But starting in the 1960s, as ethnic lines in the legal profession began to disappear, this function became obsolete, and Proskauer decided to modify its distinctive culture and become more mainstream. While Proskauer continues to have a Jewish orientation, the firm no longer has a franchise either on the top Jewish recruits or on the "Our Crowd" clients that characterized the firm's earlier years. As one prominent litigator observes, when he thinks of Proskauer, he "doesn't have a sense of persona." Today's Proskauer is in transition, trying to secure a new, institutional client base and more top associates for a firm already renowned for its consistently excellent work product.

Most recently, the firm has tried to expand its client base by acquiring many key partners laterally, particularly in the corporate and litigation areas. Explains a headhunter, "For lateral partners, bringing business is important—not so much how much, but who." Proskauer's lateral game plan has upset some. "The quality of people is not as high since the firm resorted to lateral hirings," says a corporate partner, "but the new acquisitions are better business-getters." Contrariwise in the view of a legal consultant, the new laterals are of a high level and have integrated well into the firm. And, as an important corporate lateral states, "The Proskauer selectivity process—which is sometimes maddening—works to ensure that the firm's traditions of excellence, professionalism and community are maintained not only intact but stronger than ever."

The firm's lead name is that of the late Justice Joseph Proskauer, a justice of the New York State Appellate Division, First Department, a close political advisor to Al Smith and a highly regarded litigator. When Proskauer joined the firm in 1930, he gave vitality to the firm's litigation department and was its leader until 1971. William Rose founded the firm in 1875. Norman Goetz joined the firm in 1925 and Walter Mendelsohn, the lone surviving name partner, came aboard in 1921. The firm's

*As I was a partner of the firm for a year commencing July 1, 1988, I leave for the reader to determine whether my stay was a benefit or a handicap or both in preparing this profile.

name has remained the same since 1942. During its 115-year history, the firm has had three principal offices: 11 Broadway until 1955, when it moved to 300 Park Avenue (15,000 square feet initially, 175,000 square feet by 1989) and then to 1585 Broadway (400,000 square feet), where it moved in August 1990. The firm maintains a relatively large office in Los Angeles and smaller offices in Washington, Boca Raton, Palm Beach, Clifton, New Jersey, San Francisco and London. It recently opened small offices in Paris and Brussels.

Traditionally, Proskauer's major problem, despite the universally acknowledged excellence of its lawyers, has been attracting institutional corporate clients. As one leading litigator phrases it, the firm has "no inherited powers." While many other firms of similar size and age can depend on banks and investment banking houses to constitute 10–15% of their revenue, Proskauer has no Citibank or Merrill Lynch to anchor it. Although many of these corporations use individual Proskauer departments—particularly the labor practice—the firm has not secured them across the board.

Because of Proskauer's lack of major institutional clients and lack of premium billings in the M & A field, the firm has not made the financial jump into the first tier. In 1988, according to *The American Lawyer*, Proskauer entered the top forty firms in the country in gross revenue ($97,500,000), but did not keep pace with comparable firms in either revenue per lawyer or profits per partner; the firm's ranking was 37th in the former category ($335,000) and 43rd in the latter ($340,000). In 1989 the firm improved its financial results and rose in ranking in two of the three categories: gross revenue increased to $120,000,000 (37th); revenue per lawyer, $355,000 (33rd); and profits per partner, $360,000 (47th).

Proskauer is divided into six departments: corporate, labor, litigation, real estate, tax and personal planning. The firm's management-oriented labor and employment practice is the jewel in the crown and for many years has been acknowledged to be the best and most successful in New York. In this area the firm represents many of the country's largest and most prominent corporations as well as New York City non-profit cultural and civic organizations. The firm's labor client roster includes

United Parcel Service, Inc., Republic National Bank, Home Box Office, Inc. and the Metropolitan Opera Association. The department, which is composed of seventy-two lawyers, including twenty-eight partners, is headed by Ed Silver, who also leads the entire firm. He has a national reputation as a premier negotiator. Other key labor partners include Martin Oppenheimer, Marvin Dicker, Saul Kramer and Betsy Plevan.

The largest department in the firm (115 lawyers), by virtue of the recent lateral acquisitions, is corporate, which is co-headed by Stanley Komaroff and Klaus Eppler. The practice encompasses every aspect of corporate and commercial law, representing a numerous and diverse group of medium-size and large corporate clients. Key partners include Eppler, a leading securities lawyer; Robert Kaufman, a former president of the Bar Association of the City of New York, who heads the hospital and health law practice; and Komaroff and Bert Abrams, who are prodigious business originators. Alan Hyman, the head of the bankruptcy group, created this flourishing practice several years ago *ex nihilo*. In the fall of 1988, Arnold I. Burns, former deputy attorney general in the Reagan administration, joined the firm; prior to joining the Justice Department he had been instrumental in transforming a nine-person firm in New York into one of one hundred lawyers. Robert Kafin heads up an environmental regulation specialty within the department, and Gabe Perle and Jon Baumgarten are key lawyers in the intellectual property specialty.

Stephen Kaye and Michael Cardozo co-head the litigation department, which is composed of ninety lawyers, including nineteen partners. The litigation practice is extremely diverse and, besides representing its own clients, frequently is retained by other law firms and corporations engaged in a multiplicity of disputes. Jeffrey Mishkin is extensively engaged in sports and entertainment law, including representation of the National Basketball League. Other key litigators include Larry Lavinsky, Mort Maneker, Ron Rauschberg and Frank Bonem.

The tax department is co-headed by Alan Rosenberg and Ron Schact. Key lawyers in this department include Robert Levinsohn, Ruth Schapiro and Jay Friedman. The real estate department is co-headed by Bernard Tannenbaum and Herbert

Weinstein. Phil Hirsch heads the personal planning department.

Proskauer has a two-tier partnership and, although the firm makes a conscientious—and at times agonizing—effort to reach consensus on major decisions, ultimately power resides with the most significant members of the top tier—the managing partners. The managing partners set partner compensation and associate salaries. The full partnership votes on the admission of new partners (although associates are nominated for partnership by the partners in their department) as well as such firm-wide issues as branch offices or mergers.

One highly distinctive aspect of Proskauer's culture is its treatment of partners who reach the retirement age of 70. At most other firms, retirement-age partners leave the premises. At Proskauer, if they desire, older partners are placed on "optional service," which provides generous financial arrangements, offices, secretaries and all other firm services. Messrs. Proskauer, Rose and Goetz all remained active until their deaths at, respectively, 94, 95 and 85. At this writing, Walter Mendelsohn, 93, is still active. There are currently nine optional service partners.

While Proskauer continues to attract many top-level associates, who enjoy the intellectual atmosphere and special collegiality of the firm, its recent problems in recruiting top associates across the board have distorted the process by which it turns out work product. "The firm does high quality work," says one Proskauer corporate partner, "but it's done primarily by partners." Proskauer, seconds a former house counsel, is "missing in quality high-up associates." This, in turn, means that partners have less time for training associates; in *American Lawyer* surveys of mid-level associates in 1986 and 1988, erratic training is mentioned as a source of associate discontent, notwithstanding a senior lateral's observation that he had "never seen the likes of . . . the time, effort, money and resources which are committed to continuing legal education both on a structured and an informal basis." Moreover, this convoluted distribution of labor may have caused the tension and testiness evident in certain partner-associate relationships. These factors taken together may explain why Proskauer's acceptance rate by summer associates of permanent jobs is below that of compa-

Note

rable firms, or why there are frequent gaps in mid-level associates (three–five years) in certain departments. In the 1989 survey the firm ranked 34th out of 35 in New York in overall ranking, and while the firm rated high in client contact, court appearances, drafting of court documents and *pro bono* commitment, it received low scores in interest level of the work, training and partner-associate relations.

The firm's most recent move to more spacious quarters indicates Proskauer's keen determination to modernize, refine and expand its practice. While there is tremendous pressure to discard many cultural aspects that have sustained the firm, senior partners and administrators continue to wrestle with what to preserve, what to modify and what to abandon.

REID & PRIEST

40 West 57th Street • New York, New York 10019 • (212) 603-2000

Rating: 💼💼💼💼

Direction: ?

*LAWYERS	PARTNERS	ASSOCIATES
1990: 152	49	93
1989: 114	39	69
1988: 105	37	64
1987: 84	33	46
1986: 84	30	52

	Paralegals	Support
1990:	20	175
1989:	17	140
1988:	24	NA
1987:	22	150
1986:	30	NA

*LATERAL HIRES
1989: 18
1988: 5
1987: NA
1986: 10

*MANAGING PARTNER: Daniel L. Bernstein

*REPRESENTATIVE CLIENTS:
Florida Power & Light, Mitsubishi Corporation, Hitachi Zosen Corporation, Kansas Gas & Electric Company

*BRANCHES: Washington (40)

*AVERAGE ANNUAL BILLING HOURS (1989):
Partners: NA
Associates: 1767

*NUMBER OF WOMEN

	Partners	Associates
1990:	4	38
1989:	3	28
1988:	3	25
1987:	2	21
1986:	1	16

*PARTNERSHIP TRACK: 8–9 years

*NUMBER OF LAWYERS FROM ENTERING CLASS TO MAKE PARTNER:
1981: 2 of 10
1980: 0 of 9
1979: 2 of 8
1978: 5 of 6

*GROSS REVENUE
1989: NA
1988: NA
1987: NA
1986: NA

*REVENUE PER LAWYER
1989: NA
1988: NA
1987: NA
1986: NA

*PROFITS PER PARTNER
1989: NA
1988: NA
1987: NA
1986: NA

*STARTING ASSOCIATE SALARY
1990: NA
1989: $77,000
1988: $73,000
1987: NA
1986: $62,000

*PRO BONO: 4–7% of total time

*HOURLY RATES (1989)
Partners: NA
Associates: NA

*PRINCIPAL LAW SCHOOLS
(Associates): Fordham (7), NYU (6), Columbia (5), Georgetown (5)

*NUMBER OF MINORITIES

	Partners	Associates
1990:	1	9
1989:	0	4
1988:	1	2
1987:	0	1
1986:	0	3

*SUMMER ASSOCIATES
1990: 18
1989: 15
1988: 19
1987: 12
1986: 16

Reid & Priest was built on a foundation of utility work. Recently, the firm embarked on an aggressive expansion drive, trying to diversify its practice primarily through lateral acquisitions. One senior litigator sardonically refers to the firm as "a junior Finley Kumble." Despite successfully attracting some top quality laterals, Reid & Priest's broadening effort has faltered. Its rent expense doubled when it moved from Wall Street to midtown in 1985. And the firm failed to rate among the top 100 firms nationally in gross revenues, revenue per lawyer or profits per partner between 1986 and 1989 according to *The American Lawyer*. Poor management decisions plus no financial dynamism has put Reid & Priest in a position where, as a legal consultant put it with some hyperbole, the firm "would merge with anyone who'd offer."

In 1935, Frank Reid, Samuel Murphy and A. J. F. Priest founded the firm then called Reid & Murphy. All three of the firm's founders came from the legal department of Electric Bond and Share Company, which in the 1930s was affiliated with General Electric and was one of the largest companies in the world. When Murphy became the president of Electric Bond and Share in 1936, the firm's name changed to its present form, Reid & Priest. In 1952, Priest retired to teach, although he remained of counsel to the firm.

A nine-partner Executive Committee, elected by the full partnership for three-year terms, governs Reid & Priest. The Executive Committee appoints a managing partner, currently Daniel Bernstein, who chairs the committee. The committee also makes recommendations on the admission of new partners, handles partner compensation and associate salaries and chooses members for the firm's other committees: Office Operations, Lawyer and Paraprofessional Personnel, Finances and Accounting, Client and Professional Development, Firm Development and Expansion, Fringe Benefits and Taxes and Office Location.

Reid & Priest is divided into five departments: corporate (which is by far the largest), litigation, tax, real estate and trusts and estates. The corporate department has three subdivisions: financing, international and general business law. Reid & Priest has done transactional financial work primarily for utilities such as Duke Power Company, Florida Power & Light and the Kansas

Gas and Electric Company. Japan has been the site of much of the firm's international work, and Reid & Priest's Japanese clients include Mitsubishi Corporation and Hitachi Zosen Corporation. Banking, M & A and labor are just some of the specialties under the umbrella of general business law. Corporate department head William Baker focuses primarily on financing, as does Robert Schuur. David LeFevre does international work but has also developed a specialty in sports law; he represents U.S. and Japanese baseball clubs. Charles Read's practice extends to all three corporate subdivisions.

Charles Schirmeister heads the litigation department, the first function of which is to defend the corporate department's utility clients. Observers single out Gerald Aksen for praise.

The firm maintains a large branch office in Washington (34, 1948), which merged in 1979 with the Washington-based firm of Colby, Miller & Hanes. All the name partners of that firm went to Reid & Priest, including William Colby, a former head of the CIA (1973–1976).

Associates gave Reid & Priest high marks in the 1988 survey of *The American Lawyer*, ranking the firm fourth out of 37. This represented a remarkable turnaround from the 1986 survey when the firm placed 39th among 41 firms. The key differences between Reid & Priest '86 and Reid & Priest '88: improved training and better partnership chances. The firm had gone a demoralizing two and a half years before electing a non-lateral partner in late 1986 (post-survey). Moreover, although associates had a below-average workload, they received even more below-average salaries. While in the 1988 survey associates reported good relations within the firm, a headhunter believes that Reid & Priest attracts and nurtures "some of the worst people [she's] ever met—cold." The atmosphere is "unhelpful, testing . . . [the attitude is] 'See if you're tough enough.' "

ROGERS & WELLS

200 Park Avenue • New York, New York 10166 • (212) 878-8000

Rating: 💼💼💼💼

Direction: ?

*LAWYERS

	PARTNERS	ASSOCIATES
1990: 223	73	135
1989: 200	71	126
1988: 192	67	114
1987: 158	55	92
1986: 145	48	83

	Paralegals	Support
1990:	40	345
1989:	30	334
1988:	NA	NA
1987:	24	249
1986:	NA	NA

*LATERAL HIRES

1989: 6
1988: 3
1987: NA
1986: 4

*SUPERVISING PARTNER: James M. Asher

*REPRESENTATIVE CLIENTS:

Merrill Lynch, Newsweek, Inc., Associated Press, Dreyfus Corporation, Oppenheimer & Co., Ladies Professional Golf Association

*BRANCHES: Washington (31), Los Angeles (40), Paris (7), London (6)
Total: 84 lawyers (34p and 50a)

*AVERAGE ANNUAL BILLING HOURS (1989):

Partners: NA
Associates: 2000

*NUMBER OF WOMEN

	Partners	Associates
1990:	6	51
1989:	6	47
1988:	6	41
1987:	6	30
1986:	5	26

*PARTNERSHIP TRACK: 8 years

*NUMBER OF LAWYERS FROM ENTERING CLASS TO MAKE PARTNER:

1980: 2 of 11
1979: 4 of 11
1978: 5 of 14
1977: 2 of 12

*GROSS REVENUE

1989: $99,000,000
1988: $87,000,000
1987: $66,000,000
1986: $55,000,000

*REVENUE PER LAWYER

1989: $355,000
1988: $350,000
1987: $310,000
1986: $260,000

*PROFITS PER PARTNER

1989: $320,000
1988: $315,000
1987: $275,000
1986: $280,000

*STARTING ASSOCIATE SALARY

1990: $82,000
1989: $82,000
1988: $77,000
1987: $66,000
1986: $66,000

*PRO BONO: more than 10% of total time

*HOURLY RATES

Partners: NA
Associates: NA

*PRINCIPAL LAW SCHOOLS
(Associates): NYU (12%), Columbia (9%), Harvard (8%), Georgetown (7%), Cornell (7%)

*NUMBER OF MINORITIES

	Partners	Associates
1990:	1	16
1989:	1	7
1988:	1	7
1987:	1	5
1986:	1	3

*SUMMER ASSOCIATES

1990: 36
1989: 41
1988: 38
1987: 29
1986: 26

Rogers & Wells is often portrayed as a political firm, or, as one commentator put it, the Republican counterpart to Shea & Gould. Indeed, many of its current and past leaders have been involved in politics and government: William Rogers, attorney general in the Eisenhower administration and secretary of state during the Nixon administration; John Wells, an important figure in New York Republican circles who managed campaigns for Governor Nelson Rockefeller and Senator Jacob Javits; William Casey, chairman of the SEC and undersecretary for economic affairs, Department of State in the Nixon administration, chairman and president of the Export-Import Bank in the Ford administration, and head of the CIA in the Reagan administration. Earlier, Kenneth Royall had been secretary of war during the Truman administration. Rogers & Wells acts as a registered lobbyist before the New York State legislature and state agencies. The firm also maintains a thirty-lawyer Washington office, opened in 1950, currently headed by Caspar Weinberger, secretary of defense in the Reagan administration.

Although the firm flourished from the 1950s to the 1970s, today's Rogers & Wells is viewed as having wavering leadership and producing an all-too-frequent mediocre work product. "The leadership is questionable," says a legal consultant, "and this has led to internal strife . . . and high turnover." A senior litigator calls the firm's product "no more than workmanlike," while a senior corporate lawyer judges that the firm "has a better reputation than the work merits." Observers also accuse the firm of being superficial in its hiring choices. Rogers & Wells' lawyers, says a senior litigator sarcastically, "are right out of central casting—the best-looking fellows in the business. Substance doesn't matter there." On the other hand, a legal consultant refers to the firm as "gutsy" and "scrappy."

Financially, the firm appears healthier than some observers think it is. Gross revenues and revenue per lawyer grew steadily between 1986 and 1988; the former increased from $55,000,000 to $87,000,000, the latter from $260,000 to $350,000. Rogers & Wells also moved up in *The American Lawyer* rankings in these categories. Profits per partner, by contrast, have vacillated from $280,000 in 1986 to $275,000 in 1987, then back up in 1988 to $315,000; the firm's rankings have followed suit, ranging from 41st to 56th to 51st. In 1989 revenue increased 12% to $99,000,000 while both revenue per lawyer and profits per partner increased slightly over 1% to $355,000 and $320,000, respectively. Despite the upward tilt of these figures, one prominent litigator is convinced that the firm is moving in the opposite direction.

Rogers & Wells traces its history back to 1871. The modern firm took shape, however, when what was then Hughes, Schurman & Dwight split in 1937; one faction, led by Charles Evans Hughes, Jr., re-formed as Hughes Hubbard & Reed; the other, headed first by Kenneth Royall from 1950 to 1961 (the firm was called Royall Koegel & Wells) and then by Otto Koegel, became Rogers & Wells in 1973 when William Rogers returned from government service and took over the helm. Rogers is a top business originator and has secured such clients as Merrill Lynch and 20th Century Fox. (When Marvin Davis gained control of Fox in 1981, he directed most of its legal business elsewhere.) Rogers also represented the interests of the late Shah of Iran, the Pahlavi Foundation and Air France. John Wells served as the firm's managing partner until his death in 1980; he was succeeded by Caesar Pitassy, who gave way to Victor Ganzi (who left the firm in the spring of 1990 to become general counsel to Hearst Corporation). James Asher is the current managing partner.

A six-partner Executive Committee governs Rogers & Wells. Members are appointed for terms with no fixed duration. The committee recommends appointments to the firm's other committees and, with the Personnel Committee, recommends the admission of new partners. The Executive Committee also, after consultation with partners, determines partnership shares. Most major firm decisions are put to the partnership; if a consensus is not reached, each partner votes according to his interest in the firm. The firm has two-tiers of partners—senior and junior.

Rogers & Wells has six practice areas: litigation, corporate, real estate, tax, trusts and estates and insurance. Corporate and litigation far outstrip the other practice areas. The litigation department, headed by James Weidner, showcases a powerful libel practice. The firm represents the Associated Press and Newsweek, Inc. in this capacity. The litigation department as a whole receives mixed reviews. One well-known trial lawyer opines that although Rogers & Wells is "known for strong litigation, they have never had strong litigation." Beyond Merrill Lynch, the corporate department represents clients including the Dreyfus Corporation, Oppenheimer & Co. and the Ladies Professional Golf Association. Sources disagree as to whether Rogers & Wells' corporate client roster passes muster. A senior corporate lawyer calls the firm's corporate clients "excellent," but a legal consultant says the firm lacks a large institutional base. Observers laud department head David Bernstein and James Ryan within the corporate division.

Beyond the Washington branch, the firm has a large Los Angeles office (42, 1979) and smaller offices in London (6, 1976) and Paris (7, 1965).

In *American Lawyer* surveys of New York firms in 1986 and 1988, associates placed Rogers & Wells in the middle of the pack. While the firm consistently received high marks for collegiality, associates repeatedly complained about sub-par working conditions. As a headhunter says, the firm is "pleasant, but they put three associates in one office." Associates also noted that Rogers & Wells is a firm in flux, moving toward modernity by emphasizing billings more and training and guidance less. Still, the firm's 1988 average yearly billable hours for associates is roughly 1,800—a gentlemanly pace in today's New York legal scene. While the firm moved from 21st to 17th place in the 1989 survey, substantially the same ambience appears to exist. Client contact remains light while hours billed and partner feedback, training, and guidance remain average. The firm's commitment to *pro bono* work has been perceived to have increased. Little communication appears to exist between partners and associates; as one associate put it, "Partnership is completely foggy for all associates at mid-level."

ROSENMAN & COLIN

575 Madison Avenue • New York, New York 10022 • (212) 940-8800

Rating: 💼💼💼💼

Direction: ?

*LAWYERS

	PARTNERS	ASSOCIATES
1990: 241	72	136
1989: 222	69	128
1988: 211	NA	NA
1987: 204	69	122
1986: 209	73	134

	Paralegals	Support
1990:	40	375
1989:	40	375
1988:	44	NA
1987:	48	372
1986:	35	NA

*LATERAL HIRES

1989: 25
1988: 16
1987: NA
1986: 14

*CHAIRMAN: Howard Schneider

*REPRESENTATIVE CLIENTS:

Sony Corporation, Lehman Ark Management Corp., Prudential Bache Securities, Cadillac Fairview

*BRANCHES: Washington (6)
Total: 6 lawyers (3p and 3a)

*AVERAGE ANNUAL BILLING HOURS:

Partners: NA
Associates: 1850

*NUMBER OF WOMEN

	Partners	Associates
1990:	5	70
1989:	6	69
1988:	NA	NA
1987:	4	63
1986:	3	63

*PARTNERSHIP TRACK: 8 years

*NUMBER OF LAWYERS FROM ENTERING CLASS TO MAKE PARTNER:

1981: NA of 14
1980: 3 of 16
1979: 3 of 15
1978: 4 of 16

*GROSS REVENUE

1989: $80,000,000
1988: $65,000,000
1987: $54,000,000
1986: $63,000,000

*REVENUE PER LAWYER

1989: $355,000
1988: $305,000
1987: $250,000
1986: $280,000

*PROFITS PER PARTNER

1989: $360,000
1988: $255,000
1987: $210,000
1986: $275,000

*STARTING ASSOCIATE SALARY

1990: $82,000
1989: $82,000
1988: $76,000
1987: $65,000
1986: $65,000

*PRO BONO: 1–3% of total time

*HOURLY RATES (1989)

Partners: $250–$400
Associates: $100–$245

*PRINCIPAL LAW SCHOOLS
(Associates): NYU (15), Columbia (14), Georgetown (8), Harvard (4), University of Pennsylvania (4)

*NUMBER OF MINORITIES

	Partners	Associates
1989:	0	5
1988:	0	5
1987:	0	3
1986:	0	7

*SUMMER ASSOCIATES

1990: 27
1989: 27
1988: 32
1987: 25
1986: 30

Rosenman & Colin is a grand old Jewish-oriented firm that until recently had fallen on hard times. Although the firm is energetically attempting to reverse this trend and recent operating results hold out promise, financial difficulties and internal dissension have impeded the firm's efforts. Rosenman, says a legal consultant, "has all sorts of problems . . . including clients." Spoken before 1989 results were known, a senior litigator concluded, "Possibly its best days are behind it."

Rosenman's troubles can be said to have begun in 1969 when CBS chairman William Paley discharged his personal lawyer, Ralph Colin. Colin, a trustee of the Museum of Modern Art (MOMA), had protested fellow trustee Paley's dismissal of MOMA's director as "an improper procedure." As a result of the dispute between the two men, Rosenman promptly lost longtime major client CBS to Cravath. Another blow came in 1980 when the firm was named a defendant in a $10 million anti-trust suit and was investigated by the Appellate Division because lateral acquisition Jack Bronston involved the firm in a conflict of interest between two companies competing for New York City bus shelter franchises. Bronston, while a partner at Rosenman, represented one company while the firm itself represented investors in the other company. After the conflict was publicly revealed, Bronston resigned from the firm and was convicted of mail fraud; the firm, although left financially unscathed by the lawsuit and investigation, suffered unfavorable publicity that raised questions about its ethical standards and the efficacy of its internal operations. In 1986, five partners and more than thirty associates left the firm. "We became a little too loose in our management," concluded senior partner Mendes Hershman.

Led by lateral partners Donald Siskind and Howard Schneider with senior litigation partner Gerald Walpin, the firm addressed its financial problems and, in early 1987, implemented four basic decisions: over 25% of the partners' draws were reduced or frozen; three partners (two young, one middle-aged) were asked to leave; a compensation system that considers work quality, area of specialty, business origination and productivity replaced lockstep seniority compensation; and the firm began to search for lateral acquisitions or a merger.

Financially, these measures brought the firm back at the end of 1988, after a disastrous 1987, roughly to where it was before the crisis. According to *The American Lawyer*, gross revenues had dropped from $63 million in 1986 to $54 million in 1987; in 1988, the firm recouped the loss with revenues of $65 million. Similarly, revenue per lawyer went down from $280,000 to $250,000 then back up to $305,000, in the same three-year span. The figures most affected by the Rosenman program (and most indicative of its progress) are those for profits per partner. Typically, the numbers drop from $275,000 to $210,000 between 1986 and 1987. In 1988, however, profits per partner rose only to $255,000, reflecting the decision to reduce or freeze many partnership draws. In 1989 the firm recorded substantial increments in revenue (20% increase to $80,000,000), revenue per lawyer (15% increase to $355,000) and, most significantly, profits per partner (a 40% increase to $360,000), suggesting that management's decisions are being properly maintained.

Although Rosenman's roots extend back to 1912, the modern firm took shape in 1946, led by Judge Samuel Rosenman, Ralph Colin and two other lawyers. Rosenman, a former New York Supreme Court justice and leader of the New York bar, headed the firm from 1946 until his death in 1973. He is perhaps best remembered as a confidant of Franklin Delano Roosevelt. Rosenman actually coined the term "New Deal" and wrote the memorable words "The only thing we have to fear is fear itself" in Roosevelt's first Inaugural Address. The firm name changed three times between 1946 and 1986 before it was institutionalized to Rosenman & Colin in 1987.

A seven-member Management Committee, chosen for three-year terms from a top tier of senior partners, governs the firm. The committee can propose changes in partner compensation which senior partners must approve. The entire partnership votes on the admittance of new partners.

The firm has five major practice areas: litigation, corporate and securities, real estate, tax and trusts and estates. Litigation has traditionally been the strongest and still constitutes a disproportionately large portion of its business. Observers single out Walpin, Hershman, Robert Gottlieb and Asa Sokolow as the firm's outstanding litigators. Howard Schneider is universally acknowledged as Rosenman's corporate leader—"the one good guy," says a corporate lawyer at another leading New York firm. Attracting star lawyers and big-name clients has become a chronic problem for Rosenman. As put by a former partner, "Historically, there has not been the senior-level renowned corporate partner who you have in most major law firms."

The real estate department acquired twenty lawyers from the now-dissolved Marshall Bratter Greene Allison & Tucker and is led by former Marshall partner Donald Siskind. Beyond Siskind, sources laud Samuel Lindenbaum in this department.

Associates at Rosenman have clearly and frequently expressed their discontent with the firm. In the 1988 *American Lawyer* survey, Rosenman ranked dead last among thirty-seven firms and was lambasted for not giving associates interesting work, handing out little responsibility, what one headhunter calls "hit-and-miss training" and rocky partner-associate relations. Says a former house counsel of Rosenman's internal dealings, "It can be like a . . . dog house." Associates logged many of the same complaints in 1986, when the firm further damaged morale by issuing a press release stating that Cravath's $12,000 per year increase in associates' salaries was "perverse and self-destructive." Rosenman reversed its position after receiving numerous complaints from its associates. However, in 1989 the firm's ranking increased to 13th, the turnaround being attributed to improving associate training and responding to associate concerns, including installation of computers in all offices, renovating the office and creating an associate relations committee. There was no perceived improvement in associate-partner relations, hands-on litigation experience or firm demands for increased billings.

SCHULTE ROTH & ZABEL

900 Third Avenue • New York, New York 10022 • (212) 758-0404

Rating: 💼💼💼💼   *Direction:* ↑

*LAWYERS	PARTNERS	ASSOCIATES
1990: 156	40	116
1989: 132	37	92
1988: 130	36	89
1987: 124	29	95
1986: 120	28	92

	Paralegals	Support
1990:	34	212
1989:	32	195
1988:	30	NA
1987:	32	NA
1986:	33	NA

*LATERAL HIRES

1989: 17
1988: 17
1987: NA
1986: 26

*MANAGING PARTNER: Howard Sharfstein

*REPRESENTATIVE CLIENTS:

Morgan Stanley & Co., Nomura Securities, Citibank

*BRANCHES: Palm Beach (1)
Total: 1 lawyer (1p)

*AVERAGE ANNUAL BILLING HOURS (1989):

Partners: NA
Associates: 1900

*NUMBER OF WOMEN

	Partners	Associates
1990:	4	49
1989:	4	39
1988:	3	45
1987:	NA	NA
1986:	NA	NA

*PARTNERSHIP TRACK: 6–8 years

*NUMBER OF LAWYERS FROM ENTERING CLASS TO MAKE PARTNER:

1981: 3 of NA
1980: 2 of NA
1979: 3 of NA
1978: 3 of NA

*GROSS REVENUE

1989: NA
1988: NA
1987: NA
1986: NA

*REVENUE PER LAWYER

1989: NA
1988: NA
1987: NA
1986: NA

*PROFITS PER PARTNER

1989: NA
1988: NA
1987: NA
1986: NA

*STARTING ASSOCIATE SALARY

1990: $77,000
1989: $76,000
1988: $73,000
1987: $68,000
1986: $62,000

*PRO BONO: 3–5% of total time

*HOURLY RATES

Partners: NA
Associates: $90–$210

*PRINCIPAL LAW SCHOOLS
(Associates): NYU (15), Harvard (7), Columbia (6), Fordham (6), Brooklyn (5), Hofstra (5), University of Pennsylvania (5)

*NUMBER OF MINORITIES

	Partners	Associates
1990:	0	10
1989:	0	8
1988:	0	7
1987:	NA	NA
1986:	NA	NA

*SUMMER ASSOCIATES

1990: 25
1989: 24
1988: 20
1987: NA
1986: NA

One headhunter's view of Schulte Roth—"aggressive, aggressive, aggressive"—may be the key ingredient in the firm's success to date. Although Schulte did not register in the top 100 firms nationally in gross revenue, revenue per lawyer or profits per partner between 1986 and 1989 according to *The American Lawyer*, the firm still has grown ahead of schedule. In 1985, when Schulte had ninety-eight lawyers, the firm projected it would have 125–135 lawyers within five years. By 1990, Schulte had 156 lawyers. As a legal consultant concludes, "Schulte Roth is one of the stronger mid-size firms in New York" which, another legal consultant noted, was ethnically balanced.

The reason for Schulte's lagging financial results is the lack of major corporate clients, a condition that plagues many younger, mid-sized firms. In fact, the firm may appear more profitable than it is in real terms, because, as a corporate lawyer points out, its lawyers "are younger and can be paid less." A legal consultant agrees, noting that while the firm "makes very good money" now, when the associates become partners, there could be problems. "I wouldn't bet on them in the early nineties."

Schulte Roth & Zabel was founded in 1969 by solo practitioner Thomas Baer and six associates from three leading New York firms: John McGoldrick (Kaye Scholer); Charles Goldstein and Steven Schulte (Fried Frank); and Paul Roth, Dan Shapiro and William Zabel (Cleary Gottlieb). Known initially as Baer & McGoldrick (1969–1978), the firm changed its name first to Schulte & McGoldrick (1978–1980) and then—when McGoldrick became counsel to New York governor Hugh Carey—to its present name. McGoldrick returned to the firm after completing his government service.

A nine-member Executive Committee governs the firm. Paul Roth functions as de facto head of the committee and has been the partner most extensively involved in all facets of the firm's operations. Stephen Schulte oversees recruiting, Burton Lehman controls the budget and Howard Sharfstein handles the firm's day-to-day administration. Four seats on the Executive Committee are customarily reserved for younger partners. A special committee, larger than the Executive Committee, determines partnership shares. The full partnership votes—on a one-partner, one-vote principle—to admit new partners.

The firm is composed of five departments: corporate, real estate, litigation, trusts and estates and tax. Schulte was compelled to diversify when the business it was built upon disappeared. Great Western United, a conglomerate primarily serviced by Baer, was supposed to provide the fledgling firm with significant real estate, corporate and tax work. When the Hunt brothers acquired Great Western in 1973, however, the firm lost the client which had contributed 25% of its revenues since inception.

Observers' comments on Schulte's lawyers and work product are uniformly favorable, despite much personnel shuffling. In 1979 the firm's litigation head left under an unsuccessful three-year experiment with the firm. Then John Madden became the head of the department but left in 1980 when he was appointed as the U.S. attorney for the Southern District of New York. Current litigation head David Brodsky, a lateral acquired from Guggenheim & Untermeyer, receives plaudits, as does former U.S. attorney for the Southern District of New York, John Martin (who left in 1990 to become a federal judge in the Southern District of New York). One senior litigator calls the firm "a comer" and its litigation practice "the tops"; another, that Schulte's litigators "show a high degree of intelligence and produce very good work."

Paul Roth, who leads the corporate department, built Schulte's municipal finance practice virtually by himself. Roth was also consistently one of the firm's top three business originators between 1980 and 1985 whose clients include Morgan Stanley & Co., Dillon Read & Co., Oppenheimer & Co., Weiss, Peck & Greer and HPB Associates. Jeffrey Sabin, who spearheads the firm's bankruptcy practice, also wins accolades.

In 1979 Charles Goldstein and his six-lawyer real estate department departed for Weil Gotshal over a dispute concerning the emphasis to be placed on his department compared to other departments in the firm. Paul Nussbaum joined the firm as Goldstein's successor. Sources laud Nussbaum and the department as a whole. William Zabel (trusts and estates) and Daniel Shapiro (tax) are also cited as key lawyers.

The firm maintains a small office in Palm Beach (1, 1974).

Schulte associates seem to have soured on the firm in the recent past. The firm ranked first in a 1986 *American Lawyer* survey; Schulte then was reported to provide its associates with excellent training, interesting work and responsibility without overworking them. The firm also was responsive to associates' input. In 1988, however, Schulte placed only 29th among 37 firms as associates offered widely varying responses. One associate stated that "the supposed good-feeling-all-around attitude is often contradicted by partners' treatment of associates as fungible, unthinking hired lackeys." An increasing number of associates left or contemplated leaving. This could also be due (partially) to what one headhunter termed "an associate glut" in the real estate department, which was causing the firm to "place a lot of people out."

SHEA & GOULD

1251 Avenue of the Americas • New York, New York 10020 • (212) 827-3000

Rating: 💼💼💼💼　　　　　*Direction:* ↓

*LAWYERS

	PARTNERS	ASSOCIATES
1990: 262	87	170
1989: 272	93	160
1988: 265	85	155
1987: 253	84	150
1986: 242	77	132

	Paralegals	Support
1990:	69	384
1989:	76	348
1988:	77	NA
1987:	56	295
1986:	47	NA

*LATERAL HIRES

1989: 22
1988: 16
1987: NA
1986: 28

*CHAIRMAN: None

*REPRESENTATIVE CLIENTS:

Toys 'R' Us, Madison Square Garden, British Petroleum, TCI, Touche Ross & Co., LILCO, Bear, Stearns & Co., Inc., Rupert Murdoch

*BRANCHES: Washington (9), Los Angeles (3), Miami (22), Bradenton, Fla. (6), Albany (2)
Total: 42 lawyers (17p and 25a)

*AVERAGE ANNUAL BILLING HOURS:
Partners: NA
Associates: 1779

*NUMBER OF WOMEN

	Partners	Associates
1990:	8	65
1989:	10	62
1988:	9	57
1987:	6	56
1986:	3	42

*PARTNERSHIP TRACK: 8 years

*NUMBER OF LAWYERS FROM ENTERING CLASS TO MAKE PARTNER:

1981: 5 of 11
1980: 11 of 16
1979: 3 of 10
1978: 7 of 9

*GROSS REVENUE

1989: $123,000,000
1988: $125,000,000
1987: $90,000,000
1986: $64,000,000

*REVENUE PER LAWYER

1989: $405,000
1988: $355,000
1987: $255,000
1986: $225,000

*PROFITS PER PARTNER

1989: $345,000
1988: $315,000
1987: $270,000
1986: $240,000

*STARTING ASSOCIATE SALARY

1990: $80,000
1989: $76,000
1988: $71,000
1987: $65,000
1986: $65,000

*PRO BONO: 1–3% of total time

*HOURLY RATES (1989)
Partners: $250–$350
Associates: $115–$250

*PRINCIPAL LAW SCHOOLS
(Associates): Fordham (15), NYU (10), University of Pennsylvania (10), New York Law School (9), Georgetown (9), Columbia (8), Harvard (7)

*NUMBER OF MINORITIES

	Partners	Associates
1990:	2	7
1989:	2	10
1988:	2	6
1987:	1	5
1986:	1	5

*SUMMER ASSOCIATES

1990: 24
1989: 37
1988: 37
1987: 27
1986: 29

Shea & Gould is a firm in the throes of a leadership crisis. Its legendary and autocratic founders, William Shea and Milton Gould, have passed on their power to the firm's next generation. That generation, however, predominantly Jerome Kern and Thomas Constance, have transformed Shea & Gould into a colder, more bottom-line oriented organization, seeking to homogenize its rough edges and hardball attitude and make it into a national corporate law firm.

As illustrated recently in the firm's branch office crack-ups in Miami and then Los Angeles, Shea & Gould increasingly is a firm where lawyers are unhappy with their circumstances. In mid-1988, when a compensation dispute arose in Miami and four partners filed a suit against the firm, Shea & Gould's reaction was fast and bloody; it fired ten partners and five associates. In 1989, partners in the firm's seventy-lawyer Los Angeles branch felt shortchanged in the distribution-of-profits schedule. When they asked the firm to revise the schedule, they were rebuffed. In early March, eighteen lawyers from the branch left to join Myerson & Kuhn (which has since disbanded). Again, Shea & Gould's management reacted explosively, announcing that the entire branch would close. Two days later, the Executive Committee changed its mind and decided that instead of closing, the branch would merely shrink to a "small nucleus" of lawyers. None too surprisingly, the firm could not coax back any partners—and only four associates—to be part of the nucleus.

Observers see today's Shea & Gould as extremely segmented. "It's hard to think of it as a firm—there is no central definition to them. Instead, it is a collection of individuals," says a senior litigator. Another litigator views the firm even more harshly: "Individualistic lawyers who worry more about their image than about the client."

Despite all these problems, Shea & Gould has become more profitable in recent years. The firm's financial growth, however, lags far behind its growth in size. Between 1985 and 1989, the firm expanded from 174 to 385 lawyers and by 1988, became the sixteenth largest firm in the nation. Although from 1985 through 1988 Shea & Gould quadrupled its gross revenues from $36.4 million to $125 million, it ranked only 28th on *The*

American Lawyer list of the top 100 firms nationally in gross revenue. Similarly, the firm's profits per partner increased from $240,000 in 1986 to $315,000, but this was only enough to move Shea & Gould up from 63rd place to 51st. (Shea & Gould's vastly expensive move and stark minimalist furnishing of its Exxon Building facilities in 1985, estimated at $8 million over the $14–17 million budget originally set, have not buoyed up partners' spirits or pocketbooks.) The firm did make a big leap forward in revenue per lawyer with an increase from $225,000 (1986) to $350,000 (1988) and an upward swing from 78th place to 28th in *The American Lawyer* survey. While revenue in 1989 decreased about 2% to $123,000,000, the firm was able to increase its revenue per lawyer 15% to $405,000 and its profits per partner to $345,000.

The firm was initially the result of a 1964 merger between Manning Hollinger & Shea and Gallop Climenko & Gould. Manning Hollinger, founded in 1950, had strong real estate, trusts and estates, and corporate practices; Gallop Climenko had been Kaufman Gallop Climenko & Gould—litigation specialists led by trial lawyer Samuel Kaufman until 1948 when he became a federal district judge. Both William Shea and Milton Gould soon emerged as two of New York's most well-known and high-profile lawyers. "Gould is a terrific lawyer, Shea, a great promoter," says a prominent trial lawyer. William Shea, 84, after whom Shea Stadium is named, has long been a powerhouse behind the scenes in city and state Democratic circles. Gould, 82, is a front-line litigator, a law school teacher, a prolific writer and a raconteur of the first rank. Both Shea and Gould cultivated a reputation for themselves and the firm generally as being street fighters and brokers, definitely not the genteel, white shoe "statesmen" (as Shea likes to say) generally found in law firms Shea & Gould's size.

After the 1964 merger, the firm was called Shea Gallop Climenko & Gould and then, in 1971, changed to Shea Gould Climenko & Kramer. In 1974, the firm merged with the five-lawyer Casey Craig & Constance and became Shea Gould Climenko & Casey. The period between 1978 and 1980 was a time of particularly rapid expansion for Shea & Gould as it absorbed three smaller firms—six-lawyer Bartel Engelman &

Fishman in 1978, seven-lawyer Amend & Amend, estate specialists, in 1979 and six-lawyer Lynton & Klein in 1980. Not
all of these pairings yielded favorable results: Miles Amend
passed away before the merger could begin to produce results
and five other Amend & Amend partners departed from Shea
& Gould soon after the deal, because, it is rumored, they did
not generate the expected billings. In 1978–79 alone, the
firm added nineteen lateral partners. The most notable of these
was Benjamin Bartel, both a corporate/real estate attorney and
longtime chairman of the board of Alexander's department
stores. In 1979, Robert Casey and John Craig, the firm's star
tax lawyers, left to join Finley Kumble because of a dispute
concerning fees; also in 1979, Jesse Climenko took of counsel
status. The firm name was then shortened and, as Gould noted
wryly, made honest, when it became Shea & Gould.

Despite all the mergers and dramatic expansion in the 1970s,
this decade proved relatively steady compared to the rocky
1980s. In 1984, Milton Gould had triple bypass surgery, which
convinced the firm elders that the time had come to turn over
the reins to younger partners. Messrs. Shea and Gould gave
teeth to the Executive Committee they had created in 1979,
relinquishing their veto power. Corporate partner Allan Tessler
emerged as the heir apparent (and basically crowned himself in
a 1985 *American Lawyer* article) because of his client roster,
strong personality and reputation as Gould's protégé. Under
Tessler, the firm became even more ambitious and more expansive. First, Tessler wooed over Charles Goldstein and his
billion-dollar real estate clientele from Weil Gotshal. Then,
Tessler led the way toward the firm's ill-fated California mergers, with the eight-lawyer Gold, Herscher, Marks & Pepper
in early 1985 and then with the forty-three-lawyer Pacht, Ross,
Warne, Bernhard & Sears later that same year. As both the Los
Angeles and Miami branches fell apart, Tessler essentially withdrew from the firm; by 1989, he was living in Wyoming, being
of counsel and a principal of the International Finance Group,
a merchant banking group and Shea & Gould client.

The governing power at Shea & Gould now rests with a seven-
member Executive Committee which selects its own members,
sets partner compensation and decides on associate salaries. The

committee also approves the department heads' nominations of associates for partner. Before 1984, Shea and Gould had veto power over all Executive Committee decisions. Currently, the members of the Executive Committee are Jerome Kern, Thomas Constance, Charles Goldstein, Bernard Ruggieri, Arnold Jacobs, Leon Gold and Martin Shelton. Observers are highly critical of the firm's recent management. *The American Lawyer* opined: "The dramas in Miami and Los Angeles show a Shea & Gould in transition from a firm run by a pair of patriarchs to one led by seven men who are no less dictatorial but a lot less effective."

The firm has three primary practice areas: (the traditional) litigation, (the more recent emphasis) corporate/banking and (the imported) real estate. Shea & Gould also has several small service departments: tax, trusts and estates, labor, bankruptcy and "other." Observers agree that the firm's quality of work and lawyers are inconsistent. "Spotty," comments a judge pithily. "The work product, in my experience, is average at best," says a senior litigator. "It ranges the extremes in terms of work level and personality," says a former house counsel. Gould, Gold and Shelton are the key figures in litigation; Kern, Constance and Jacobs lead the corporate practice. Kern, in particular, has broken new ground for the firm by focusing on acquisitions and by having (largely) transactional clients. Observers note that Shea & Gould has developed a "top corporate practice but it is not institutional," in the words of a legal consultant. Many view Jacobs, though he is not a rainmaker like Kern, as the best pure lawyer among the heavy hitters on the Executive Committee. Lawrence Lipson is a standout in real estate, as well as the department's co-chairman (with Goldstein). A real estate lawyer at another leading New York firm calls the department "very impressive. It has a lot of depth." The bankruptcy division declined in the eyes of observers when Stanley Hirschfeld left recently for Dewey Ballantine.

Shea & Gould has long held the reputation of taking on any and every type of case, large or small, in litigation. The firm's longstanding clients include Toys 'R' Us, Madison Square Garden and British Petroleum. More recently the firm has had such clients as TCI (Kern), Touche Ross & Co., Equimark Corporation, LILCO, Bear, Stearns and Co., Inc., Crossland Savings Bank, Metromedia, Inc. and in real estate, Tishman Speyer Properties, Rupert Murdoch, Mendik Realty Company, Inc. and The Equitable Life Assurance Society of the United States.

The firm maintains small branch offices in Los Angeles (3, 1985), Washington (7, 1975), Miami (15, 1985), Bradenton (6, 1986), Albany (2, 1977) and London (1, 1976). The branch in Albany is devoted to lobbying and is guided by partners Bernard Ruggieri and Kevin McGrath.

Associates are none too enchanted with Shea & Gould. In a 1986 *Amerian Lawyer* survey, mid-level associates ranked the firm 27th of 41 firms. They complained that the firm demanded long hours but did not necessarily provide interesting work, that the facilities were inadequate and that there was internal tension between associates, some of it because associates felt their real estate peers who came over from Weil Gotshal with Goldstein received preferential treatment. Interestingly, Shea & Gould was not among the firms rated in *The American Lawyer* 1988 survey. Recently, the firm, led by Kern, has taken measures to make fewer partners, possibly in reaction to a *New York Law Journal* poll which revealed that it was easier to make partner at Shea & Gould than at any other of the city's thirty largest firms. On the positive side for associates, Shea & Gould raised its associate salaries to near the top going rate for the first time in 1989. Observers characterize the firm's recruiting as sub-par. "They hire in a scattered way," says a headhunter. "Shea & Gould doesn't get as good law school graduates as the top firms," adds a corporate lawyer.

SHEARMAN & STERLING

599 Lexington Avenue • New York, New York 10022 • (212) 848-4000

Rating: 💼💼💼💼💼   *Direction:* ↑

*LAWYERS

	PARTNERS	ASSOCIATES
1990: 440	109	310 2.84
1989: 422	110	294
1988: 494	125	347
1987: 395	115	272
1986: NA	112	304

	Paralegals	Support
1990:	105	919
1989:	87	898
1988:	89	NA
1987:	74	850
1986:	NA	NA

*LATERAL HIRES

1989: 24
1988: 31
1987: NA
1986: 25

*CHAIRMAN: Robert Carswell

*REPRESENTATIVE CLIENTS:

Citibank, Fuji Bank, Bank of Montreal, Georgia Pacific, Owens Corning Fiberglass

*BRANCHES: Abu Dhabi (1), London (9), Los Angeles (37), Paris (27), San Francisco (33), Tokyo (5), Toronto (3), Washington (8)
Total: 123 lawyers (NAp and NAa)

*AVERAGE ANNUAL BILLING HOURS:

Partners: NA
Associates: NA

*NUMBER OF WOMEN

	Partners	Associates
1990:	11	149
1989:	10	120
1988:	10	118
1987:	6	110
1986:	6	119

*PARTNERSHIP TRACK: 8 years

*NUMBER OF LAWYERS FROM ENTERING CLASS TO MAKE PARTNER:

1981: 4 of 43
1980: 5 of 41
1979: 9 of 34
1978: 7 of 34

*GROSS REVENUE

1989: $281,000,000
1988: $228,000,000
1987: $180,000,000
1986: $137,000,000

*REVENUE PER LAWYER

1989: $575,000
1988: $485,000
1987: $435,000
1986: $335,000

*PROFITS PER PARTNER

1989: $800,000
1988: $630,000
1987: $550,000
1986: $480,000

*STARTING ASSOCIATE SALARY

1990: $83,000
1989: $83,000
1988: $77,000
1987: $67,000
1986: $67,000

*PRO BONO: 4-7% of total time

*HOURLY RATES

Partners: $250–$350
Associates: $105–$230

*PRINCIPAL LAW SCHOOLS
(Associates): Columbia (67), NYU (64), Harvard (60)

*NUMBER OF MINORITIES

	Partners	Associates
1990:	2	34
1989:	2	22
1988:	2	17
1987:	2	17
1986:	2	19

*SUMMER ASSOCIATES

1990: 62
1989: 80
1988: 73
1987: 62
1986: 43

Shearman & Sterling, states a legal consultant, is simply "the consummate banking firm." Since the late 19th century, Shearman & Sterling has meant Citibank, and on this foundation the firm has built perhaps the most institutional practice in New York.

Clients—not star lawyers—dominate the firm's formula for success, and financially, the firm is a dramatic success. According to *The American Lawyer*, Shearman & Sterling's gross revenues have ballooned from $137,000,000 in 1986 to $228,000,000 in 1988, an increase that moved the firm into the top five firms nationally in this category. That the firm ranks lower in revenues per lawyer (tenth in 1988 with revenue per lawyer of $485,000) and profits per partner (sixteenth, with profits per partner of $630,000), reflects the sheer size of the firm—in 1988, the firm had 494 lawyers. In 1989 the firm continued its impressive growth; revenue increased $53,000,000 to $281,000,000 (a 23% increase), revenue per lawyer, $90,000, to $575,000 (19%) and profits per partner, $170,000, to $800,000 (27%).

The history of the firm begins in 1864 when prominent New York attorney David Dudley Field (compiler of the Field Code—New York's first code of civil procedure) hired Thomas Shearman as his managing clerk. In 1873, five years after John Sterling signed on as an unpaid clerk at what was then Field & Shearman, the firm became Shearman & Sterling. During its early years, the firm represented such robber barons as Jay Gould, James Stillman, and John D. Rockefeller in their internecine and other battles. Through Stillman the firm first secured business from National Citibank, the forerunner of Citibank.

In 1918, the firm merged its two partners and eleven associates with Carey & Carroll. After World War II, General Boykin Wright and several of his colleagues left what would become Cahill Gordon and joined Shearman & Sterling. Due in large measure to Wright's prodigious business origination, the firm experienced substantial growth and for a time added his name to the firm name. In 1961, the name reverted to Shearman & Sterling.

Currently, the firm is divided into seven departments: corporate, litigation, bank financing, tax, real estate, individual clients and anti-trust. The corporate department is by far the largest, and is involved in M & A, public and private financings, workouts (for defaulting debtors) and various contractual matters. Within the department, lawyers separate into teams by client, not by specialty, so that the firm can respond directly and efficiently to various clients' requirements.

Observers differ on the quality of the firm's work product. A legal consultant says Shearman & Sterling is in the "top five nationally." "You're not going to find any better," concurs a senior corporate lawyer. However, a litigator notes that "the chatter says they're bureaucratic and mediocre." Beyond their mixed reviews as a group, Shearman & Sterling's lawyers lack individual visibility. "It does not have heavyweights to fight for business and has not grown its own stars," says a legal consultant. Laterals have not provided an antidote; while the firm brought in seventy-five lawyers between 1986 and 1988, another legal consultant says the acquisitions are "momentary and narrowly targeted to specific gaps; they are not open-ended."

Citibank continues to be Shearman & Sterling's most significant client, providing roughly 20% of the firm's revenues. The side effects of this relationship, however, have begun to outstrip the relationship itself. The Citibank work has given Shearman & Sterling exposure to foreign banks such as the Bank of Montreal and Fuji Bank, which have become clients. The firm's international work in Eurodollar financing and transactions has introduced it to foreign governments and corporations which also have become clients of the firm. It is estimated that 60% of the firm's work is international in nature. Shearman & Sterling also represents the New York offices of over thirty U.S. banks as well as major corporations including Georgia Pacific, Owens Corning Fiberglass and Corning Glass.

The firm today maintains offices in Paris, Los Angeles, San Francisco, London, Tokyo and Abu Dhabi. It does not have a Washington office, preferring to use independent counsel there.

Since the 1970s, the firm has been headed successively by three senior partners, Robert Clare, Robert Knight and Robert Carswell, who head its twelve-member Management Committee. Knight was the former counsel to the U.S. Treasury Department and Carswell was its former Deputy Secretary.

Associates at Shearman & Sterling vacillate about the firm in

American Lawyer surveys from 1986 to 1988. In 1986, the firm ranked 10th in New York, and mid-level associates judged that Shearman & Sterling's smooth administration, interesting, challenging work and commitment to *pro bono* outweighed the firm's propensity to bury junior associates under mountains of paper. In 1987, summer associates rated the firm 33rd out of 50 even though they had the city's highest pay. Some complained of long hours and work "little better than stapling." The firm did better in 1988 when mid-level associates voted it 19th, but again there were complaints of too much work, too many hours and too much understaffing. More importantly, associates called Shearman & Sterling unresponsive to their concerns and said that the firm tries to solve morale problems by "throwing money" at them. In 1989 Shearman & Sterling moved from 19th to 16th in the survey, echoing the comment of one associate that, "I don't think the firm is the worst place to work, but it is probably not the best either." Unhappiness is expressed over the lack of knowledge of the chances to make partner and concern is voiced over the training program, partner-associate relations (an "us-against-them" attitude), rigid firm rules and sexist attitudes.

SIMPSON THACHER & BARTLETT

425 Lexington Avenue • New York, New York 10017 • (212) 455-2000

Rating: 💼💼💼💼💼   *Direction:* ↑

*LAWYERS

	PARTNERS	ASSOCIATES
1990: 448	97	334
1989: 401	95	287
1988: 363	85	263
1987: 325	83	229
1986: NA	79	201

3.4

	Paralegals	Support
1990:	128	749
1989:	125	726
1988:	NA	NA
1987:	88	527
1986:	NA	NA

*LATERAL HIRES

1989: 14
1988: 22
1987: NA
1986: 9

*MANAGING PARTNER: ~~Cyrus Vance~~ *RICHARD BEATTIE*

*REPRESENTATIVE CLIENTS:

Manufacturers Hanover, Burmah Oil, Joseph E. Seagram & Sons, General Motors Corporation, Atlas Corp., Kohlberg Kravis Roberts

*BRANCHES: Columbus (4), London (5)
Total: 9 lawyers (3p and 6a)

*AVERAGE ANNUAL BILLING HOURS (1989):
Partners: NA
Associates: 1968

*NUMBER OF WOMEN

	Partners	Associates
1990:	5	119
1989:	5	104
1988:	3	91
1987:	2	83
1986:	3	74

*PARTNERSHIP TRACK: 7–9 years

*NUMBER OF LAWYERS FROM ENTERING CLASS TO MAKE PARTNER:

1982: 2 of 40
1981: 6 of 31
1980: 6 of 36
1979: 5 of 27
1978: 4 of 25

*GROSS REVENUE
1989: $201,000,000
1988: $151,000,000
1987: $122,000,000
1986: $103,000,000

*REVENUE PER LAWYER
1989: $525,000
1988: $440,000
1987: $390,000
1986: $375,000

*PROFITS PER PARTNER
1989: $1,015,000
1988: $ 790,000
1987: $ 645,000
1986: $ 570,000

*STARTING ASSOCIATE SALARY
1990: $83,000
1989: NA
1988: $77,000
1987: $66,000
1986: $66,000

*PRO BONO: 3% of total time

*HOURLY RATES (1988)
Partners: NA
Associates: NA

*PRINCIPAL LAW SCHOOLS
(Associates): Columbia (43), Harvard (30), NYU (29), Georgetown (13), University of Pennsylvania (10), Fordham (6)

*NUMBER OF MINORITIES

	Partners	Associates
1990:	2	27
1989:	2	22
1988:	2	15
1987:	2	11
1986:	2	9

*SUMMER ASSOCIATES
1990: 48
1989: 61
1988: 57
1987: 40
1986: 57

Simpson Thacher is an old-line Wall Street firm built on the foundation of its longstanding relationship with Manufacturers Hanover. Despite its substantially expanded client base and ultra-modern corporate practice, the firm has not completely lost its genteel, low-key atmosphere and old-world values. "I'd be proud to be a partner there," says a prominent trial lawyer.

Simpson Thacher also has not suffered on the bottom line. Gross revenues have increased between 1986 and 1988 from $103,000,000 to $151,000,000, revenue per lawyer has grown from $375,000 to $440,000 and profits per partner have risen from $570,000 to $790,000. The firm has also been the epitome of consistency in *The American Lawyer* rankings of the top 100 firms nationally in these categories. In both gross revenue and profits per partner, the firm has held steady at the exact same place between 1986 and 1988—eighteenth place and eighth place, respectively. The firm slipped from ninth place to thirteenth in revenue per lawyer for the same time span. Its 1989 results are a continuation of its impressive growth: revenue rose by $50,000,000, to $201,000,000 (a 33% increase), revenue per lawyer, $85,000, to $525,000 (19%) and profits per partner, $225,000, to $1,015,000 (28%).

John Simpson, Thomas Thacher and William Barnum founded the firm in 1884. Philip Bartlett, an associate with the firm since its start, became a name partner in 1904 when Barnum retired. Edwin Weisl, who joined the firm in the 1940s, expanded its client base to include Paramount Communications (then Gulf & Western) and what was then Lehman Brothers. Simpson Thacher, despite the prevalence of no-nepotism rules on Wall Street, has always been something of a family business; three generations of Thachers, Edwin Weisl, Jr. and Whitney North Seymour, Jr.—son of the prominent, flamboyant Whitney North Seymour—all practiced at the firm. A rare blot on the firm's standing resulted from the 1974 disbarment and imprisonment of former Simpson Thacher partner Joel Dolkart for stealing hundreds of thousands of dollars in fees paid to Simpson Thacher by Gulf & Western. On the positive side, Gulf & Western remained a client of the firm.

Today, the firm's best-known lawyer is Cyrus Vance, a former president of the Association of the Bar of the City of New

York, U.S. attorney for the Southern District of New York and—most notably—secretary of state (1977–1980) in the Carter administration. Vance originally came to Simpson Thacher in 1947, where he became Weisl's protégé. He left the firm to follow Weisl to Washington and into government service in the late 1950s, not to return until 1969.

A self-perpetuating Policy Committee governs the firm. There are no limits to length of terms on the committee; the existing members occasionally select new members. This system replaced a two-tiered partnership, but allowed the top tier—senior partners—to keep their influence as they became the Policy Committee. The Policy Committee makes all decisions concerning partner compensation and approves associate salaries upon the recommendation of the Personnel Committee. The full partnership votes to admit new partners. Votes are weighted according to partners' shares in the firm.

The firm is divided into seven principal practice areas: corporate/banking, litigation/labor, tax, real estate, bankruptcy, ERISA and personal planning. Observers agree that corporate is by far the strongest department and single out Joel Hoffman, Richard Beattie (general counsel of HEW in the Carter administration), William Murphy and Michael Siegal. "Simpson Thacher is one of the great dealmaking firms in town," says a senior litigator. Roy Reardon is the litigation department's lone undisputed star. "He's as good as anyone," says a former house counsel. Beyond Reardon, however, the department lacks marquee names. A prominent trial lawyer calls Simpson Thacher "weak in litigation despite Roy Reardon's recent success." Conrad Harper, a litigator with the firm since 1971 and a partner since 1974, recently was elected as the first black president of the Association of the Bar of the City of New York.

Beyond its relationship to Manufacturers Hanover (which is managed by Edgar Mecinter, a strong leader in the firm during the 1980s), Simpson Thacher represents such clients as Joseph E. Seagram & Sons, American Electric Power Company, Burmah Oil, General Motors Corporation, Atlas Corp. and Kohlberg Kravis Roberts.

The firm currently maintains branch offices in London (3, 1978) and Columbus, Ohio (5, 1980). Branches in Washington

(1946), Hong Kong (1980) and Singapore (1981) have since closed.

Associates have generally found Simpson Thacher an interesting and pleasant place to work. The firm placed 15th in New York in 1986 and 1988 *American Lawyer* surveys. Associates agreed that the firm had a relaxed atmosphere and smooth internal relations. Corporate associates receive more responsibility than those in litigation, to whom little trial experience is available. The only negative point made consistently was that although associates get good training, there is a paucity of feedback from partners. In 1989 Simpson Thacher moved from 15th to 10th position, despite continuing dissatisfaction with partner feedback and chances to make partner and a pronounced division on whether it can still be considered a "kinder, gentler" law firm.

SKADDEN, ARPS, SLATE, MEAGHER & FLOM
• •
919 Third Avenue • New York, New York 10022 • (212) 735-3000

Rating: 💼💼💼💼💼   *Direction:* ↑

*LAWYERS	PARTNERS	ASSOCIATES
1990: 550	114	404 3.54
1989: 537	106	406
1988: 475	100	359
1987: 412	93	309
1986: 329	84	245

	Paralegals	Support
1990:	NA	NA
1989:	NA	NA
1988:	221	NA
1987:	209	711
1986:	138	657

*LATERAL HIRES

1989: 93
1988: NA
1987: NA
1986: NA

*EXECUTIVE PARTNER: Peter P. Mullen

*REPRESENTATIVE CLIENTS:

Anheuser-Busch, Marine Midland Bank, Aetna, Grey Advertising, Home Insurance

*BRANCHES: Boston (30), Chicago (86), Washington (160), Los Angeles (122), London (4), Brussels (6), San Francisco (35), Tokyo (5), Wilmington, Del. (44), Sydney (3), Hong Kong (4)
Total: 535 lawyers (NAp and NAa)

*AVERAGE ANNUAL BILLING HOURS (1989):
Partners: NA
Associates: NA

*NUMBER OF WOMEN

	Partners	Associates
1990:	14	143
1989:	12	135
1988:	8	118
1987:	5	96
1986:	5	76

*PARTNERSHIP TRACK: 7.5 years

*NUMBER OF LAWYERS FROM ENTERING CLASS TO MAKE PARTNER:

1981: 10 of 31
1980: 6 of 20
1979: 11 of 20
1978: 5 of 21

*GROSS REVENUE

1989: $517,500,000
1988: $440,000,000
1987: $290,000,000
1986: $228,000,000

*REVENUE PER LAWYER

1989: $545,000
1988: $520,000
1987: $350,000
1986: $320,000

*PROFITS PER PARTNER

1989: $1,195,000
1988: $1,155,000
1987: $885,000
1986: $780,000

*STARTING ASSOCIATE SALARY

1990: $83,000
1989: $77,000
1988: $73,000
1987: $71,000
1986: $63,000

*PRO BONO: 4–7% of total time

*HOURLY RATES (1989)
Partners: NA
Associates: NA

*PRINCIPAL LAW SCHOOLS (Associates): Harvard (26.5%), NYU (19.6%), Chicago (16.7%)

*NUMBER OF MINORITIES

	Partners	Associates
1990:	1	35
1989:	1	23
1988:	1	19
1987:	1	11
1986:	1	8

*SUMMER ASSOCIATES

1990: 83
1989: 72
1988: 52
1987: 87
1986: 46

The Skadden Arps success story seems made for Hollywood. The firm's meteoric rise in the last twenty years, spurred by its ground-breaking M & A practice, has left it towering above all other leading New York firms, both in number of lawyers and in annual revenue. As one legal consultant proclaims, "It is the most successful law firm in the world."

Skadden Arps now has about 1,000 lawyers, over five hundred located in New York (more than the total of any other New York firm combined with its branch offices). Perhaps even more impressive is Skadden Arps' rate of growth; the firm jumped from forty lawyers in 1970 to over two hundred in 1980 to over five hundred in 1986. With 1988 revenues of $440,000,000 Skadden widened the gap between itself and its nearest competitors ($110,000,000 separated Skadden from Davis Polk in 1987 and $212,000,000 separated Skadden from Shearman & Sterling in 1988) and thus reaffirmed the fiscal dominance that has become its trademark.

In 1948, when the firm was founded by Messrs. Skadden, Arps and Slate, no one could envision what destiny had in store for this small midtown firm. However, the seeds of growth had been planted when, at the outset, the founding partners had the good sense to hire as their first associate Brooklyn-born Harvard Law School graduate Joseph Flom. Still, more than twenty years would elapse before the firm, utilizing Flom's growing reputation as a savvy proxy solicitation lawyer, would begin its transformation into a sucessful giant enterprise.

Flom—with the disdain, if not the enmity, of larger New York firms which refused to soil their hands in such unseemly sport—almost single-handedly developed the practice and methodology for hostile takeovers in the early 1970s. Flom's great contribution was to make the art of leverage into a science. His approach led naturally into formulating defensive techniques (poison pills, greater-than-majority votes required by the certificate of incorporation of the target company, etc.).

Flom had the vision to see that the firm could use its takeover and defensive techniques as the base for building a full-service firm. Because of his fame—or notoriety—he was able to persuade major U.S. corporations to enter into retainer agreements with Skadden Arps (which were unique at the time, and still may be) under which a corporation paid a negotiated minimum annual fee (in the high five and six figures) which entitled it to call on Skadden Arps in the event of a hostile takeover or the desire by the client itself to commence a hostile takeover. (Concurrently, the client agreed that if Skadden Arps were to represent other clients in takeover litigation directed at them, they would not raise the issue of conflict of interest to disqualify the firm.) These retainers provided Skadden Arps with a base of millions of dollars in fees at the commencement of each fiscal year without actually doing any work.

Flom put together a final piece of the puzzle by recommending that clients use up their retainers by employing Skadden Arps' services in a variety of specialties having little to do with takeovers: anti-trust, tax and pension, ERISA, real estate, labor and employment law, debtors and creditors rights, product liability, etc. As clients were won over to Flom's system, Skadden brought in top-quality lateral partners—a method it relies upon to this day—to staff these specialties and to extend the firm's reach. Thus, in effect, Flom took a unique franchise in a narrow area and expanded it into a supermarket instead of a boutique.

Successful expansion has bought Skadden the ability to pick and choose among cases and clients. "Skadden has the luxury of doing what it wants without really worrying about immediate returns," says a former house counsel. More importantly, however, Flom's expansion has brought the firm a stability and respect within the legal community that the M & A franchise alone could not. As a senior partner of a medium-sized New York firm explains, "While M & A is the keystone and is very definitely top of the line, the breadth of the practice is there."

Skadden has large branch offices in Washington, Los Angeles and Chicago and smaller ones in Wilmington, San Francisco, Boston, Tokyo, London, Brussels, Sydney and Hong Kong.

Most observers believe Skadden has become fully institutionalized. The firm appears able to weather a down cycle in its takeover business because of a bedrock of hefty clients like Anheuser-Busch, Marine Midland Bank, Aetna, Grey Advertising and Home Insurance Co. Nor is Skadden dependent on the 65-year-old Flom; the firm seems capable of moving ahead on the talent it has recruited to assist him. Observers single out Peter Atkins, who administers the corporate and securities department, as well as litigators Ken Pleavitt and Steve Axinn.

Skadden has paid the price of "going big." First, while the firm overwhelmingly outranks other New York firms in revenue in 1988, according to *The American Lawyer* Skadden drops to seventh in revenue per lawyer and to fifth in profits per partner for that year.

More importantly, the size of Skadden's business and the crisis nature of much of its practice has led to criticism of the firm's work product. Various corporate partners and litigators have noted that, in their personal experience, Skadden partners have been too busy to do the kind of homework which is necessary to understand various matters. Several litigators have noted that associates in various cases appear to be in over their heads and that Skadden's work is not particularly outstanding unless it is supervised by "bigger names."

On a more positive note, Skadden Arps' management remarkably has improved despite the speed and extent of the firm's growth. In the early 1980s, Flom replaced a rather democratic firm governance, under which policy was decided by all partners, with a structure in which he was the chairman, Peter Mullen, the executive partner and Earle Yaffa (who had been a partner at Arthur Young), the managing director. This basic division of responsibility emulates big business operations: Chairman of the Board for policy and long-range planning; CEO for supervising a broad base of executive and administrative decisions; and a Chief Operating Officer and Chief Financial Officer for internal management and financial oversight.

For Skadden Arps, the redistribution of power and function has enabled management to move decisively, without the burden of a cumbersome bureaucracy. The senior partner at a medium-size New York firm observes of their internal workings: "The flow of information within the firm is almost unbelievably good." All in all, as one headhunter says, "It's the best big law firm in terms of how it is managed."

If Skadden has broken ground with its method of administration, the firm has been equally creative, conscious and corporate about establishing a distinctive firm atmosphere. The firm depends enormously on its "troops" to grind out emergency jobs; as one headhunter put it, Skadden is "like a trading floor—as frantic as law firms go." Therefore, the firm emphasizes rewards, monetary and otherwise. "Skadden pays their associates extremely well and works them extremely hard," says a corporate partner at another New York firm, but Skadden Arps does more than that. The firm specializes in finding alternative incentives. A place as big as Skadden could easily become impersonal, but the firm has worked hard to give lawyers a place to blow off steam. Skadden has its very own internal health club/torture chamber, complete with exercise equipment, trainers, a snack bar and, of course, a selection of postworkout grooming products.

More importantly, the firm has applied its ingenuity to encouraging and sponsoring *pro bono* work. In 1988, Skadden launched a ground-breaking Fellowship Program. At a cost of $2 million per year, the firm funds as many as fifty lawyers for two-year stints in legal aid offices and other such institutions that assist the poor. Ronald Tabak, brought over from Hughes Hubbard & Reed in 1985, coordinates the firm's *pro bono* programs and personally spends 40% of his time on *pro bono* cases.

Associates seem to appreciate the firm's efforts. They ranked Skadden fourth in 1986 and fifth in 1988 in *American Lawyer* surveys of New York firms. Those polled agreed that the firm demands long hours and heaps on the work. But in return, associates get good training and support from partners, responsibility and interesting assignments. One associate wrote that "in many ways, Skadden is like a microcosm of New York City—noisy, intense, often assaulting, but if you love it, there's no place better. It's got something for everybody. The only problem is, it often has too much of that something." In 1989 Skadden slipped to 15th position in the survey, much of the drop fueled by perceptions—perhaps misperceptions—that work was slowing down and layoffs were near. Concerns also were voiced that, despite its efforts to the contrary, the firm was becoming more of a "corporation" or "business."

Notwithstanding, whatever Skadden has done, it seems to

be working. Indeed, one headhunter says she has never placed a lawyer from the firm for any reason except failure to make partner or the firm's long hours and constant pressures. Whatever doubts may exist concerning the pace of future expansion and the institutional stability of this relatively young firm, it is and should continue to be a powerful and influential force not only in New York but on the national and international scene.

STROOCK & STROOCK & LAVAN

7 Hanover Square • New York, New York 10004 • (212) 806-5400

Rating: 💼💼💼💼

Direction: ↑

*LAWYERS	PARTNERS	ASSOCIATES
1990: 245	76	151
1989: 243	75	152
1988: 240	76	152
1987: 222	NA	NA
1986: 180	NA	NA

	Paralegals	Support
1990:	29	454
1989:	56	395
1988:	52	NA
1987:	48	NA
1986:	46	NA

*LATERAL HIRES

1989: 14
1988: 3
1987: NA
1986: NA

*CHAIRMAN: Erwin Millimet

*REPRESENTATIVE CLIENTS:

Goldman, Sachs & Co., Bank Hapoalim, Irving Trust, Bear Stearns & Co., Inc., International Harvester, Chemical Bank, PepsiCo.

*BRANCHES: Washington (14), Los Angeles (51), Miami (29)
Total: 94 lawyers (32p and 62a)

*AVERAGE ANNUAL BILLING HOURS (1989):
Partners: NA
Associates: 1950

*NUMBER OF WOMEN

	Partners	Associates
1990:	9	61
1989:	9	62
1988:	9	66
1987:	NA	NA
1986:	NA	NA

*PARTNERSHIP TRACK: 8 years

*NUMBER OF LAWYERS FROM ENTERING CLASS TO MAKE PARTNER:

1981: 3 of 21
1980: 1 of 14
1979: 7 of 9
1978: 3 of 11

*GROSS REVENUE

1989: $120,000,000
1988: $108,000,000
1987: $91,000,000
1986: $68,500,000

*REVENUE PER LAWYER

1989: $365,000
1988: $350,000
1987: $340,000
1986: $295,000

*PROFITS PER PARTNER

1989: $460,000
1988: $435,000
1987: $415,000
1986: $350,000

*STARTING ASSOCIATE SALARY

1990: $82,000
1989: $82,000
1988: $76,000
1987: $65,000
1986: $65,000

*PRO BONO: NA

*HOURLY RATES (1989)

Partners: NA
Associates: NA

*PRINCIPAL LAW SCHOOLS
(Associates): NYU (40), Brooklyn (19), Columbia (8), Fordham (8), Yeshiva (4)

*NUMBER OF MINORITIES

	Partners	Associates
1990:	0	2
1989:	0	4
1988:	0	1
1987:	NA	NA
1986:	NA	NA

*SUMMER ASSOCIATES

1990: 27
1989: 38
1988: 25
1987: NA
1986: NA

Stroock & Stroock & Lavan began as an old-line Jewish firm that represented many "Our Crowd" families. On the strength of its client base and a number of important lawyers, the firm expanded dramatically from fewer than twenty lawyers in the mid-1950s to 332 lawyers in 1989. Expansion, however, has proved a mixed blessing; today, the firm lacks cohesion. One senior corporate lawyer calls Stroock "a collection of duchies" and "a firm seeking to define itself enough to become a firm." Stroock is "not a law firm," says a former house counsel, "but a proprietorship with a very small group of equity partners." Although observers consider the aggregate work product to be good, most agree that, as one senior litigator says, it "ranges the extremes" and is "uneven."

On the other hand, expansion has meant steadily increasing revenues. According to *The American Lawyer*, between 1986 and 1988, Stroock's gross revenues have grown from $68,500,000 to $108,000,000 and its revenue per lawyer from $295,000 to $350,000. During the same time span, profits per partner rose from $350,000 to $435,000. Despite this absolute growth, however, Stroock has dropped in the rankings in both revenue per lawyer (from 24th to 30th) and profits per partner (from 26th to 28th). In 1989 the firm's revenues rose $12,000,000, to $120,000,000 (an 11% increase); revenue per lawyer, $15,000, to $365,000 (4%) and profits per partner, $25,000, to $460,000 (6%). Relative to firms of comparable size, Stroock is getting less mileage from its lawyers.

Although the firm that would become Stroock & Stroock & Lavan was founded in 1876, it did not include the Stroock name until 1895, when it was placed second. After this milestone, the firm began to achieve acclaim by representing the Loebs, Rosenwalds, Ittelsons and Warburgs. The firm adopted the name Stroock & Stroock in 1906. Peter Lavan (originally Levine) joined the firm in 1918. He cultivated the firm's commercial practice, which included the representation of the Julius Rosenwald interests, and became the senior partner. His name was added to the firm's in 1946. (The unusual firm name with two ampersands was necessitated by New York law at the time that permitted having two ampersands but not altering a partnership name when other name partners were deceased.) Following Lavan's death, leadership of the firm passed to a series of lawyers until the late 1960s when Stroock converted to an Executive Committee system.

The Stroock Executive Committee is the controlling body in a two-tier partnership. It is elected for five-year terms by and from the top-tier senior partners who thereby control the firm. The senior partners adjust their percentage share interest in the firm every five years; young partnership shares are adjusted annually by the Executive Committee. Upon recommendation from each department, the Executive Committee selects new partners subject to partnership approval, which is customarily given.

The firm is divided into six departments: corporate, litigation, insolvency, real estate, tax and employee benefits, and trusts and estates.

Charles Moerdler, who left Cravath to join Stroock, heads the litigation department and has emerged as the firm's top gun. "Charles Moerdler is a star," says a former house counsel. From 1966–67, he served as buildings commissioner in the Lindsay administration. Observers also laud Alvin Hellerstein. Viviene Nearing, also an accomplished litigator, earned a place in history as the contestant who defeated Charles Van Doren in the quiz program called "21."

Although Stroock's corporate client roster is extremely diverse, one focal point has become M & A transactions. The firm does periodic work for Goldman, Sachs & Co., Shearson Lehman/American Express and Bear, Stearns & Co. among other investment banking concerns. A headhunter noted that one of Stroock's central attractions is its "sexy corporate work." William Perlmuth, Bruce Rabb and Lewis Cole, observers agree, lead the way in the corporate department. Cole also represents the Dreyfus Group.

Rita Hauser is a prominent Republican and acclaimed international lawyer who represents Bank Hapoalim, one of Israel's largest banks. She also plays an active and important role in various Jewish organizationas and frequently has been mentioned as a possible Supreme Court nominee. In 1979 Stroock acquired Bach & McAuliffe and thereby became engaged in various facets of municipal bond work.

The insolvency department was established in 1980 when Stroock acquired Krause Hirsch & Gross, a fifty-year-old bankruptcy firm. Lawrence Handelsman now leads a department which a senior bankruptcy partner at another leading New York firm calls "one of the real bankruptcy players in New York." The firm represents a number of important creditors such as Manufacturers Hanover, Irving Trust, Pepsico and International Harvester.

Observers rate Stroock's large real estate department highly. Lateral Leonard Boxer characterizes the pattern of good acquisitions that has lifted this department. The firm's most notable regular real estate client is Chemical Bank.

Stroock has branch offices in Washington (14, 1967), Los Angeles (51, 1976) and Miami (29, 1977).

In recent years, the firm has experienced difficulty in recruiting and retaining associates. Top Jewish law graduates who previously had been barred from joining white shoe firms are now hired by most of them, thus decreasing the talent pool available to Stroock. Relations between certain key partners and associates are sometimes testy; verbal harangues expressing criticisms of associates' work and demanding the expenditure of more time are not out of character. "Interrelations in the firm are terrible," claims a former house counsel. A legal consultant cites an abundance of "internal competition." Still, another legal consultant attributes this ambience to just one corporate partner who is "out of sync," not to firm-wide problems. Mid-level associates polled in a 1988 *American Lawyer* survey ranked the firm 22nd of 37 and said there was only a 50% chance that they would be at Stroock in two years. Associates also complained that they had to choose specialties according to "economics," not vocation, because of extremely dim partnership chances in litigation. A 1986 survey of mid-level associates also emphasized pessimism vis-à-vis partnership chances and noted that, although the firm provided guidance for first- and second-year associates, afterward they were left to sink or swim.

SULLIVAN & CROMWELL

125 Broad Street • New York, New York 10004 • (212) 558-4000

Rating: 💼💼💼💼💼   *Direction:* ↑

*LAWYERS	PARTNERS	ASSOCIATES
1990: 292	81	211 2.6
1989: 275	77	199
1988: 293	82	194
1987: 300	76	224
1986: NA	NA	NA

	Paralegals	Support
1990:	60	841
1989:	64	NA
1988:	49	NA
1987:	48	NA
1986:	37	NA

*LATERAL HIRES
1989: 7
1988: 4
1987: 5
1986: 2

*CHAIRMAN: John E. Merow

*REPRESENTATIVE CLIENTS:
Bank of New York, Allied Stores Corporation, Eastman Kodak Company, First Boston Corporation, Gulf Oil Corporation, McGraw-Hill, Inc., Prudential Bache Securities Inc.

*BRANCHES: Los Angeles (14), Washington (21), London (7), Paris (4), Melbourne (4), Tokyo (2)
Total: 52 lawyers (13p and 39a)

*AVERAGE ANNUAL BILLING HOURS:
Partners: NA
Associates: NA

*NUMBER OF WOMEN
	Partners	Associates
1990:	3	60
1989:	4	60
1988:	4	58
1987:	4	59
1986:	3	55

*PARTNERSHIP TRACK: 6–8 years

*NUMBER OF LAWYERS FROM ENTERING CLASS TO MAKE PARTNER:
1981: 5 of 42
1980: 2 of 19
1979: 9 of 30
1978: 4 of 30

*GROSS REVENUE
1989: $230,000,000
1988: $210,000,000
1987: $159,000,000
1986: $115,000,000

*REVENUE PER LAWYER
1989: $665,000
1988: $675,000
1987: $500,000
1986: $435,000

*PROFITS PER PARTNER
1989: $1,210,000
1988: $1,375,000
1987: $785,000
1986: $665,000

*STARTING ASSOCIATE SALARY
1990: $83,000
1989: $78,000
1988: $77,000
1987: $65,000
1986: $65,000

*PRO BONO: 4–7% of total time

*HOURLY RATES
Partners: NA
Associates: NA

*PRINCIPAL LAW SCHOOLS
(Associates): NYU (31), Columbia (31), Harvard (22), Yale (17)

*NUMBER OF MINORITIES
	Partners	Associates
1990:	2	17
1989:	2	18
1988:	2	15
1987:	2	11
1986:	2	8

*SUMMER ASSOCIATES
1989: 65
1988: 56
1987: 61
1986: 48

Pride dominates the Sullivan & Cromwell story—the well-deserved pride of a firm with a highly successful past and a sky-high standard of excellence, and the foolish pride of a firm so ingrown and inflexible that it cannot admit to mistakes. "We're Sullivan & Cromwell, and you're not," summarizes one head-hunter, and this attitude explains how the firm can attract star lawyers, star clients and produce a top work product while facing numerous charges of legal and ethical impropriety.

Strength characterized Sullivan & Cromwell from the start when Algernon Sullivan and William Nelson Cromwell founded the firm in 1879. Its mystique grew as eminences with reputations far beyond Sullivan & Cromwell chose to work there: Cromwell himself; Supreme Court Justice Harlan Fisk Stone; international lawyer and secretary of state John Foster Dulles; top litigators William Piel and David Peck; and securities lawyer and statesman Arthur Dean.

Today, Sullivan & Cromwell still applies much of the formula originally responsible for the firm's success. The firm is divided into four major practice groups, each headed by a managing partner: general practice (Robert M. Thomas, Jr., managing partner); litigation (John L. Warden); tax (Willard B. Taylor); and trusts and estates (Henry Christensen III). Of the Sullivan & Cromwell litigators, Marvin Schwartz and former department head Michael Cooper are repeatedly singled out as outstanding by observers. Neil Anderson has emerged as an up-and-coming litigation star. Led by George Kern, Jr., the firm has also built a powerful M & A practice with lawyers from both the litigation and the tax departments. A senior litigating partner states that it is "one of the few firms that just handles important matters very well and seems to have a never-ending succession of outstanding lawyers. It is an extremely smooth operation." Virtually all observers praise what one senior called Sullivan & Cromwell's "first-rate work product."

Another Sullivan & Cromwell signature holdover is its billing system. Since the firm's founding no invoice ever has been prepared for a client based on the aggregate time charges accrued in a particular matter, which is the norm for other firms. Although Sullivan & Cromwell maintains time data for internal statistical purposes and to establish billing norms for different types of matters, this information is not made available to clients. The trick for the Sullivan & Cromwell billing partner is to balance the value of the work done with the going rate of other large New York firms in similar instances. Accordingly, if Sullivan & Cromwell can staff a matter with fewer lawyers or younger associates, it can directly increase its revenue per lawyer and profits per partner ratios. To take advantage of this, a legal consultant notes, the firm "hires the best and the brightest and doesn't let clients push them around." The system seems to work; few clients try to nickel-and-dime the firm and in 1988 Sullivan & Cromwell was third in New York in revenue per lawyer ($675,000) and third in profits per partner ($1,375,000). In 1989 the firm's revenue per lawyer slipped to $665,000 (again third in New York) and its profits per partner declined to $1,210,000 (a drop to fourth in New York).

What appears to be missing from Sullivan & Cromwell are the superstars like Messrs. Dulles and Dean who, between them, guided the firm for almost a half-century from 1926 to 1972. Today, although Chairman John Merow, a corporate lawyer, wields great power—Merow alone sets individual partners' draws (which are not circulated to others)—he, nevertheless, works closely with the firm's eight-man Executive Committee and just is not cut from the same charismatic cloth as many of his predecessors. While the firm may simply have grown too large to sustain an autocracy, Sullivan & Cromwell now endures the problems endemic to the diffusion of power (e.g., logrolling by Executive Committee members in selecting partners from different departments and placing loyalty to the firm above responding promptly and properly to outside criticism of various actions taken by its lawyers).

Some observers have claimed that a leadership vacuum is responsible for the ethical problems that have plagued Sullivan & Cromwell in the last several years. During this time, the firm has been accused of (a) becoming involved in a conflict of interest by representing a corporation in a hostile takeover when it had been involved a year earlier in counseling relating to the target company's concerns about a takeover or proxy fight (AB Electrolux); (b) making a frivolous motion to reverse a judge's decision against a defendant because of stock owned by the judge's mother-in-law although the two sets of lawyers earlier representing the defendant had not moved to disqualify the judge when that stock interest was disclosed prior to a seventy-five-day trial (Polaroid v. Kodak); (c) improperly attempting to influence or suppress the testimony of witnesses in a will contest (the Johnson estate); (d) improperly obtaining pre-trial information from a third-party witness by misleading the witness and by failing, as required by law, to give notice thereof to opposing counsel (the Wynyard case); (e) failing to advise plaintiffs in a stock fraud case in response to a discovery request that the New York Stock Exchange was investigating its client-defendant (Prudential-Bache); and (f) failing to amend an SEC filing in a takeover contest to disclose material negotiations with third parties (Allied Stores). In the AB Electrolux and Wynyard cases, the courts refused to believe the testimony of Sullivan & Cromwell lawyers and held against the firm. As a result of Wynyard, two Sullivan & Cromwell lawyers also face disciplinary proceedings for their conduct.

These matters require substantially more exposition in order to more fully understand the situations present, but Sullivan & Cromwell contends that it is the victim of the amimus of adversaries and judges who were out to get a highly visible, aggressive firm and who thereby provided a field day for journalists all too happy to jump on the bandwagon. These critics and journalists have countered by saying that Sullivan & Cromwell's problems are thoroughly attributable not only to its weak-willed internal governance but to its arrogance.

The term "arrogant" comes up frequently when sources describe Sullivan & Cromwell. Even a senior partner who lauded the firm's work product could not help adding, "Sullivan & Cromwell tends to be a bit pompous." In part, this is due to the firm's clubby "us-against-them" nature. Lawyers connected to the firm—even those "passed over" for partner or retired—retain a strong sense of superiority, pride and loyalty to the firm. They consider themselves special and are treated that way by the firm. Associates assimilate quickly to the ambience and "leave with a heavy heart," says a headhunter. The firm received highly consistent reviews from mid-level associates surveyed by *The American Lawyer* in 1986 (when it ranked fifth out of forty-one New York firms) and 1988 (when it placed sixth of thirty-seven). Sullivan & Cromwell works its associates long and hard (in 1986, the firm placed first for hours worked), but rewarded them with great responsibility and interesting work. Associates get rather ad hoc, on-the-job training and little support from partners; some associates respond well to this program and enjoy their autonomy, while others deplore the sink-or-swim atmosphere. The 1989 survey reports basically the same associate reactions, but the firm dropped to 27th place out of 35 firms.

Clearly, the accusations of impropriety have not reinforced the Sullivan & Cromwell image. On the other hand, one legal consultant notes that it is the only such firm that could have suffered such a barrage of bad publicity and remain basically unaffected by it. This is no small tribute to the long and illustrious history of the firm, the good will and good work generated by it during all the years and the high standing of the lawyers at Sullivan & Cromwell.

THACHER PROFFITT & WOOD
Two World Trade Center • New York, New York 10048 • (212) 912-7400

Rating: 💼💼💼💼

Direction:?

*LAWYERS

	PARTNERS	ASSOCIATES
1990: 124	28	90
1989: 132	29	95
1988: 141	33	102
1987: 118	27	83
1986: 119	27	87

	Paralegals	Support
1990:	19	123
1989:	17	125
1988:	19	NA
1987:	18	130
1986:	18	NA

*LATERAL HIRES
1989: 2
1988: 1
1987: NA
1986: 6

*CHAIRMAN: Phillip C. Broughton

*REPRESENTATIVE CLIENTS:
NA

*BRANCHES: Washington (7), White Plains, N.Y. (3)
Total: 10 lawyers (6p and 4a)

*AVERAGE ANNUAL BILLING HOURS:

Partners: 1535
Associates: 1670

*NUMBER OF WOMEN

	Partners	Associates
1990:	3	36
1989:	3	34
1988:	3	39
1987:	3	40
1986:	2	33

*PARTNERSHIP TRACK: 8 years

*NUMBER OF LAWYERS FROM ENTERING CLASS TO MAKE PARTNER:
1981: 1 of 8
1980: 4 of 6
1979: 0 of 11
1978: 1 of 3

*GROSS REVENUE
1989: NA
1988: $32,259,000*
1987: $31,271,000*
1986: $25,971,000*

*REVENUE PER LAWYER
1989: NA
1988: NA
1987: NA
1986: NA

*PROFITS PER PARTNER
1989: NA
1988: $254,000
1987: $294,000
1986: $236,000

*STARTING ASSOCIATE SALARY
1990: $83,000
1989: $75,000
1988: $73,000
1987: $70,000
1986: $57,000

*PRO BONO: 1–3% of total time

*HOURLY RATES (1989)
Partners: $215–$350
Associates: $125–$220

*PRINCIPAL LAW SCHOOLS
(Associates): NYU (14%), Fordham (13%), University of Virginia (15%)

*NUMBER OF MINORITIES

	Partners	Associates
1990:	0	6
1989:	0	5
1988:	0	5
1987:	0	3
1986:	0	3

*SUMMER ASSOCIATES
1990: 13
1989: 14
1988: 23
1987: 22
1986: 26

Thacher Proffitt, says a legal consultant, is "a good, solid mid-size firm that must decide its direction." With a corporate practice top-heavy with savings and loan clients and a large number of lawyers in real estate litigation, Thacher Proffitt has assumed a somewhat unlikely configuration. Gentlemanly, at times even sleepy, the firm has little turnover, takes in few laterals and places slight (though recently more) emphasis on billable hours.

Concludes a headhunter, "It is not one of the most profitable—possibly on purpose." The firm had gross revenues of $25,971,000 in 1986, $31,271,000 in 1987 and $32,259,000 in 1988; each year produced a modest increase but not enough relative to other leading New York firms to earn Thacher Proffitt a spot in *The American Lawyer* listing of the top 100 firms in this category. Thacher Proffitt's profits are somewhat erratic, but by the firm's own count, it would have made the bottom third of the top 100 firms ranked by profits per partner, with $236,000 in 1986, $294,000 in 1987 and (even after a significant drop to) $254,000 in 1988.

Thacher Proffit's roots extend back as far as 1838, but the modern firm began to take shape in 1913, when it became Barry, Wainwright, Thacher & Symmers. The name changed to Thacher, Proffitt, Prizer, Crawley & Wood in 1951. In 1973, the name was shortened to its present form. Also in 1973, the firm merged with Townsend & Lewis.

Philip Broughton is the firm's managing partner. The Legal Personnel Committee sets associate salaries.

The firm is divided into five departments: corporate—by far the largest, double the size of the next largest practice area, real estate, litigation, tax and legislative/regulatory. Observers give the firm's work product mixed reviews. "The work is not super-duper, cutting edge," says a headhunter. "Great benefits practice—Doug McClintock. Solid litigation." A senior trial litigator disagrees, however, saying that the firm has "no reputation as litigators."

The firm maintains branch offices in Washington (7, 1983) and White Plains (3, 1989). Thacher Proffitt also became affiliated with Whittenburg Whittenburg & Schacter of Amarillo and Dallas, Texas, in 1989. The firms share clients but bill and pay expenses separately.

Associates have improved their opinion of the firm in recent years. Thacher Proffitt ranked 31st of 41 firms in a 1986 *American Lawyer* survey of mid-level associates; in the 1988 survey, the firm placed seventh. Associates praise the firm's positive atmosphere and interesting work, particularly in corporate. Although those polled predicted they would stay with Thacher Proffitt long-term, most knew little about their partnership chances. Neither partners nor associates have felt much billing pressure; the average annual billable hours for partners was 1,392 and for associates was 1,497 in 1986. In 1987 the numbers increased, respectively, to 1,620 and 1,613 and in 1988 to 1,535 and 1,670. The firm attracts "nice, thoughtful, more well-rounded people than elsewhere," sums up a headhunter. "Partners don't leave for more money but associates do." Partnership chances are "slimmer" than at other leading New York firms. Between 1985 and 1988, six associates who started at the firm made partner.

WACHTELL, LIPTON, ROSEN & KATZ

299 Park Avenue • New York, New York 10171 • (212) 371-9200

Rating: 💼💼💼💼💼   Direction: ↑

*LAWYERS

	PARTNERS	ASSOCIATES
1989: 96	52	42
1988: 85	46	38
1987: 85	43	41
1986: 92	42	49

	Paralegals	Support
1989:	27	244
1988:	NA	NA
1987:	18	234
1986:	NA	NA

*LATERAL HIRES
1989: NA
1988: 2
1987: NA
1986: 0

*MANAGING PARTNER: Meyer Koplow

*REPRESENTATIVE CLIENTS:
Firm does only transactional work

*BRANCHES: None

*AVERAGE ANNUAL BILLING HOURS (1987):
Partners and associates averaged 2,041

*NUMBER OF WOMEN

	Partners	Associates
1989:	4	5
1988:	2	8
1987:	0	10
1986:	0	13

*PARTNERSHIP TRACK: 6 years

*NUMBER OF LAWYERS FROM ENTERING CLASS TO MAKE PARTNER:
1982: 6 of 8
1981: 1 of 4
1980: 5 of 6
1979: 3 of 8

*GROSS REVENUE
1989: $115,000,000
1988: $89,500,000
1987: $86,500,000
1986: $81,000,000

*REVENUE PER LAWYER
1989: $1,225,000
1988: $1,090,000
1987: $985,000
1986: $930,000

*PROFITS PER PARTNER
1989: $1,590,000
1988: $1,350,000
1987: $1,405,000
1986: $1,440,000

*STARTING ASSOCIATE SALARY
1990: $83,000
1989: $83,000
1988: $77,000
1987: NA
1986: $65,000

*PRO BONO: 1–3% of total time

*HOURLY RATES
Partners: NA
Associates: NA

*PRINCIPAL LAW SCHOOLS
(Associates): Harvard (10), Yale (8), NYU (5), University of Pennsylvania (4)

*NUMBER OF MINORITIES

	Partners	Associates
1989:	0	0
1988:	0	0
1987:	0	0
1986:	0	0

*SUMMER ASSOCIATES
1989: 19
1988: 10
1987: 25
1986: 10

If there is any firm in New York which is *sui generis*, it is Wachtell, Lipton, Rosen & Katz. Smaller, more focused and more consistent than other leading New York firms, Wachtell has simply become, as one legal consultant says, "the best at whatever they've tried."

The firm was founded in 1965 by its four name partners. (George Katz died in 1989). Herbert Wachtell, who wrote a leading treatise on New York civil procedure, leads the litigation department; he is a higly visible, aggressive and successful litigator. Martin Lipton, who together with his wife (who is a partner of the firm) wrote the bible on takeovers and freezeouts, heads the corporate department and is arguably one of the top two M & A lawyers in the country (with Joseph Flom of Skadden Arps). Leonard Rosen, who heads the creditors' rights department, is regarded as one of the country's leading lawyers in this specialty.

Wachtell has succeeded largely by going against the grain. Compared to other leading New York firms, Wachtell Lipton is rather modest in size with about ninety lawyers. But its revenue per lawyer ($1,090,000 in 1988) as reported in *The American Lawyer* exceeds that of all other New York firms; in 1987, Wachtell also ranked first in profits per partner ($1,405,000). These financial results take on even greater significance when they are compared to the next leading firm in each category: $720,000 revenue per lawyer (Cravath, 1988) and $1,220,000 profits per partner (Cravath, 1987).

The firm deals almost solely in transactional work: the defense of hostile takeovers and related litigation, tax, anti-trust and reorganization work. And in each of these departments the firm has recognized stars; among them are Bernard Nussbaum (litigation), James Fogelson (corporate/securities) and Lawrence King (creditors' rights). Charles Mederrick leads the tax department.

Yet, unlike fellow M & A specialist Skadden Arps, Wachtell Lipton has no interest in becoming a "full service" firm and representing clients on a continuing, general basis. In fact, one senior litigating partner notes that "in very routine litigation, they are very routine—they make no secret of the fact that they find that work boring." However, he adds, "they are preeminent in their specialties." Echoes a legal consultant, "They are the most intellectually astute lawyers to be found anywhere. They have esoteric but usable solutions to many problems. There are none more expert in the field than them."

Wachtell Lipton generates revenue primarily from premium fees related to the "fair value" of the firm's work in classic You-Bet-Your-Company crisis situations. While this is uncommon compensation, it also is uncommon to obtain the great majority of a firm's revenue through this approach. If a client protests the firm's lump-sum invoices, Wachtell's policy is to ask the client to pay what it thinks is fair and then cut its ties with that client.

Experience and practice have combined to make Wachtell "the leanest firm of all," according to a former litigator. "There is no deadwood." The firm exercises quality control by hiring only the top law school graduates and hardly ever makes lateral hirings. Associates, once chosen by the firm, have a solid chance to make partner. Wachtell's peculiar 1:1 ratio of partners to associates reflects the firm's de-emphasis of hourly charges in favor of premium fees. Under those circumstances, there is no need for the firm to pad itself with associates to generate profit. If anything, a former house counsel notes, because of the potential for upward mobility "everyone who is there over two years loves it."

While most other New York firms have rescinded lockstep, seniority-based compensation to partners, Wachtell Lipton again differentiates itself by retaining this approach; the firm separates partners into broad, seniority-derived tiers (the founding partners being in the first tier) and pays accordingly. In addition, the firm rewards its associates with the "going rate" plus a substantial "profit-sharing" year-end bonus.

This approach at Wachtell, however, is less a reflection of inflexibility or traditionalism than of the firm's top-to-bottom, across-the-board strength. As one legal consultant observes, the firm is composed of "the best and the brightest. They're all good down to the associates." Adds a senior litigator, "They have a real sense of cohesiveness and a uniformity of quality."

Because of its small size, Wachtell has been able to establish a true firm identity and to recruit those who fit its requirements.

The firm, which is predominantly Jewish, consists of lawyers who are, one headhunter marvels, "to a person, well-rounded." She also perceives that at Wachtell, "They all see themselves as knights in shining armor with a very moralistic point of view against hostile takeovers."

Associates share this dedication. In a 1988 *American Lawyer* survey of mid-level associates, the firm ranked first among thirty-seven New York firms (up from the 1986 survey, in which it ran third). Wachtell was praised for everything from its partners' treatment of associates to its crack support staff. Even the associates' chronic overwork has become a point of pride. As one respondent explained, Wachtell is "obsessed with its own excellence." The 1989 survey revealed substantially the same high grades from associates.

Consistent with the firm's general philosophy of being "different but better," Wachtell has a less formal governing structure. The firm is, for partners, a participatory democracy. There is no written partnership agreement. While all partners vote on all matters of any consequence, formal voting is a rarity. The entire partnership decides on admitting new partners; any partner may recommend an associate for partnership without prior screenings of any committee. A loose administrative committee, staffed by any partner who desires to serve, controls matters of administration. The firm is more stringent about outside liaisons. Partners can neither own stock in a client corporation nor sit on any of its boards.

Wachtell Lipton is doing precisely what it wants to do. In a relatively short time it has reached almost legendary status for its proficiency and achievements. Although the flow of hostile takeovers and M & A work has abated, the sheer intellectual strength of this relatively young firm should enable it to adapt to whatever legal crises may arise.

WEBSTER & SHEFFIELD
237 Park Avenue • New York, New York 10071 • (212) 808-6000

Rating: 💼💼💼   *Direction:* ↓

*LAWYERS

	LAWYERS	PARTNERS	ASSOCIATES
1990:	108	39	62
1989:	109	34	67
1988:	113	36	71
1987:	105	37	62
1986:	100	36	52

	Paralegals	Support
1990:	18	119
1989:	18	125
1988:	NA	NA
1987:	19	136
1986:	15	NA

*LATERAL HIRES
1989: 2
1988: 2
1987: NA
1986: 3

*MANAGING PARTNERS: Donald Elliott and Eugene Harper, Jr.

*REPRESENTATIVE CLIENTS:
State of New York, State of Michigan, ICC Industries, Inc., Liggett Group, Inc., Mazda Motors of America, Inc., Carnegie Hall Corporation, Sumitomo Bank Ltd.

*BRANCHES: Washington (9), Houston (8)
Total: 17 lawyers (NAp and NAa)

*AVERAGE ANNUAL BILLING HOURS (1989):
Partners: NA
Associates: 1900

*NUMBER OF WOMEN

	Partners	Associates
1990:	4	25
1989:	2	24
1988:	0	25
1987:	1	20
1986:	1	12

*PARTNERSHIP TRACK: 8 years

*NUMBER OF LAWYERS FROM ENTERING CLASS TO MAKE PARTNER:
1981: 4 of 16
1980: 1 of 11
1979: 0 of 10
1978: 2 of 8
1977: 0 of 10

*GROSS REVENUE
1989: NA
1988: NA
1987: NA
1986: NA

*REVENUE PER LAWYER
1989: NA
1988: NA
1987: NA
1986: NA

*PROFITS PER PARTNER
1989: NA
1988: NA
1987: NA
1986: NA

*STARTING ASSOCIATE SALARY
1990: NA
1989: NA
1988: $77,000
1987: $65,000
1986: $63,000

*PRO BONO: 1–3% of total time

*HOURLY RATES
Partners: NA
Associates: NA

*PRINCIPAL LAW SCHOOLS
(Associates): NYU (7), Columbia (5), Fordham (4), Georgetown (4)

*NUMBER OF MINORITIES

	Partners	Associates
1990:	0	2
1989:	0	3
1988:	0	4
1987:	0	5
1986:	0	3

*SUMMER ASSOCIATES
1990: 12
1989: 10
1988: 11
1987: 20
1986: 15

Webster & Sheffield is a mid-size general practice firm, the history of which may be more consequential than its present status or prospects. The firm's most famous partner is John Lindsay, the former mayor of New York who, according to a headhunter, has "lots to do with the firm's outlook." That outlook, unusual among leading law firms, puts extreme emphasis on public service over profits. "They're Jesuits," says the same headhunter. "They question things but believe in the system. They have consciences." The firm takes its *pro bono* and community service work seriously. This attitude is exemplified by such key partners as Donald Elliott, a former chairman of the New York City Planning Commission. Webster partners also sit on the boards of major educational, charitable and cultural organizations, such as Barnard College, Carnegie Hall, the Children's Aid Society, Long Island University and the South Street Seaport Museum.

The perception that Webster & Sheffield is "declining," as a former house counsel believes, may be the result of the firm's unimpressive financial picture. Webster & Sheffield failed to make *The American Lawyer* list of top 100 firms nationally in gross revenue, revenue per lawyer or profits per partner between 1986 and 1988. Moreover, after steadily expanding from 1979 to 1983 at a rate of 12% per annum, growth was cut in half between 1983 and 1988, a period of accelerated growth for many other leading firms.

Bethual Webster—a prominent lawyer, former president of the Bar Association of the City of New York and trustee of the Ford Foundation—founded the firm in 1934. Webster also was to play an important role in U.S. foreign affairs. In the late 1960s, he mediated the conflict between Guatemala and the United Kingdom concerning British Honduras. After its founding, the firm added and exchanged pieces in each of the next four decades. Charles Garside joined the firm in the late 1930s; the firm became Webster & Garside. In the late 1940s, Frederick Sheffield—subsequently chairman of the Carnegie Foundation—and Frances Horan came on board, while after World War II Garside left to devote himself to public service. The firm changed its name to Webster Sheffield & Horan. The next decade was marked by the acquisition of Chrystie & Chrystie, trusts and estates specialists; the firm became known as Webster Sheffield & Chrystie. In 1961, the firm took in the New York City branch of Buffalo's Fleischmann, Gaeckle, Stokes & Hitchcock. Webster Sheffield & Chrystie became Webster Sheffield Fleischmann Hitchcock & Chrystie. Finally, in 1976, the firm institutionalized its name as Webster & Sheffield.

A Management Committee with a varying number of members elected by the partnership for open-ended terms governs the firm. Led by chairman Peter Heller, the committee sets billing rates for partners and associates and makes final decisions on partner compensation. The fourteen-member Work Committee handles associate training and recommends associates for partnership (although nominations can come from the general partnership as well). The full partnership votes to admit new partners and set associate salaries, the latter on the basis of proposals by the Work Committee. The Hiring Committee is the only other permanent committee; ad hoc committees are formed as needed.

Webster & Sheffield has six departments: litigation, corporate, public finance, real estate, tax and trusts and estates. Despite being the firm's largest practice area, litigation is not viewed as Webster & Sheffield's strong point. "Indifferent . . . not what they're best at," analyzes a senior litigator. A house counsel also recalls "not [being] particularly impressed" by the firm's litigators. Donald Elliot is the key partner in the department, although Harvey Myerson, who left the firm for Finley, Kumble and then Myerson & Kuhn (both now defunct), was probably the best-known litigator recently attached to the firm (although he was not well known when he was there).

What Webster is best at is public finance. Beyond Lindsay, this department, which has represented the states of New York and Michigan, includes the outstanding Eugene Harper and Thomas McGavin, a lateral from Dewey Ballantine.

Peter Heller and Eliot Cutler headline the corporate department, which represents such interests as ICC Industries Inc., Toyo Kogyo Co. Ltd. and Liggett & Myers Tobacco Company.

The firm maintains branch offices in Washington (9, 1976) and Houston (8, 1982).

Associates who are more interested in a linear, ultra-consistent environment than being on the cutting edge find a home at Webster & Sheffield. "They don't hire laterals often," says a headhunter. "There's not much attrition."

WEIL GOTSHAL & MANGES
767 Fifth Avenue • New York, New York 10153 • (212) 310-8000

Rating: 💼💼💼💼💼   *Direction:* ↑

*LAWYERS	PARTNERS	ASSOCIATES
1990: 391	90	291
1989: 353	85	261
1988: 334	73	251
1987: 316	73	236
1986: 280	69	204

	Paralegals	Support
1990:	108	803
1989:	65	742
1988:	NA	NA
1987:	61	470
1986:	NA	NA

*LATERAL HIRES
1989: 28
1988: 40
1987: NA
1986: 37

*CO-MANAGING PARTNERS: Todd Lang, Harvey Miller, Ira M. Millstein

*REPRESENTATIVE CLIENTS:
General Electric Credit Corp., Citibank, General Motors, TWA, American Airlines, Prudential, Drexel Burnham (in reorganization), Carl Icahn, Odyssey Partners

*BRANCHES: Washington (42), Miami (23), Houston (58), Dallas (28), London (1) Total: 131 lawyers (NAp and NAa)

*AVERAGE ANNUAL BILLING HOURS:
Partners: NA
Associates: NA

*NUMBER OF WOMEN
	Partners	Associates
1990:	13	114
1989:	12	105
1988:	8	94
1987:	8	91
1986:	7	79

*PARTNERSHIP TRACK: 7.5 years

*NUMBER OF LAWYERS FROM ENTERING CLASS TO MAKE PARTNER:
1982: 9 of NA
1981: 14 of NA
1980: 2 of NA
1979: 6 of NA
1978: 8 of NA

*GROSS REVENUE
1989: $200,000,000
1988: $160,000,000
1987: $134,000,000
1986: $120,000,000

*REVENUE PER LAWYER
1989: $440,000
1988: $385,000
1987: $355,000
1986: $365,000

*PROFITS PER PARTNER
1989: $690,000
1988: $675,000
1987: $555,000
1986: $605,000

*STARTING ASSOCIATE SALARY
1990: $82,000
1989: $82,000
1988: $76,000
1987: $65,000
1986: $65,000

*PRO BONO: NA

*HOURLY RATES
Partners: NA
Associates: NA

*PRINCIPAL LAW SCHOOLS
(Associates): NYU (19), Yeshiva (13), Columbia (12), Brooklyn (11), Fordham (11), Georgetown (10), Harvard (9), University of Chicago (9)

*NUMBER OF MINORITIES
	Partners	Associates
1990:	4	17
1989:	1	13
1988:	1	13
1987:	1	13
1986:	0	15

*SUMMER ASSOCIATES
1990: 56
1989: 51
1988: 46
1987: 46
1986: 42

Weil Gotshal, a transaction-driven corporate powerhouse, began as a quiet firm in midtown. Since the advent of Ira Millstein, Todd Lang and later Harvey Miller, however, it has not remained a very quiet place. While the firm has expanded substantially beyond its Jewish base, it still retains, as one ex-house counsel puts it, "lots of Jewish angst. It is a firm where more people yell at more people than anywhere else." "Weil Gotshal has a group of highly motivated, neurotic, non-collegial lawyers who are very talented," summarizes another house counsel.

Surprisingly, the firm's rate of financial growth slacked off somewhat between 1986 and 1989. While gross revenues grew from $120,000,000 in 1986 to $200,000,000 in 1989, the firm slipped from 10th place in *The American Lawyer* ranking of the top 100 firms nationally to 16th. Similarly, while revenue per lawyer increased from $365,000 to $440,000 and profits per partner increased from $605,000 to $690,000 (in both cases after a sub-par 1987, in which revenues per lawyer dropped to $355,000 and profits per partner to $555,000), the firm dropped in the rankings for both categories. Weil Gotshal placed 12th in 1986 in revenue per lawyer; by 1989, the firm was down to 16th. In 1986, the firm had ranked 7th in profits per partner; in 1989, Weil Gotshal placed 14th.

Frank Weil, Sylvan Gotshal and Horace Manges founded the firm in 1930. In its early years, Weil Gotshal was a small midtown Jewish firm with a substantial base of factoring textile and retail clients. The firm only truly took shape and began its accelerated growth after 1958, when Ira Millstein, a litigator and anti-trust regulation lawyer, made partner. He had started at the firm as an associate in 1951. With the arrival of corporate star Todd Lang, also in the 1950s, and bankruptcy star Harvey Miller in 1970, the troika of key lawyers needed to galvanize the firm was complete.

Millstein, Lang and Miller are mainstays on the six-member Executive Committee that runs the firm. The partnership elects four of the members for two-year terms, while the other two are recommended by the committee itself and are replaced annually. Members may serve consecutive terms. The Executive Committee elects a managing partner, staffs the firm's other committees, sets partner compensation (just the four regular members do this) and approves associate salaries proposed by the Legal Personnel Committee. New partners are admitted by vote of the full partnership. Millstein enjoys an extremely pungent, favorable reputation for both his leadership qualities and his intellectually aggressive style. As one wag put it, "Ira Millstein drives the consensus."

Weil Gotshal is divided into nine primary practice areas: corporate, litigation, securities litigation, trade regulation, business reorganization, tax, real estate, employment law and ERISA and trusts and estates. Virtually all of the firm's departments are highly respected; the only area of doubt is whether Weil Gotshal will be able to sustain its excellence once its superstars are no longer in active practice. Beyond Lang, the key figures in corporate are Carl Lobel, Steven Jacobs and Peter Standish. A prominent trial lawyer calls Millstein, who straddles corporate and litigation, "one of the great corporate schmoozers of all time." The litigation department produces "excellent work which is thorough and solid," according to a senior litigator, and includes such standouts as John Wing, who has a white collar criminal practice and is a former assistant U.S. attorney. In the anti-trust and trade regulation area, observers single out Paul Victor and Stuart Rosen for praise. Miller leads the firm's bankruptcy subdivision, which a bankruptcy lawyer at another leading New York firm calls "the leading bankruptcy department in New York City," while Gordon Henderson is a leading light in tax. The only practice area seen as questionable is real estate. Charles Goldstein, who made the practice explode when he came to Weil Gotshal in 1979, left for Shea & Gould in 1984 with virtually the entire Weil Gotshal real estate department in tow. In 1990 Alan Pomerantz, a real estate mover and shaker, joined the firm.

The firm maintains branch offices in Washington (42, 1975), Miami (23, 1981), Houston (58, 1985) and Dallas (28, 1987). Nancy Buc and Carla Hill are the key figures in the D.C. office.

Associates' life at Weil Gotshal is not smooth sailing, primarily because of the firm's well-documented abrasive internal relations, sink-or-swim approach to training and endless hours. "There is stridency and stress which affects the quality of life for both partners and associates," says a senior litigator. Weil

Gotshal ranked low in 1986, 1988 and 1989 *American Lawyer* associate surveys in New York—35th of 41 firms in 1986, 29th of 37 in 1988 and 23rd of 35 in 1989. "People either love it or hate it—more hate it," says a headhunter, summarizing much of what associates themselves reported. "The partners can be very abusive. There's a real 'in' club—you have to give your life to the firm. People leave because they are crying miserable." Some associates accentuated the positive, and noted that the firm always provides interesting work and is trying to alleviate its personnel problems. Says a headhunter, "The people who thrive there are people who take absolutely nothing personally." Nonetheless, one legal consultant believes that the purported long hours and difficult interpersonal relations are more mythical than real and in any event are quite exaggerated.

WHITE & CASE
....
1155 Avenue of the Americas • New York, New York 10036 • (212) 819-8200

Rating: 💼💼💼💼   *Direction:* ↑ ?

*LAWYERS

	LAWYERS	PARTNERS	ASSOCIATES
1990:	304	NA	NA
1989:	269	72	186
1988:	260	NA	NA
1987:	209	59	148
1986:	169	NA	NA

	Paralegals	Support
1989:	57	550
1988:	63	NA
1987:	36	375
1986:	39	NA

*LATERAL HIRES

1989: NA
1988: 10
1987: NA
1986: 20

*CHAIRMAN: James B. Hurlock

*REPRESENTATIVE CLIENTS:

Bankers Trust, U.S. Steel, GE, the central banks of Indonesia and Turkey, Cigna Corporation

*BRANCHES: Washington (20), Los Angeles (31), Miami (15), London (5), Paris (15), Hong Kong (4), Stockholm (8), Singapore (3), Tokyo (2), Ankara (2), Istanbul (4), Jedda (9)
Total: 118 lawyers (33p and 85a)

*AVERAGE ANNUAL BILLING HOURS (1988):
Partners: NA
Associates: NA

*NUMBER OF WOMEN

	Partners	Associates
1989:	NA	NA
1988:	NA	NA
1987:	NA	NA
1986:	NA	NA

*PARTNERSHIP TRACK: 7–9 years

*NUMBER OF LAWYERS FROM ENTERING CLASS TO MAKE PARTNER:

1981: 4 of 27
1980: 4 of 23
1979: 2 of 11
1978: 3 of 17

*GROSS REVENUE

1989: $144,000,000
1988: $120,000,000
1987: $104,000,000
1986: $77,000,000

*REVENUE PER LAWYER

1989: $380,000
1988: $375,000
1987: $355,000
1986: $310,000

*PROFITS PER PARTNER

1989: $425,000
1988: $460,000
1987: $435,000
1986: $390,000

*STARTING ASSOCIATE SALARY

1990: $83,000
1989: $81,000
1988: $77,000
1987: $66,000
1986: $66,000

*PRO BONO: 3% of total time

*HOURLY RATES
Partners: NA
Associates: NA

*PRINCIPAL LAW SCHOOLS
(Associates): Harvard (27), Columbia (27), NYU (27)

*NUMBER OF MINORITIES

	Partners	Associates
1989:	NA	NA
1988:	NA	NA
1987:	NA	NA
1986:	NA	NA

*SUMMER ASSOCIATES

1989: 40
1988: 44
1987: 65
1986: 59

Today's White & Case scarcely resembles the prototypically white shoe firm which went by that name fifteen years ago. Business connections and a gentleman's club atmosphere have given way to the hustle and bustle of a firm on the cutting edge, particularly in its international banking practice.

More than other firms its size, White & Case has become an extension of one man's talents and idiosyncrasies. James Hurlock has run White & Case since he was elected chairman of the Management Committee in 1980. He receives the lion's share of credit for what some observers refer to as "raising White & Case from the dead." At the same time, however, Hurlock's distinctive, domineering style of decision-making continues to raise its own set of problems.

The firm traces its roots to 1901 when it was established by J. Du Pratt White and George Case, who both had important social, banking and commercial connections. For many years White & Case defined white shoe: senior partners decided who would join the partnership, there was lockstep seniority compensation, and the firm was suitably genteel in ambience and areas of practice. Notwithstanding, during this period White & Case ranked high among New York firms, both in number of lawyers and prestige.

For fifteen years until his death in 1964, the firm was run by Joseph Mandel Hartfield, Jewish by birth but totally assimilated. The Colonel—a Kentucky appellation—was a 4'10"-tall bachelor who always wore a black suit, black string tie and black hat and squired around town chorus girls a foot taller and many years younger than himself. He also was a significant business originator. After Hartfield's death, first Henry Mannix and then Orson Marden, a leading litigator who headed the American Bar Association, New York State Bar Association, and Bar Association of the City of New York, ran the firm until 1975. Hal Fales led the firm until Hurlock took over the reins.

Although there were rumblings of discontent in the late 1960s, White & Case did not confront the problems facing it (and many other old-line firms) until Hurlock was elected chairman. The firm had recently lost a major account because of haphazard billing procedure, suffered the withdrawal of business from many old-line corporations which had started to enlarge their own in-house staff and endured the unfortunate *National Student Marketing* case brought by the SEC against the firm which was settled in 1977 for almost $2 million. It cost the firm far more by way of prestige and standing than dollars expended.

At the outset, Hurlock dedicated himself to finding new areas of strength for the firm. His personal success in representing the central bank of Indonesia and later the central banks of Turkey, Gabon, Zaire, Peru, Costa Rica, Panama and Honduras persuaded him to emphasize building up White & Case's overseas branches. While the great preponderance of the firm's activities are still domestic, Hurlock has expended much energy in staffing the foreign branches with the best associates; this, in turn, has engendered much criticism from within that this approach depletes the supply of talent in New York.

On the up side, White & Case's international practice has indeed brought back a measure of the firm's old prestige and has given it new financial life. White & Case has kept pace in explosive times with other leading New York firms; in *American Lawyer* surveys it consistently ranks around 30th in gross revenues, with numbers that have grown from $77,000,000 in 1986 to $104,000,000 in 1987 to $120,000,000 in 1988. Moreover, the firm has held steady in the rankings for revenue per lawyer and profits per partner despite much internal turmoil. Nonetheless, 1989 broke the continuing progress across the financial board; while revenue increased $24,000,000, to $144,000,000, revenue per lawyer increased only $5,000, to $380,000 and profits per partner actually dropped $35,000, to $425,000.

White & Case always has had a steady banking practice and what one former house counsel calls a "stellar client list" to fall back on. In its early years, the firm represented what became Bankers Trust, which has always been the firm's largest client. Bankers Trust once accounted for 20–25% of White & Case's revenue; now it amounts to a still significant 10%. The firm also has represented U.S. Steel, Prudential, General Electric and General Electric Credit Corporation, Indonesia, Turkey, Deutsche Bank, Swiss Bank Corp, Aetna and Cigna Corp.

Beyond banking, White & Case has become synonymous for

what the same house counsel calls "adequate work with adequate people." The tax department is "good, but not tremendous," says a tax lawyer from another leading New York firm. Although the real estate department has acquired laterals, it remains, as one observer summarizes, "second rate." While the firm's corporate and M & A practice has grown of late, most observers agree that litigation, while technically proficient, lags behind both in terms of high-powered litigators and business originators. Paul Bschorr, a leader in securities litigation, and John Barnum, a former deputy secretary of transportation and the head of the firm's Washington office, are two notable exceptions to this rule. Jeffrey Barist has emerged as the firm's most outstanding younger litigator.

Hurlock's ability to be an effective, judicious manager of both individuals and the firm as a whole has been continually questioned. Unhappiness with his leadership was a factor in persuading at least four significant partners to leave the firm in the early 1980s. Another significant corporate partner left in 1985 to start an institutional finance department at Skadden Arps. Although substantial additional compensation was one of the attractions inducing the move, the question remained as to the extent to which unhappiness with Hurlock played a role in that decision. The decision in 1984 to move the firm's downtown and midtown offices to Sixth Avenue, while resolving many office problems, increased rent from $14 per square foot to more than $37 per square foot, entailed $14 million of capital improvements and made many partners extremely unhappy.

The most openly dramatic example of Hurlock's leadership and judgment relates to the Evan Dawson matter. In 1988 Hurlock decided to dissolve the firm and reorganize it simultaneously without Dawson when Dawson, a senior trusts and estates partner who had fallen into disfavor, refused to acquiesce in a retirement program structured for him by Hurlock. At this writing, there is a substantial question whether the decision to dissolve and reorganize the firm as a method of ousting Dawson was legally and financially supportable under the circumstances. There also is a substantial question as to the extent to which the litigation brought by Dawson against the firm will hurt it both financially and from a public relations point of view.

Another recent Hurlock decision came into play when White & Case selected <u>Rudolph Giuliani</u> as a partner prior to his run for the New York mayoralty. Although there was much competition among leading New York firms to take in Giuliani, White & Case's choice became questionable after taking into consideration the estimated $1,000,000 compensation package granted to Giuliani and his associate at the U.S. attorney's office, particularly after the firm's connection to Panama emerged in the mayoralty campaign and became a public relations disaster. Giuliani left White & Case in May 1990 to become a partner in a more litigation-oriented New York firm.

Notwithstanding, White & Case remains a popular place to work. In both 1986 and 1988 *American Lawyer* mid-level associate surveys the firm placed a strong eighth in New York. Lawyers lauded the firm for its excellent training, good internal relations and attractive travel opportunities. Associates in 1988 also noted the firm's unforced sincerity in committing to *pro bono* work. However, in the 1989 survey the firm dropped to 25th position, the result of a perceived decline in each of the components of the overall evaluation, including interest in the work, training, treatment by partners and camaraderie. Concern also was expressed about the firm's policies on a variety of family and parental matters.

Under Hurlock's leadership White & Case has transformed itself into a modern firm. It seeks top talent from all quarters, broader fields of expertise and an expanded client base while it encourages and rewards hard work and business productivity. Although this approach has placed the firm on the upswing, it still has not regained the standing it once enjoyed. Hurlock seeks to do so and more, but the question is whether the firm has the capability of achieving these goals, taking into consideration the spirited competition from other similarly situated firms.

WHITMAN & RANSOM

200 Park Avenue • New York, New York 10166 • (212) 351-3000

Rating: 💼💼💼💼

Direction: ?

*LAWYERS

	PARTNERS	ASSOCIATES
1990: 141	64	66
1989: 117	54	51
1988: 109	52	46
1987: 81	40	32
1986: 96	47	39

	Paralegals	Support
1990:	24	189
1989:	16	132
1988:	NA	NA
1987:	16	115
1986:	NA	NA

*LATERAL HIRES

1989: 30
1988: 11
1987: NA
1986: 3

*MANAGING PARTNER: Maged F. Riad

*REPRESENTATIVE CLIENTS: NA

*BRANCHES: Los Angeles (24), Greenwich, Conn. (40), Newark (8), London (6), Palo Alto (4), Sacramento (2)
Total: 84 lawyers (NAp and NAa)

*AVERAGE ANNUAL BILLING HOURS:

Partners: NA
Associates: 2000

*NUMBER OF WOMEN

	Partners	Associates
1990:	5	30
1989:	3	20
1988:	3	17
1987:	2	9
1986:	2	9

*PARTNERSHIP TRACK: 8–10 years

*NUMBER OF LAWYERS FROM ENTERING CLASS TO MAKE PARTNER:

1981: 2 of 4
1980: 1 of 2
1979: 3 of 5
1978: 1 of 7

*GROSS REVENUE

1989: NA
1988: NA
1987: NA
1986: NA

*REVENUE PER LAWYER

1989: NA
1988: NA
1987: NA
1986: NA

*PROFITS PER PARTNER

1989: NA
1988: NA
1987: NA
1986: NA

*STARTING ASSOCIATE SALARY

1990: $78,000
1989: $75,000
1988: $70,000
1987: NA
1986: $57,000

*PRO BONO: 1–3% of total time

*HOURLY RATES

Partners: NA
Associates: NA

*PRINCIPAL LAW SCHOOLS
(Associates): Fordham (13), NYU (5), St. John's (5)

*NUMBER OF MINORITIES

	Partners	Associates
1990:	4	9
1989:	4	7
1988:	3	3
1987:	1	3
1986:	2	5

*SUMMER ASSOCIATES

1990: 7
1989: 7
1988: 6
1987: 7
1986: 5

Whitman & Ransom, a senior corporate lawyer states flatly, is "a good example of bad expansion." That the firm did not, according to *The American Lawyer*, qualify as one of the top 100 firms nationally in gross revenue, revenue per lawyer or profits per partner confirms that although Whitman & Ransom is bigger, it's not better. The consequence of the firm's determined expansion campaign is a lack of cohesion—what a leading litigator calls "an amalgam of nothing" and what a judge calls "quality problems."

Since its inception in 1919, the firm has adopted the names of its founding partners, Charles Whitman and William Ransom. Whitman was a former governor of New York; Ransom had been counsel to the New York State Public Service Commission. Both men became presidents of the American Bar Association. Whitman & Ransom frequently has used mergers to grow. First, the firm joined with the twenty-lawyer Parr, Doherty, Polk & Sargent in 1970. In 1976, it merged with the ten-lawyer firm of Havens, Wandless, Stitt & Tighe. Finally, in 1978, Whitman & Ransom acquired the twenty-eight-lawyer Connecticut firm Hirshberg, Pettengill, Strong & Nagle. Another means of expansion relied on heavily by the firm is lateral acquisitions. Peter Leisure left Curtis Mallet and jumped to Whitman & Ransom in 1979, where he led the litigation department. John Dowd came to the firm from the Department of Justice to bolster the firm's white-collar criminal practice. (Neither man is currently with the firm; Leisure has since become a judge.) In 1981, Frank Church, formerly a U.S. Senator from Idaho and chairman of the Senate Foreign Relations Committee, came to the firm, where he now conducts a substantial Far East practice.

The firm has a two-tiered partnership, with capital and non-capital partners. The capital partners elect a six-member Management Committee for two-year terms, with no limitations on the number of consecutive terms. The Management Committee recommends partnership compensation to the capital partners and makes final decisions on this matter. Also finalized by the Management Committee are recommendations made by the Associate Committee on the admission of non-capital partners and associate compensation. Currently, the firm's managing partner is Maged Riad. New capital and non-capital partners are elected by the capital partners. The non-capital partnership track is typically nine years; another twelve years pass before the non-capital partner is considered for election as a capital partner.

Whitman & Ransom's two central practice areas are corporate/international and litigation. The firm has smaller real estate, trusts and estates, tax, bankruptcy and municipal finance departments. In April 1989, Whitman & Ransom's insurance department left the firm and went to Mound, Cotton & Wollan. Herbert Polk, an insurance litigator at Whitman & Ransom for forty-three years, became of counsel to both firms rather than leave. Observers single out Polk, real estate lawyer Neil Underberg and partially retired litigator Robert Newman for praise. John Oram, Jr., is considered a power in the corporate area.

The firm maintains a relatively large branch office in Greenwich, Connecticut, inherited from the merger with Hircshberg, Pettengill. It also has a medium-size office in Los Angeles and small offices in Palo Alto, Sacramento and London. The Connecticut office functions largely independently from New York. It has its own management committee, recruits separately from the New York branch and maintains a different pay scale. In certain locations, such as Tokyo and Beirut, instead of having a branch, Whitman & Ransom is affiliated with a local firm. Lateral acquisition James Anderson, the first American lawyer to establish a practice in post-war Japan, is of counsel in the firm's New York office. He remains one of a small number of attorneys from outside Japan authorized to practice there. Certain young associates train abroad for several years in Whitman & Ransom's Tokyo affiliate; the New York firm, in turn, trains Japanese, Korean, European and Middle Eastern lawyers in American law.

Associates at Whitman & Ransom lead what one headhunter calls a "pretty civilized" existence. The workload and hours are no more than average. Atmosphere, however, may be a trouble spot. The firm is "very social," according to a former house counsel, "and has lots of stuffed shirts."

WILLKIE FARR & GALLAGHER

153 East 53rd Street • New York, New York 10022 • (212) 935-8000

Rating: 💼💼💼💼   *Direction:* ↑

*LAWYERS	PARTNERS	ASSOCIATES
1990: 279	79	190
1989: 265	72	183
1988: 240	NA	NA
1987: 228	67	156
1986: 212	64	143

	Paralegals	Support
1990:	58	493
1989:	51	487
1988:	NA	NA
1987:	51	355
1986:	NA	NA

*LATERAL HIRES
1989: 25
1988: 19
1987: NA
1986: 19

Jack Nussbaum

*MANAGING PARTNER: Susan P. Thomases

*REPRESENTATIVE CLIENTS:
Shearson Lehman, Willis Corroon, plc, Yamaha, Prudential Life, Major League Baseball

*BRANCHES: Washington (56), Paris (9), London (3)
Total: 68 lawyers (14p and 54a)

*AVERAGE ANNUAL BILLING HOURS:
Partners: NA
Associates: NA

*NUMBER OF WOMEN

	Partners	Associates
1990:	7	70
1989:	10	63
1988:	10	70
1987:	8	59
1986:	6	61

*PARTNERSHIP TRACK: 8 years

*NUMBER OF LAWYERS FROM ENTERING CLASS TO MAKE PARTNER:
1981: 4 of 23
1980: 5 of 17
1979: 3 of 10
1978: NA of 12

*GROSS REVENUE
1989: $142,500,000
1988: $135,000,000
1987: $102,000,000
1986: $85,000,000

*REVENUE PER LAWYER
1989: $460,000
1988: $460,000
1987: $390,000
1986: $375,000

*PROFITS PER PARTNER
1989: $805,000
1988: $785,000
1987: $640,000
1986: $500,000

*STARTING ASSOCIATE SALARY
1990: $82,000
1989: $82,000
1988: $77,000
1987: $65,000
1986: $65,000

*PRO BONO: 2% of total time

*HOURLY RATES
Partners: NA
Associates: NA

*PRINCIPAL LAW SCHOOLS
(Associates): Harvard (39), NYU (39), Columbia (28)

*NUMBER OF MINORITIES

	Partners	Associates
1990:	1	9
1989:	1	8
1988:	1	9
1987:	1	6
1986:	1	7

*SUMMER ASSOCIATES
1990: 76
1989: 38
1988: 34
1987: 51
1986: 32

For a firm apparently so solid across the board, Willkie Farr draws unusually mixed reactions from observers and fellow lawyers. One legal consultant says that the firm is "struggling for identity . . . is conservative on growth . . . and behind the times"; yet a headhunter counters that Willkie Farr is "forward-thinking" and "on the way up." A senior litigator thinks that the firm is "medium-to-good overall" but that in his personal experience he "expected them to be better." A former house counsel, however, concludes that "this firm always seems to be better than I think it should be." A leading trial lawyer states that Willkie Farr has a "good litigation department but could use a few trial lawyers." Another senior litigator says that the "dynamism is in corporate, not litigation." One legal consultant attempts to reconcile these disparate opinions by explaining that the firm is "one of the most underrated by lawyers, one of the most respected by clients." The 1989 departure of Kenneth Bialkin, a firm leader and corporate securities superstar, to Skadden Arps further confuses the issue: there is dispute both as to the reasons for Bialkin's move and its effects on Willkie Farr.

Willkie's financial success, however, is uncontestable. Largely due to its tremendous M & A business, the firm has hovered in and around the national top 10 for revenue per lawyer and profits per partner according to *The American Lawyer*. Between 1986 and 1988, Willkie's revenue per lawyer grew from $375,000 to $460,000 and its profits per partner increased from an already-impressive $500,000 to $785,000. During the same time period, the firm's gross revenues ranked somewhat lower but have grown swiftly from $85,000,000 in 1986 to $135,000,000 in 1988. The firm experienced a relatively flat 1989: revenues increased $7,500,000, to $142,500,000, revenue per lawyer remained at $460,000 while profits per partner increased $20,000, to $805,000.

Willkie has origins in the firm of Hornblower & Byrne—founded in 1888. Between 1890 and 1941, this firm experienced several permutations. William Chadbourne left to found what would become Chadbourne & Parke; Elihu Root, Jr. left to head what is now Dewey, Ballantine. Harold Gallagher, who was a former president of the American Bar Association and who had a critical hand in bringing Wendell Willkie into the firm in 1941, led the firm for forty years. Willkie joined up following the 1940 election when he lost his bid to become President of the United States to the then two-term incumbent Franklin D. Roosevelt. Although Willkie became the firm's lead name, he was too busy with politics and the war effort to spend much time at the firm. He did argue a significant case before the Supreme Court in 1943 in which he succeeded in blocking the effort of the United States government to deport an immigrant who had joined the Communist party when he came to the United States. Wendell Willkie died in 1944.

In the 1970s the firm was a defendant in two actions which were damaging both from a professional and a monetary standpoint. In one, a stockholder's action was brought against Leasco Data (a Saul Steinberg–controlled company) following its takeover of Reliance Insurance Co. and liquidation of the insurance company's $30 million "surplus surplus." The court found a registration statement prepared by the firm designed "to obscure, rather than to reveal in plain English, the critical elements of a proposed deal." A judgment of $100,000 was entered against Leasco of which the firm's portion was $5,000. (In 1986, Reliance severed its relationship with Willkie because of a disagreement with the firm's defense of a class action and derivative suits brought by shareholders of the Walt Disney Company. That litigation, in which Reliance and Disney are co-defendants, arises from greenmail payments made by Disney to Reliance in 1984.)

Promptly after the Leasco case, the SEC instituted an action against the firm in which Willkie lawyers were charged with having "lent their skills and services" to helping Robert Vesco bilk $60 million from Investors Overseas' Fund of Funds. Willkie Farr settled out of court for an undisclosed amount. In 1980 a jury found against Willkie Farr's co-defendant, Bank of New York, for 42% of the loss, the other 58% being valued at $34.8 million had the firm continued as a defendant.

The firm is governed by a ten-partner Executive Committee chosen by the partnership for three-year terms. Susan Thomases has been the administrative partner in charge of day-to-day operations since 1982 when the position was first created. The firm has a network of committees, including a Compensation Committee which determines partner compensation. Willkie's system is one of "absolutely merit compensation," says a legal consultant. There is also a Professional Personnel Committee which handles associate compensation, and a Business Committee that deals with firm-wide financial issues as well as billing and rates.

Willkie has seven departments: corporate, litigation, public finance, tax, real estate, trusts and estates/personal services and employment relations. The corporate department, headed by Jack Nusbaum, is substantially larger than the others and has enjoyed great success with a variety of M & A transactions. Bialkin and Nusbaum—whom one headhunter refers to as "the tops"—represented Shearson Loeb Rhodes Inc. in its 1981 merger with American Express Co.

Observers single out Louis Craco and David Foster among Willkie's litigators, the latter specifically for his anti-trust work. Craco's most well-known client is Major League Baseball. Recently Benito Romano, Rudolph Giuliani's successor as U.S. attorney, decided to join the firm and not return to Dewey Ballantine.

In 1976 the firm acquired the eleven-lawyer municipal bond firm of Sykes Galloway & Dikeman and entered into that specialty.

Willkie has branch offices in Washington (56, 1981), London (3, 1988) and Paris (6, 1971); it maintained a Paris office between 1924 and 1932.

Associates, seemingly, have also found their impressions of Willkie difficult to reconcile. A 1986 *American Lawyer* survey of mid-level associates placed the firm 6th among 41; the 1988 survey ranked Willkie 31st of 37; the 1989 survey, 33rd of 35. In 1986, associates found the work interesting and believed they received a substantial amount of responsibility. By 1988, one associate described the work as administrative and "beyond boring." Similarly, the problem cited most in a 1987 survey of summer associates was that the expansion of the firm's summer program caused a shortage of interesting work. The firm also ranked below the 1988 New York average in associates' view of their treatment by partners. Office space and support staff were both designated inadequate. In 1989 the firm received the worst scores in the nation for partner-associate and inter-associate relations. On the other hand, a legal consultant observes that Willkie associates are "quite happy" and "do not burn out" while a headhunter refers to them as "wholesome, NYU business-type people."

WILSON, ELSER, MOSKOWITZ, EDELMAN & DICKER

420 Lexington Avenue • New York, New York 10170 • (212) 490-3000

Rating: 💼💼💼💼   *Direction:* ↑

*LAWYERS	PARTNERS	ASSOCIATES
1990: 217	66	151
1989: 203	60	143
1988: 175	49	126
1987: 170	46	124
1986: 184	NA	NA

	Paralegals	Support
1989:	30	NA
1988:	36	NA
1987:	NA	NA
1986:	30	NA

*LATERAL HIRES
1989: 46
1988: 27
1987: NA
1986: 5

*SENIOR MANAGING PARTNER: Thomas W. Wilson

*CHIEF EXECUTIVE OFFICER: Albert J. Caro

*REPRESENTATIVE CLIENTS:
Utica National Insurance Group, Shand, Morahan and Company, Lloyd's of London

*BRANCHES: Los Angeles (44), Newark (25), Philadelphia (24), San Francisco (17), Baltimore (11), Washington (9), Miami (6), Chicago (9), Tokyo (2), London (1)
Total: 148 lawyers (NAp and NAa)

*AVERAGE ANNUAL BILLING HOURS:
Partners: NA
Associates: NA

*NUMBER OF WOMEN

	Partners	Associates
1989:	NA	NA
1988:	NA	NA
1987:	NA	NA
1986:	NA	NA

*PARTNERSHIP TRACK: NA

*NUMBER OF LAWYERS FROM ENTERING CLASS TO MAKE PARTNER:
1981: NA
1980: NA
1979: NA
1978: NA

*GROSS REVENUE
1989: $82,000,000
1988: $69,000,000
1987: $60,000,000
1986: NA

*REVENUE PER LAWYER
1989: $260,000
1988: $250,000
1987: $240,000
1986: NA

*PROFITS PER PARTNER
1989: $460,000
1988: $415,000
1987: $450,000
1986: NA

*STARTING ASSOCIATE SALARY
1990: NA
1989: $45,000
1988: NA
1987: NA
1986: NA

*PRO BONO: NA

*HOURLY RATES
Partners: NA
Associates: NA

*PRINCIPAL LAW SCHOOLS (Associates): Fordham (17), New York Law School (16), Pace (14), St. John's (13)

*NUMBER OF MINORITIES

	Partners	Associates
1989:	NA	NA
1988:	NA	NA
1987:	NA	NA
1986:	NA	NA

*SUMMER ASSOCIATES
1989: NA
1988: NA
1987: NA
1986: NA

Wilson Elser, the biggest insurance defense firm in the country, demonstrates the advantages of knowing your customers and keeping them happy. The firm is a supermarket for insurance companies, largely handling litigation and litigation resolution in a variety of fields, including product liabililty, professional liability, corporate and securities liability and life, accident and health liability. While the firm handles commercial matters for non-insurance clients, Wilson Elser's focus is on work for insurance company clients and on supervising insurance litigation carried out by other, usually local, counsel—small cases compared to those ordinarily handled by other leading firms, but an extraordinarily high volume of them. "As insurance lawyers go," says one senior litigator, "they're good."

This cottage industry, as well as tight management policies, have made Wilson Elser steadily more profitable. According to *The American Lawyer*, the firm's gross revenue in 1988 was $69,000,000, up slightly from $60,000,000 in 1987. Similarly, the firm's revenue per lawyer edged upward from $240,000 to $250,000 in the same time span. In 1989 gross revenue rose to $82,000,000 while revenue per lawyer rose modestly again to $260,000. The firm ranked in the bottom half of the nation's top 100 firms in these categories. Profits per partner, however, are the true measure of Wilson Elser's success. In 1987, the firm had profits per partner of $450,000 and ranked a remarkable 20th in this respect country-wide. While profits per partner dropped to $415,000 in 1988, in 1989 profits per partner increased to $460,000, which was 25th in the country. These results reflect the firm's two-tier partnership system; in 1988, Wilson Elser had thirty-eight equity partners and thirty contract partners—as well as the highest lawyer/partner ratio (6.6:1) in the country. Also, Wilson Elser's associates are not recruited from the top law schools and are paid between $45,000 and $80,000 per annum—substantially less than their counterparts at other leading New York firms. Thus, in classic style—lower overhead and a pie sliced into fewer pieces—the firm generates handsome profits.

Wilson Elser emerged out of a split within Kroll, Edelman, Elser & Wilson in late 1978. Name partners Thomas Wilson, John Elser and Max Edelman left Kroll Edelman due to a dispute over financial management and partnership shares. They were joined in exile by principal partners Harold Moskowitz and Herbert Dicker as well as nearly all of Kroll Edelman's junior partners and two major clients—Shand, Morahan and Company and various underwriters of Lloyd's of London. In 1980, the sixty-lawyer firm founded by the departees was christened Wilson, Elser, Edelman & Dicker; in 1985 Moskowitz' name was added to the firm's. Since its founding, Wilson Elser has grown at an accelerated rate. By 1982, the firm had over one hundred lawyers and was adding twenty-five to thirty lawyers per year to the New York office alone. The firm blossomed to 212 lawyers by 1988.

In 1983, the firm instituted its two-tier partnership structure. A seven-partner Executive Committee that has been called "omnipotent" handles matters of firm policy. Otherwise, Wilson Elser's governance remains rather loosely defined; there is no specific policy on when associates may expect to be considered for contract partnership or on when the step from contract to equity partner ordinarily occurs. In 1986, twelve associates were made contract partners; in 1987, only one was.

Wilson is undisputably the firm's leader, managerially and otherwise. Wilson Elser, however, thrives not on the excellence or creativity of individual stars but on a consistent work product delivered at a moderate cost. Cost control—imposed by lower hourly rates and by the efficient distribution of foot soldiers—combined with the firm's specialization has attracted such clients as Utica National Insurance Group. In all respects, Wilson Elser defines itself by the needs of its clients.

At its founding, Wilson Elser inherited offices in New York, Washington, D.C., San Francisco, Los Angeles and London. In 1983, it opened offices in Newark; in 1984, Philadelphia; in 1987, Tokyo, Baltimore and Miami; and in 1988, Chicago.

The working conditions for Wilson Elser associates have always been rather severe. The firm presses its associates to accumulate the goal of fifty billable hours per week and more than 1,900 billable hours per year. Partnership chances—whether contract or equity—exist but are more sparse than at other leading firms because of Wilson Elser's emphasis on keeping overhead low. Those associates involved with direct litigation tend to have interesting assignments and receive much responsibility; those who specialize in supervisory work often find it tedious and disappointing. These negatives, combined with the firm's lower pay scale, have led to a high turnover rate among associates; ten leave, ten more are hired. Associates at Wilson Elser are perceived—and perceive themselves—as utterly replaceable.

WINTHROP, STIMSON, PUTNAM & ROBERTS

One Battery Park Plaza • New York, New York 10004 • (212) 858-1000

Rating:

Direction: ↑ ?

*LAWYERS

	PARTNERS	ASSOCIATES
1990: 212	55	145
1989: 204	50	144
1988: 180	48	124
1987: 161	49	96
1986: 140	47	93

	Paralegals	Support
1989:	30	485
1988:	25	426
1987:	20	320
1986:	13	NA

*LATERAL HIRES

1989: 8
1988: 19
1987: 18
1986: 17

*MANAGEMENT COMMITTEE CHAIRMAN:
William M. Evarts, Jr.

*REPRESENTATIVE CLIENTS:
Bank of New York, American Express, Travelers, Credit Suisse, Toronto Dominion Bank

*BRANCHES: Washington (21), Stamford (18), Palm Beach (5), London (3), Brussels (2)
Total: 56 lawyers (12p and 34a)

*AVERAGE ANNUAL BILLING HOURS (1989):
Partners: NA
Associates: 1834

*NUMBER OF WOMEN

	Partners	Associates
1990:	7	74
1989:	7	NA
1988:	6	NA
1987:	6	NA
1986:	4	NA

*PARTNERSHIP TRACK: 7–8 years

*NUMBER OF LAWYERS FROM ENTERING CLASS TO MAKE PARTNER:
1982: 1 of 17
1981: 0 of 15
1980: 4 of 13
1979: 2 of 13
1978: 2 of 6

*GROSS REVENUE
1989: $88,000,000
1988: $72,000,000
1987: $61,000,000
1986: $47,500,000

*REVENUE PER LAWYER
1989: $340,000
1988: $345,000
1987: $300,000
1986: $265,000

*PROFITS PER PARTNER
1989: $385,000
1988: $400,000
1987: $355,000
1986: $320,000

*STARTING ASSOCIATE SALARY
1990: $83,000
1989: $80,000
1988: $75,000
1987: $67,000
1986: $55,000

*PRO BONO: 1–3% of total time

*HOURLY RATES
Partners: NA
Associates: NA

*PRINCIPAL LAW SCHOOLS
(Associates): Brooklyn (12), NYU (12), Columbia (10), Georgetown (9), Harvard (9), University of Virginia (9)

*NUMBER OF MINORITIES

	Partners	Associates
1990:	0	17
1989:	0	12
1988:	0	13
1987:	0	6
1986:	0	7

*SUMMER ASSOCIATES
1990: 41
1989: 36
1988: 20
1987: 44
1986: 34

Until the mid-1980s, Winthrop Stimson was a model white shoe firm. It had longstanding institutional clients, a conservative old-world demeanor and a reserved, gentlemanly—some might even say smug—air about it. Even now, the firm continues to pay partners in accordance with lockstep seniority which reaches its maximum after a nine-year period; the firm also continues to stress the importance of collegiality and to abhor unseemly behavior, such as partners' raising their voices to associates. Some at the firm may still harbor fond feelings for the firm's old gentlemanly schedule. "Our expressed and actual desire," Henry Stimson once said, "is to conduct our law practice during office hours, which are 9:30 to 5:30 and, under pressure of unfinished business, if necessary, Saturday morning."

Around 1985, however, Winthrop Stimson got tough. That was the year the firm acquired the forty-lawyer Hale Russell & Gray, with its strong Scandinavian practice, thereby gaining twenty-five clients and generating annual fees of about $13 million. Also in 1985, the firm opened a Washington office that included both lobbying and more ordinary practice activities such as trade matters and governmental contracts (the latter specialty has proved particularly successful). In 1989, the firm acquired two partners from LeBoeuf Lamb specializing in utility finance.

Among observers, there are still non-believers. "The blood has run thin," says one senior litigator; "they have not kept up," says another. The firm's operating results, however, show progress. Between 1986 and 1988, Winthrop Stimson's gross revenue grew from $47,500,000 to $72,000,000. Revenue per lawyer increased from $265,000 to $345,000 and profits per partner increased from $320,000 to $400,000. Perhaps more importantly, the firm also moved up in *The American Lawyer* ranking of the top 100 firms nationally in each category—from 73rd place to 60th in gross revenue, 44th to 33rd in revenue per lawyer and 31st to 30th in profits per partner. Winthrop Stimson not only kept up but also surpassed its competition in a period of accelerated growth for the entire profession. However, the firm did not maintain its steady growth in 1989. While gross revenue increased $16,000,000, to $88,000,000, there was a $5,000 drop in revenue per lawyer to $340,000 and a $15,000 drop in profits per partner to $385,000.

Winthrop Stimson's origins trace back to 1868 and the firm Root & Compton, where, in 1891, Bronson Winthrop and Henry Stimson became clerks. The firm evolved into Winthrop & Stimson in 1897 and adopted its current name in 1927. Stimson, the firm's most renowned partner, was a quintessential establishment Republican. He served as secretary of war in the Taft administration, secretary of state in the Hoover administration and secretary of war in both the Roosevelt and Truman administrations. Winthrop was a direct descendent of John Winthrop, the colonial governor of Massachusetts. Albert Putnam and George Roberts became partners in the early 1900s.

A nine-member Management Committee, elected by the partnership for staggered terms of up to four years, governs the firm. Currently, William Evarts, Jr. is the chairman of the Management Committee and thereby the firm's managing partner. The Management Committee appoints members to three other committees—Associates, Administrative Personnel and Facilities—which are led by younger partners. Partners are compensated strictly by seniority. The Associates Committee makes recommendations on associate compensation to the full partnership, which votes on a one-partner, one-vote basis. Any partner may propose a candidate for admission to the partnership; all new partners must be unanimously approved by the partnership.

Winthrop Stimson is divided into five departments: corporate, litigation, tax, trusts and estates and real estate. All receive mixed reviews. "Their work product is 'iffy'," says a senior corporate lawyer. Observers do not single out many star-caliber individual lawyers. In corporate, the key figures are Evarts and Merrell "Ted" Clark, who, says a former house counsel, is a "big gun." Litigator Ed Wesley and tax lawyer Peter Faber also receive praise.

The firm at least has partially lost two major clients because of takeovers. It had represented Singer Company, but when Singer was taken over by Bilzerian in 1988, Winthrop Stimson lost all its Singer business outside of the sewing machine division. The firm had also represented Irving Trust for over forty years; Irving Trust work led to over half of the billings of the firm's thirty-five banking lawyers. Since Irving Trust was taken over by Bank of New York, it remains unclear what legal business will be going to Winthrop as opposed to Bank of New York's counsel, Sullivan & Cromwell.

Winthrop Stimson maintains branch offices in Stamford, Conn. (17, 1977), Palm Beach (5, 1976), London (3, 1972) and Washington (21, 1985).

Associates recently have revised and improved their opinions of Winthrop Stimson. In a 1986 *American Lawyer* survey of mid-level associates in New York, the firm ranked 23rd among 41 firms; in 1988, the firm shot up to second place. The most important area of improvement was training. The firm also instituted a rotation system that has proved extremely popular and effective. Its internal relations remain good, and associates continue to receive adequate levels of responsibility. Winthrop Stimson's facilities and support staff received complaints, but these may have evaporated with the firm's October 1989 move to One Battery Park Plaza. Nonetheless, in the 1989 survey the firm dropped to 18th place, which is attributable largely to a perceived lack of direct information about partnership chances (lowest in the country) and partner feedback (fifth worst in the country). There is also disgruntlement with the varying workloads resulting from the firm's associate assignment system.

The Next Twenty-Five Leading New York Firms

ANDERSON KILL OLICK & OSHINSKY, P.C.
. . . .
666 Third Avenue • New York, New York 10017 • (212) 850-0700

*LAWYERS†
1990: 148
1989: 124
1988: 95
1987: NA

	Paralegals	Support
1990:	100	183
1989:	83	137
1988:	61	NA
1987:	31	NA

*LATERAL HIRES
1990: 41
1989: 38
1988: 28
1987: NA

*MANAGING PARTNER: Eugene R. Anderson

*NUMBER OF WOMEN
1990: 50
1989: 39
1988: NA
1987: NA

*STARTING SALARY
1990: $82,000
1989: $77,000
1988: $70,000
1987: $65,000

*BRANCHES: Washington (32), Philadelphia (2)
Total: 34 lawyers

*PRINCIPAL LAW SCHOOLS
NYU (27), Fordham (19), Columbia (16)

*PRO BONO: NA

*NUMBER OF MINORITIES
1990: 10
1989: 13
1988: NA
1987: NA

*SUMMER ASSOCIATES
1990: 22
1989: 18
1988: 13
1987: 9

†There is no breakdown of partners and associates, as all lawyers of the firm are considered partners.

BAER MARKS & UPHAM

805 Third Avenue • New York, New York 10022 • (212) 702-5700

*LAWYERS	PARTNERS	ASSOCIATES
1989: 97	37	55
1988: 91	40	46
1987: 77	33	44
1986: 96	37	57

	Paralegals	Support
1989:	15	100
1988:	15	100
1987:	15	100
1986:	15	109

*LATERAL HIRES

1989: 16
1988: 12
1987: 12
1986: 7

*MANAGING PARTNERS: Joel M. Handel, Donald J. Bezahler, Barry J. Mandel

*NUMBER OF WOMEN

	Partners	Associates
1989:	1	14
1988:	1	12
1987:	1	18
1986:	1	17

*PARTNERSHIP TRACK: 8.5 years

*NUMBER OF LAWYERS FROM ENTERING CLASS TO MAKE PARTNER:

1980: 3 of 8
1979: 1 of 8

*STARTING ASSOCIATE SALARY

1989: $77,500
1988: $75,000
1987: $70,000
1986: $65,000

*PRINCIPAL LAW SCHOOLS

NYU (9), Brooklyn (5), Boston (4), Columb
Georgetown (3), Fordham (3)

*PRO BONO: NA

*NUMBER OF MINORITIES

	Partners	Associates
1989:	0	5
1988:	0	1
1987:	0	0
1986:	0	0

*SUMMER ASSOCIATES

1989: 7
1988: 6
1987: 6
1986: 7

BATTLE FOWLER

280 Park Avenue • New York, New York 10017 • (212) 856-7000

*LAWYERS	PARTNERS	ASSOCIATES
1990: 105	38	64
1989: 105	38	64
1988: 90	33	57
1987: NA	NA	NA
1986: NA	NA	NA

	Paralegals	Support
1990:	21	140
1989:	22	155
1988:	NA	NA
1987:	NA	NA
1986:	NA	NA

*LATERAL HIRES

1989: 9
1988: NA
1987: NA
1986: NA

*MANAGING PARTNER: Thomas V. Glynn

*NUMBER OF WOMEN

	Partners	Associates
1990:	2	25
1989:	2	27
1988:	NA	NA
1987:	NA	NA
1986:	NA	NA

*PARTNERSHIP TRACK: 7.5 years

*NUMBER OF LAWYERS FROM ENTERING
CLASS TO MAKE PARTNER:

1982: 3 of 8
1981: 4 of 12
1980: 1 of 4
1979: 4 of 6

*STARTING ASSOCIATE
SALARY

1990: $80,000
1989: $80,000
1988: $76,000
1987: $71,000
1986: $55,000

*PRINCIPAL LAW SCHOOLS
Cornell (5), Fordham (5), NYU (5),
St. John's (5), Harvard (4)

*PRO BONO: NA

*NUMBER OF MINORITIES

	Partners	Associates
1990:	2	3
1989:	3	2
1988:	NA	NA
1987:	NA	NA
1986:	NA	NA

*SUMMER ASSOCIATES

1990: 9
1989: 14
1988: 13
1987: 12
1986: 4

CARTER, LEDYARD & MILBURN

2 Wall Street • New York, New York 10005 • (212) 732-3200

*LAWYERS	PARTNERS	ASSOCIATES
1990: 96	35	58
1989: 84	32	52
1988: 77	30	49
1987: 56	24	32
1986: 57	25	32

	Paralegals	Support
1990:	27	120
1989:	23	109
1988:	18	96
1987:	10	89
1986:	8	78

*LATERAL HIRES

1989: 3
1988: 12
1987: 16
1986: 5

*CHAIRMAN: None

*NUMBER OF WOMEN

	Partners	Associates
1990:	1	22
1989:	1	19
1988:	1	23
1987:	0	12
1986:	0	10

*PARTNERSHIP TRACK: 8 years

*NUMBER OF LAWYERS FROM ENTERING CLASS TO MAKE PARTNER:

1981: 1 of 13
1980: 1 of 7
1979: 1 of 9
1979: NA

*STARTING ASSOCIATE SALARY

1989: $81,000
1988: $76,000
1987: $65,000
1986: $65,000

*PRINCIPAL LAW SCHOOLS

Columbia, Yale, Harvard, NYU, Fordham

*PRO BONO: 5% of total time

*NUMBER OF MINORITIES

	Partners	Associates
1990:	0	9
1989:	0	7
1988:	0	4
1987:	0	2
1986:	0	2

*SUMMER ASSOCIATES

1990: 11
1989: 12
1988: 10
1987: 4
1986: 4

244

CULLEN & DYKMAN
· ·
177 Montague Street • Brooklyn, New York 11201 • (718) 855-9000

*LAWYERS	PARTNERS	ASSOCIATES
1990: 103	27	72
1989: 104	24	80
1988: 100	26	74
1987: 93	25	78
1986: 91	23	68

	Paralegals	Support
1989:	39	173
1988:	44	148
1987:	54	144
1986:	43	104

*LATERAL HIRES
1989: 8
1988: 0
1987: 2
1986: 0

*CHAIRMAN: F. Peter O'Hara

*NUMBER OF WOMEN

	Partners	Associates
1989:	1	10
1988:	1	4
1987:	1	11
1986:	1	20

*PARTNERSHIP TRACK: NA

*NUMBER OF LAWYERS FROM ENTERING CLASS TO MAKE PARTNER:
1981: 0 of 3
1980: 0 of 3
1979: 1 of 4
1978: 2 of 4

*STARTING ASSOCIATE SALARY
1990: $55,000
1989: $52,000
1988: $48,000
1987: $44,000
1986: $40,000

*PRINCIPAL LAW SCHOOLS
St. John's, Brooklyn

*PRO BONO: 3–4% of total 1989 time

*NUMBER OF MINORITIES

	Partners	Associates
1989:	0	6
1988:	0	8
1987:	0	2
1986:	0	2

*SUMMER ASSOCIATES
1989: 5
1988: 4
1987: 4
1986: 9

DREYER and TRAUB

101 Park Avenue • New York, New York 10178 • (212) 661-8800

*LAWYERS	PARTNERS	ASSOCIATES
1989: 100	35	60
1988: 81	NA	NA
1987: 85	29	56
1986: 74	NA	NA

	Paralegals	Support
1989:	NA	NA
1988:	NA	NA
1987:	NA	NA
1986:	NA	NA

*LATERAL HIRES

1989: NA
1988: NA
1987: NA
1986: NA

*CHAIRMAN: NA

*NUMBER OF WOMEN

	Partners	Associates
1989:	NA	NA
1988:	NA	NA
1987:	NA	NA
1986:	NA	NA

*PARTNERSHIP TRACK: NA

*NUMBER OF LAWYERS FROM ENTERING CLASS TO MAKE PARTNER:

1980: NA
1979: NA

*STARTING ASSOCIATE SALARY

1989: NA
1988: NA
1987: NA
1986: NA

*PRINCIPAL LAW SCHOOLS

NA

*PRO BONO: NA

*NUMBER OF MINORITIES

	Partners	Associates
1989:	NA	NA
1988:	NA	NA
1987:	NA	NA
1986:	NA	NA

*SUMMER ASSOCIATES

1989: NA
1988: NA
1987: NA
1986: NA

FISH & NEAVE

875 Third Avenue • New York, New York 10022 • (212) 715-0600

*LAWYERS	PARTNERS	ASSOCIATES
1990: 102	31	71
1989: 92	29	62
1988: 83	26	57
1987: 74	25	49
1986: 69	23	45

	Paralegals	Support
1990:	35	130
1989:	31	100
1988:	29	100
1987:	22	100
1986:	25	100

*LATERAL HIRES

1989: 2
1988: 4
1987: 6
1986: 3

*MANAGING PARTNER: Herbert Schwartz

*NUMBER OF WOMEN

	Partners	Associates
1990:	3	20
1989:	1	18
1988:	1	14
1987:	1	12
1986:	1	11

*PARTNERSHIP TRACK: 8 years

*NUMBER OF LAWYERS FROM ENTERING CLASS TO MAKE PARTNER:

1981: 1 of 4
1980: 2 of 5
1979: 0 of 6
1978: 3 of 6
1977: 2 of 5

*STARTING ASSOCIATE SALARY

1989: $83,000
1988: $76,000
1987: $68,500
1986: $65,000

*PRINCIPAL LAW SCHOOLS

University of Michigan (6), Harvard (5), Georgetown (4), University of Pennsylvania (4), University of Virginia (3), Yale (2)

*PRO BONO: 1–3% of total time

*NUMBER OF MINORITIES

	Partners	Associates
1990:	0	4
1989:	0	5
1988:	0	4
1987:	0	2
1986:	0	2

*SUMMER ASSOCIATES

1990: 20
1989: 21
1988: 17
1987: 16
1986: 13

HAIGHT, GARDNER, POOR & HAVENS
195 Broadway • New York, New York 10005 • (212) 341-7000

*LAWYERS	PARTNERS	ASSOCIATES
1990: 96	39	52
1989: 84	37	59
1988: 77	NA	NA
1987: 95	NA	NA
1986: 87	NA	NA

	Paralegals	Support
1990:	16	147
1989:	NA	NA
1988:	NA	NA
1987:	NA	NA
1986:	NA	NA

*LATERAL HIRES

1989: 3
1988: 3
1987: NA
1986: 1

*MANAGING PARTNER: Richard G. Ashworth

*NUMBER OF WOMEN

	Partners	Associates
1990:	1	14
1989:	1	14
1988:	NA	NA
1987:	NA	NA
1986:	NA	NA

*PARTNERSHIP TRACK: 6–9 years

*NUMBER OF LAWYERS FROM ENTERING CLASS TO MAKE PARTNER:

1980: 2 of 9
1979: 1 of 9

*STARTING ASSOCIATE SALARY

1989: NA
1988: NA
1987: NA
1986: NA

*PRINCIPAL LAW SCHOOLS
NA

*PRO BONO: NA

*BRANCHES: Washington (5), Houston (10), San Francisco (2), Hong Kong (1)
Total: 18 lawyers (8p and 10a)

*NUMBER OF MINORITIES

	Partners	Associates
1990:	1	7
1989:	1	6
1988:	NA	NA
1987:	NA	NA
1986:	NA	NA

*SUMMER ASSOCIATES

1990: 11
1989: 9
1988: NA
1987: NA
1986: NA

HERZFELD & RUBIN, P.C.

195 Broadway • New York, New York 10005 • (212) 344-5500

*LAWYERS†	PARTNERS	ASSOCIATES
1990: 132	47	73
1989: 137	46	78
1988: 117	40	61
1987: 110	41	57
1986: 110	39	62

	Paralegals	Support
1989:	32	140
1988:	27	149
1987:	24	124
1986:	21	117

*LATERAL HIRES

1989: 4
1988: NA
1987: NA
1986: NA

*SENIOR MEMBER: Herbert Rubin

*NUMBER OF WOMEN

	Partners	Associates
1989:	1	16
1988:	1	16
1987:	1	15
1986:	NA	NA

*PARTNERSHIP TRACK: NA

*NUMBER OF LAWYERS FROM ENTERING CLASS TO MAKE PARTNER:

1982: NA
1981: NA
1980: NA
1979: NA

†Includes branches.

*STARTING ASSOCIATE SALARY

1989: NA
1988: NA
1987: NA
1986: NA

*PRINCIPAL LAW SCHOOLS

Fordham, NYU, St. John's

*PRO BONO: NA

*BRANCHES: Los Angeles, Edison, N.J., Miami, Southfield, Mich, El Paso

*NUMBER OF MINORITIES

	Partners	Associates
1989:	0	3
1988:	NA	NA
1987:	NA	NA
1986:	NA	NA

*SUMMER ASSOCIATES

1989: NA
1988: NA
1987: NA
1986: NA

KENYON & KENYON

One Broadway • New York, New York 10004 • (212) 425-7200

*LAWYERS	PARTNERS	ASSOCIATES
1990: 79	32	47
1989: 77	32	45
1988: 79	31	48
1987: 76	31	45
1986: 71	30	41

	Paralegals	Support
1990:	18	150
1989:	18	157
1988:	21	152
1987:	20	146
1986:	21	122

*LATERAL HIRES

1989: 5
1988: 2
1987: 7
1986: 2

*CHAIRMAN: None

*NUMBER OF WOMEN

	Partners	Associates
1990:	0	9
1989:	0	8
1988:	0	10
1987:	0	8
1986:	0	7

*PARTNERSHIP TRACK: 8–9 years

*NUMBER OF LAWYERS FROM ENTERING CLASS TO MAKE PARTNER:

1981: NA of 5
1980: 1 of 2
1979: 1 of 3
1978: 1 of NA

*STARTING ASSOCIATE SALARY

1990: $80,000
1989: $80,000
1988: $75,000
1987: $71,000
1986: $65,000

*PRINCIPAL LAW SCHOOLS

Fordham (8), Georgetown (6), St. John's (6), Boston University (4), George Washington (4), Rutgers (4)

*PRO BONO: NA

*BRANCHES: Washington (15)

*NUMBER OF MINORITIES

	Partners	Associates
1990:	0	3
1989:	0	3
1988:	0	2
1987:	0	3
1986:	0	4

*SUMMER ASSOCIATES

1990: 19
1989: 13
1988: NA
1987: NA
1986: NA

KRONISH, LIEB, WEINER & HELLMAN

1345 Avenue of the Americas • New York, New York 10105 • (212) 841-6000

*LAWYERS	PARTNERS	ASSOCIATES
1990: 75	27	44
1989: 74	31	43
1988: 76	31	45
1987: 75	32	43
1986: 77	30	47

	Paralegals	Support
1990:	15	125
1989:	15	125
1988:	17	125
1987:	17	125
1986:	14	127

*LATERAL HIRES

1989: 9
1988: 6
1987: 9
1986: 12

*MANAGING PARTNER: Stephen D. Gardner

*NUMBER OF WOMEN

	Partners	Associates
1990:	2	19
1989:	0	23
1988:	0	22
1987:	0	20
1986:	1	20

*PARTNERSHIP TRACK: 8 years

*NUMBER OF LAWYERS FROM ENTERING CLASS TO MAKE PARTNER:

1981: 0 of 3
1980: 0 of 5
1979: 2 of 5
1978: 3 of 6

*STARTING ASSOCIATE SALARY

1990: $80,000
1989: $75,000
1988: $73,500
1987: $70,500
1986: $65,000

*PRINCIPAL LAW SCHOOLS

Columbia (9), NYU (7), Georgetown (5)

*PRO BONO: NA

*NUMBER OF MINORITIES

	Partners	Associates
1990:	0	3
1989:	0	2
1988:	NA	NA
1987:	NA	NA
1986:	NA	NA

*SUMMER ASSOCIATES

1990: 9
1989: 11
1988: 10
1987: 9
1986: 7

MARKS MURASE & WHITE

400 Park Avenue • New York, New York 10022 • (212) 832-3333

*LAWYERS	PARTNERS	ASSOCIATES
1990: 53	NA	NA
1989: 44	23	21
1988: 41	NA	NA
1987: 47	25	22
1986: NA	NA	NA

	Paralegals	Support
1989:	NA	NA
1988:	NA	NA
1987:	NA	NA
1986:	NA	NA

*LATERAL HIRES

1989: 19
1988: NA
1987: NA
1986: NA

*MANAGING PARTNER: Jiro Murase

*NUMBER OF WOMEN

	Partners	Associates
1989:	NA	NA
1988:	NA	NA
1987:	NA	NA
1986:	NA	NA

*PARTNERSHIP TRACK: NA

*NUMBER OF LAWYERS FROM ENTERING CLASS TO MAKE PARTNER:

1980: NA
1979: NA

*STARTING ASSOCIATE SALARY

1990: $80,000
1989: NA
1988: NA
1987: NA
1986: NA

*PRINCIPAL LAW SCHOOLS

NA

*PRO BONO: NA

*BRANCHES: Los Angeles (9), London (7), Washington (10), Tokyo (3), Hamburg (3)

*NUMBER OF MINORITIES

	Partners	Associates
1989:	NA	NA
1988:	NA	NA
1987:	NA	NA
1986:	NA	NA

*SUMMER ASSOCIATES

1989: NA
1988: NA
1987: NA
1986: NA

MENDES & MOUNT

Three Park Avenue • New York, New York 10016 • (212) 951-2200

*LAWYERS†	PARTNERS	ASSOCIATES
1990: 106	43	62
1989: 122	44	79
1988: 108	42	76
1987: 101	43	61
1986: 96	39	56

	Paralegals	Support
1989:	28	NA
1988:	21	NA
1987:	15	NA
1986:	18	NA

*LATERAL HIRES

1989: NA
1988: NA
1987: NA
1986: NA

*MANAGING PARTNER: Daniel M. Bianca

*NUMBER OF WOMEN

	Partners	Associates
1989:	NA	NA
1988:	NA	NA
1987:	NA	NA
1986:	NA	NA

*PARTNERSHIP TRACK: 8 years

*NUMBER OF LAWYERS FROM ENTERING CLASS TO MAKE PARTNER:

1982: NA
1981: NA
1980: NA
1979: NA

†Includes branch.

*STARTING ASSOCIATE SALARY

1989: NA
1988: NA
1987: NA
1986: NA

*PRINCIPAL LAW SCHOOLS

Fordham, NYU, St. John's

*PRO BONO: NA

*BRANCHES: Los Angeles (20)

*NUMBER OF MINORITIES

	Partners	Associates
1989:	NA	NA
1988:	NA	NA
1987:	NA	NA
1986:	NA	NA

*SUMMER ASSOCIATES

1989: NA
1988: NA
1987: NA
1986: NA

MILGRIM, THOMAJAN & LEE, P.C.

53 Wall Street • New York, New York 10005 • (212) 858-5300

*LAWYERS†	PARTNERS	ASSOCIATES
1990: 113	48	59
1989: 107	48	59
1988: 67	38	29
1987: NA	NA	NA
1986: NA	NA	NA

	Paralegals	Support
1990:	21	145
1989:	30	178
1988:	13	70
1987:	NA	NA
1986:	NA	NA

*LATERAL HIRES
1989: 29
1988: NA
1987: NA
1986: NA

*SENIOR PARTNER: Roger Milgrim

*NUMBER OF WOMEN

	Partners	Associates
1990:	5	21
1989:	5	12
1988:	NA	NA
1987:	NA	NA
1986:	NA	NA

*PARTNERSHIP TRACK: 6–8 years

*NUMBER OF LAWYERS FROM ENTERING CLASS TO MAKE PARTNER:
1982: 1 of 3
1981: 3 of 4
1980: 1 of 3
1979: 2 of 3
1978: 1 of NA

†Includes branches.

*STARTING ASSOCIATE SALARY
1990: $82,000
1989: $82,000
1988: $76,000
1987: $71,000
1986: $55,000

*PRINCIPAL LAW SCHOOLS
NYU (5), George Washington (5), University of Virginia (4)

*PRO BONO: NA

*BRANCHES: Austin, Tex. (7), Boston (7), Dallas (2), Los Angeles (6), Washington (7)

*NUMBER OF MINORITIES

	Partners	Associates
1990:	2	3
1989:	1	2
1988:	NA	NA
1987:	NA	NA
1986:	NA	NA

*SUMMER ASSOCIATES
1990: 6
1989: 6
1988: 10
1987: 9
1986: NA

MORGAN & FINNEGAN

345 Park Avenue • New York, New York 10154 • (212) 758-4800

*LAWYERS	PARTNERS	ASSOCIATES
1990: 76	28	46
1989: 73	25	48
1988: 58	24	34
1987: 49	23	26
1986: 39	22	17

	Paralegals	Support
1990:	34	106
1989:	34	114
1988:	30	116
1987:	25	93
1986:	20	91

*LATERAL HIRES

1989: 1
1988: 5
1987: 4
1986: 5

*MANAGING PARTNER: John C. Varsil

*NUMBER OF WOMEN

	Partners	Associates
1990:	2	7
1989:	1	12
1988:	1	12
1987:	1	7
1986:	1	5

*PARTNERSHIP TRACK: 8–10 years

*NUMBER OF LAWYERS FROM ENTERING CLASS TO MAKE PARTNER:

1982: NA
1981: NA
1980: NA
1979: NA

*STARTING ASSOCIATE SALARY

1990: $80,000
1989: $80,000
1988: $68,000
1987: $60,000
1986: $48,000

*PRINCIPAL LAW SCHOOLS

George Washington (7), St. John's (5), NYU (2)

*PRO BONO: 1–2% of total time

*NUMBER OF MINORITIES

	Partners	Associates
1990:	2	1
1989:	1	4
1988:	1	3
1987:	0	3
1986:	0	3

*SUMMER ASSOCIATES

1990: 13
1989: 14
1988: 15
1987: 7
1986: 7

255

MORRISON COHEN SINGER & WEINSTEIN
. . . .

750 Lexington Avenue • New York, New York 10022 • (212) 735-8600

*LAWYERS	PARTNERS	ASSOCIATES
1990: 45	24	21
1989: 42	24	16
1988: 28	16	12
1987: 28	16	12
1986: 22	13	9

	Paralegals	Support
1990:	9	57
1989:	7	46
1988:	5	39
1987:	5	32
1986:	NA	NA

*LATERAL HIRES

1989: 6
1988: 4
1987: 1
1986: 1

*MANAGING PARTNER: Robert Stephan Cohen

*NUMBER OF WOMEN

	Partners	Associates
1990:	4	9
1989:	4	4
1988:	2	4
1987:	3	4
1986:	3	2

*PARTNERSHIP TRACK: 7–9 years

*NUMBER OF LAWYERS FROM ENTERING CLASS TO MAKE PARTNER:

NA (firm founded in 1984)

*STARTING ASSOCIATE SALARY

1990: $77,500
1989: $65,000
1988: $63,000
1987: $55,000
1986: NA

*PRINCIPAL LAW SCHOOLS

St. John's (4), Fordham (2), Hofstra (2), Rutgers (2)

*PRO BONO: NA

*NUMBER OF MINORITIES

	Partners	Associates
1990:	0	1
1989:	0	1
1988:	0	0
1987:	0	0
1986:	0	0

*SUMMER ASSOCIATES

1990: 4
1989: 5
1988: 5
1987: 5
1986: 5

OLWINE, CONNELLY, CHASE, O'DONNELL & WEYLER

750 Seventh Avenue • New York, New York 10019 • (212) 261-8000

*LAWYERS	PARTNERS	ASSOCIATES
1990: 95	31	61
1989: 84	26	55
1988: 71	22	46
1987: 68	20	44
1986: 68	21	44

	Paralegals	Support
1990:	8	75
1989:	14	106
1988:	10	105
1987:	7	87
1986:	4	85

*LATERAL HIRES

1989: 7
1988: 14
1987: 10
1986: 4

*CHAIRMAN: None

*NUMBER OF WOMEN

	Partners	Associates
1990:	1	33
1989:	0	26
1988:	0	17
1987:	0	7
1986:	0	6

*PARTNERSHIP TRACK: 8 years

*NUMBER OF LAWYERS FROM ENTERING CLASS TO MAKE PARTNER:

1982: NA of 10
1981: 3 of 7
1980: 3 of 12
1979: 1 of 12

*STARTING ASSOCIATE SALARY

1990: $83,000
1989: $80,000
1988: $68,000
1987: $65,000
1986: $50,000

*PRINCIPAL LAW SCHOOLS

Fordham, Virginia, George Washington, Georgetown

*BRANCHES: Washington (10)

Total: 10 lawyers (4p and 6a)

*NUMBER OF MINORITIES

	Partners	Associates
1990:	0	6
1989:	0	3
1988:	0	1
1987:	0	0
1986:	0	0

*SUMMER ASSOCIATES

1990: 16
1989: 11
1988: 11
1987: 13
1986: 15

PENNIE & EDMONDS

1155 Avenue of the Americas • New York, New York 10036 • (212) 790-9090

*LAWYERS	PARTNERS	ASSOCIATES
1990: 87	30	57
1989: 73	27	42
1988: 63	NA	NA
1987: 59	23	32
1986: 60	23	33

	Paralegals	Support
1990:	13	75
1989:	NA	NA
1988:	NA	NA
1987:	NA	NA
1986:	NA	NA

*LATERAL HIRES
1989: 5
1988: 6
1987: NA
1986: 2

*CHAIRMAN: NA

*NUMBER OF WOMEN

	Partners	Associates
1990:	2	19
1989:	0	19
1988:	NA	NA
1987:	NA	NA
1986:	NA	NA

*PARTNERSHIP TRACK: 8–10 years

*NUMBER OF LAWYERS FROM ENTERING CLASS TO MAKE PARTNER:
1980: NA
1979: NA
1978: NA
1977: NA

*STARTING ASSOCIATE SALARY
1990: $82,000
1989: $71,000
1988: $65,000
1987: NA
1986: $65,000

*PRINCIPAL LAW SCHOOLS
NA

*PRO BONO: NA

*BRANCHES: Washington (6)

*NUMBER OF MINORITIES

	Partners	Associates
1990:	0	3
1989:	0	5
1988:	NA	NA
1987:	NA	NA
1986:	NA	NA

*SUMMER ASSOCIATES
1989: 12
1988: NA
1987: NA
1986: NA

258

RICHARDS & O'NEIL
885 Third Avenue • New York, New York 10022 • (212) 207-1200

*LAWYERS	PARTNERS	ASSOCIATES
1990: 80	23	55
1989: 75	24	50
1988: 60	23	37
1987: 51	22	29
1986: 45	22	23

	Paralegals	Support
1989:	20	113
1988:	27	93
1987:	32	NA
1986:	NA	NA

*LATERAL HIRES

1989: 5
1988: 1
1987: 4
1986: 3

*CHAIRMAN: Hugh J. Freund

*NUMBER OF WOMEN

	Partners	Associates
1989:	3	19
1988:	3	12
1987:	3	12
1986:	3	13

*PARTNERSHIP TRACK: 6–8 years

*NUMBER OF LAWYERS FROM ENTERING CLASS TO MAKE PARTNER:

1982: 2 of 6
1981: 0 of 3
1980: 2 of 2
1979: 2 of 3

*STARTING ASSOCIATE SALARY

1990: $80,000
1989: $80,000
1988: $76,000
1987: $70,000
1986: $52,000

*PRINCIPAL LAW SCHOOLS

Columbia (16), NYU (13), Fordham (7), Harvard (5)

*PRO BONO: 1–2% of total time

*NUMBER OF MINORITIES

	Partners	Associates
1989:	2	3
1988:	2	4
1987:	2	4
1986:	2	0

*SUMMER ASSOCIATES

1989: 9
1988: 9
1987: 8
1986: 9

ROBINSON, SILVERMAN, PEARCE, ARONSOHN & BERMAN

1290 Avenue of the Americas • New York, New York 10104 • (212) 541-2000

*LAWYERS	PARTNERS	ASSOCIATES
1990: 80	37	43
1989: 86	34	52
1988: 77	29	48
1987: 73	26	47
1986: 68	24	42

	Paralegals	Support
1989:	15	134
1988:	12	113
1987:	9	99
1986:	9	92

*LATERAL HIRES
1989: NA
1988: NA
1987: NA
1986: NA

*CHAIRMAN: Michael Rosen

*NUMBER OF WOMEN

	Partners	Associates
1989:	NA	NA
1988:	NA	NA
1987:	NA	NA
1986:	NA	NA

*PARTNERSHIP TRACK: NA

*NUMBER OF LAWYERS FROM ENTERING CLASS TO MAKE PARTNER:
1982: NA
1981: NA
1980: NA
1979: NA

*STARTING ASSOCIATE SALARY
1989: $72,000
1988: $68,000
1987: $65,000
1986: $65,000

*PRINCIPAL LAW SCHOOLS
NA

*PRO BONO: NA

*BRANCHES: Miami (1)

*NUMBER OF MINORITIES

	Partners	Associates
1989:	NA	NA
1988:	NA	NA
1987:	NA	NA
1986:	NA	NA

*SUMMER ASSOCIATES
1989: 7
1988: 9
1987: 7
1986: 6

SEWARD & KISSELL

One Battery Park Plaza • New York, New York 10004 • (212) 574-1200

*LAWYERS	PARTNERS	ASSOCIATES
1990: 80	22	54
1989: 84	25	59
1988: 73	23	50
1987: 74	21	53
1986: 69	21	48

	Paralegals	Support
1990:	17	104
1989:	14	97
1988:	12	86
1987:	12	94
1986:	8	89

*LATERAL HIRES

1989: 9
1988: 6
1987: 8
1986: 2

*MANAGING PARTNER: Eugene P. Souther

*NUMBER OF WOMEN

	Partners	Associates
1990:	2	20
1989:	2	22
1988:	2	21
1987:	2	22
1986:	2	17

*PARTNERSHIP TRACK: 8 years

*NUMBER OF LAWYERS FROM ENTERING CLASS TO MAKE PARTNER:

1981: NA of 12
1980: 3 of 7
1979: 1 of 10
1978: 1 of 10

*STARTING ASSOCIATE SALARY

1990: $76,000
1989: $73,000
1988: $71,500
1987: $67,500
1986: $62,000

*PRINCIPAL LAW SCHOOLS

Fordham (8), Boston (5), Columbia (4), NYU (4), North Carolina (4), St. John's (3), Vanderbilt (3), Hofstra (3), Northwestern (3)

*PRO BONO: 3% of total time

*BRANCHES: Washington (6)
Total: 6 lawyers (3p and 3a)

*NUMBER OF MINORITIES

	Partners	Associates
1990:	0	5
1989:	0	1
1988:	0	1
1987:	0	1
1986:	0	0

*SUMMER ASSOCIATES

1990: 10
1989: 10
1988: 10
1987: 12
1986: 7

SPENGLER CARLSON GUBAR BRODSKY & FRISCHLING

520 Madison Avenue · New York, New York, 10022 · (212) 935-5000

*LAWYERS	PARTNERS	ASSOCIATES
1990: 63	25	33
1989: 56	23	33
1988: 60	22	38
1987: 53	22	31
1986: 50	18	32

	Paralegals	Support
1990:	10	89
1989:	14	73
1988:	13	77
1987:	15	70
1986:	15	60

*LATERAL HIRES

1989: 13
1988: 3
1987: 15
1986: 6

*MANAGING PARTNER: Leonard Gubar

*NUMBER OF WOMEN

	Partners	Associates
1990:	3	13
1989:	3	13
1988:	2	12
1987:	3	13
1986:	3	10

*PARTNERSHIP TRACK: 7 years

*NUMBER OF LAWYERS FROM ENTERING
CLASS TO MAKE PARTNER:

1982: 0 of 18
1981: 1 of 16
1980: 2 of 12
1979: 2 of 10

*STARTING ASSOCIATE
SALARY

1990: $80,000
1989: $75,000
1988: $68,000
1987: $65,000
1986: $57,000

*PRINCIPAL LAW SCHOOLS

NYU (9), Yeshiva (4), Fordham
(3), Georgetown (4), Columbia
(3)

*PRO BONO: NA

*NUMBER OF MINORITIES

	Partners	Associates
1990:	0	1
1989:	0	1
1988:	0	2
1987:	0	1
1986:	0	0

*SUMMER ASSOCIATES

1990: 3
1989: 4
1988: 4
1987: 7
1986: 4

SUMMIT ROVINS & FELDESMAN

445 Park Avenue • New York, New York 10022 • (212) 702-2200

*LAWYERS

	PARTNERS	ASSOCIATES
1990: 74	38	30
1989: 108	49	42
1988: 107	52	43
1987: 99	52	35
1986: 95	46	41

	Paralegals	Support
1989:	13	133
1988:	14	116
1987:	13	119
1986:	9	95

*LATERAL HIRES

1989: 13
1988: 11
1987: 6
1986: 14

*EXECUTIVE COMMITTEE: Walter Feldesman, Richard Solomon, Stuart Summit

*NUMBER OF WOMEN

	Partners	Associates
1989:	4	14
1988:	2	14
1987:	2	12
1986:	1	17

*PARTNERSHIP TRACK: 7 years

*NUMBER OF LAWYERS FROM ENTERING CLASS TO MAKE PARTNER:

1982: 0 of 5
1981: 0 of 7
1980: 1 of 8
1979: 0 of 9

*STARTING ASSOCIATE SALARY

1990: $72,000
1989: $69,000
1988: $62,500
1987: $56,500
1986: $48,000

*PRINCIPAL LAW SCHOOLS

Fordham (7), Yeshiva (3), New York (2), St. John's (2)

*PRO BONO: NA

*NUMBER OF MINORITIES

	Partners	Associates
1989:	0	0
1988:	0	1
1987:	0	0
1986:	0	1

*SUMMER ASSOCIATES

1989: 6
1988: 6
1987: 7
1986: 8

TENZER, GREENBLATT, FALLON & KAPLAN

● ●

405 Lexington Avenue • New York, New York 10174 • (212) 573-4300

*LAWYERS	PARTNERS	ASSOCIATES
1989: 75	36	29
1988: 69	32	29
1987: 67	29	31
1986: 61	26	28

	Paralegals	Support
1989:	16	94
1988:	17	96
1987:	15	72
1986:	12	67

*LATERAL HIRES	COUNSEL
1989: 6	10
1988: 8	8
1987: 12	7
1986: 6	7

*SENIOR PARTNER: Lyonel E. Zunz

*NUMBER OF WOMEN

	Partners	Associates
1989:	1	10
1988:	1	8
1987:	1	6
1986:	0	6

*PARTNERSHIP TRACK: None

*NUMBER OF LAWYERS FROM ENTERING CLASS TO MAKE PARTNER:

1982: 0 of 4
1981: 0 of 2
1980: 1 of 2
1979: 3 of 8

*STARTING ASSOCIATE SALARY

1989: $75,000
1988: $67,000
1987: $62,000
1986: $55,000

*PRINCIPAL LAW SCHOOLS

NYU (6), Fordham (5), Columbia (3), Georgetown (2), American (2)

*PRO BONO: NA

*NUMBER OF MINORITIES

	Partners	Associates
1989:	0	2
1988:	0	1
1987:	0	0
1986:	0	0

*SUMMER ASSOCIATES

1989: 4
1988: 4
1987: 6
1986: 3

264

TOWNLEY & UPDIKE

405 Lexington Avenue • New York, New York 10174 • (212) 973-6000

*LAWYERS	PARTNERS	ASSOCIATES
1990: 84	32	44
1989: 84	30	46
1988: 89	NA	NA
1987: 88	NA	NA
1986: 73	NA	NA

	Paralegals	Support
1990:	14	120
1989:	NA	NA
1988:	NA	NA
1987:	NA	NA
1986:	NA	NA

*LATERAL HIRES

1989: 6
1988: 5
1987: NA
1986: 5

*CHAIRMAN: None

*NUMBER OF WOMEN

	Partners	Associates
1989:	5	11
1988:	NA	NA
1987:	NA	NA
1986:	NA	NA

*PARTNERSHIP TRACK: 8 years

*NUMBER OF LAWYERS FROM ENTERING CLASS TO MAKE PARTNER:

1981: 1 of 10
1980: 1 of 6
1979: 0 of 5

*STARTING ASSOCIATE SALARY

1990: $76,000
1989: NA
1988: $65,000
1987: NA
1986: $60,000

*PRINCIPAL LAW SCHOOLS

NA

*PRO BONO: NA

*NUMBER OF MINORITIES

	Partners	Associates
1990:	2	4
1989:	2	2
1988:	NA	NA
1987:	NA	NA
1986:	NA	NA

*SUMMER ASSOCIATES

1990: 10
1989: 12
1988: NA
1987: NA
1986: NA

Appendixes

Appendix A

······································

Total Number of Lawyers in New York (1990)

Firm	Total Number in New York	Total Number in New York and Branch Offices	Gross Revenue	Revenue Per Lawyer	Profits Per Partner	Starting Associate Salary
Skadden	550	1,085	$517,500,000	$545,000	$1,195,000	$83,000
Simpson	448	457	201,000,000	525,000	1,015,000	83,000
Shearman	440	563	281,000,000	575,000	800,000	83,000
Weil	391	522	200,000,000	340,000	385,000	83,000
Paul	377	410	195,000,000	535,000	915,000	83,000
Milbank	369	476	187,500,000	450,000	665,000	83,000
Davis	351	415	240,500,000	630,000	1,125,000	83,000
Proskauer	325	392	120,000,000	355,000	360,000	82,000
Cravath	305	314	213,000,000	740,000	1,765,000	82,962
White	304	422	144,000,000	380,000	425,000	83,000
Sullivan	292	344	230,000,000	665,000	1,210,000	83,000
Kaye	287	353	188,000,000	550,000	685,000	83,000
Willkie	279	347	142,500,000	460,000	805,000	82,000
Dewey	278	386	139,000,000	410,000	465,000	83,000
Debevoise	274	338	147,000,000	485,000	655,000	83,000
Cahill	273	290	146,500,000	575,000	1,515,000	83,000
Shea	262	304	123,000,000	405,000	345,000	80,000
Fried	256	397	213,000,000	580,000	815,000	82,000
Mudge	251	296	91,000,000	340,000	355,000	82,000
Stroock	245	339	120,000,000	365,000	460,000	82,000
Cleary	243	283	181,000,000	530,000	775,000	83,000

Rosenman	241	247	$80,000,000	$355,000	$360,000	$82,000
Kelley	223	388	112,500,000	300,000	365,000	83,000
Rogers	223	307	99,000,000	355,000	320,000	82,000
Wilson	217	365	82,000,000	260,000	460,000	45,000*
Chadbourne	215	272	95,000,000	405,000	505,000	83,000
Winthrop	212	268	88,000,000	340,000	385,000	83,000
LeBouef	211	384	117,000,000	330,000	305,000	83,000
Bower	200	206	NA	NA	NA	NA
Brown	198	244	77,000,000	315,000	395,000	80,000
Cadwalader	197	279	96,000,000	355,000	410,000	83,000
Lord Day	184	196	NA	NA	NA	82,000
Coudert	160	344	120,000,000	360,000	405,000	83,000
Schulte	156	157	NA	NA	NA	77,000
Patterson	154	163	NA	NA	NA	83,000
Reid	152	192	NA	NA	NA	77,000*
Whitman	141	225	NA	NA	NA	78,000
Kramer	140	140	NA	NA	NA	83,000
Hughes	131	191	76,000,000	325,000	330,000	80,000
Parker	130	134	NA	NA	NA	75,000
Thacher	124	134	32,259,000†	NA	254,000†	83,000
Breed	109	118	NA	NA	NA	80,000
Phillips	109	110	32,000,000	285,000	240,000	75,000
Webster	108	125	NA	NA	NA	NA
Curtis	104	140	NA	NA	NA	80,000
Donovan	103	160	NA	NA	NA	79,000
Wachtell	96	96	115,000,000	1,225,000	1,590,000	83,000
Epstein	80	163	48,000,000	NA	230,000	69,000
Hawkins	70	72	NA	NA	NA	NA
Jackson	31	121	NA	NA	NA	65,000

*1989
†1988 results

Total Number of Lawyers in New York and Branch Offices (1990)

Firm	Total Number in New York	Total Number in New York and Branch Offices	Gross Revenue	Revenue Per Lawyer	Profits Per Partner	Starting Associate Salary
Skadden	550	1,085	$517,500,000	$545,000	$1,195,000	$83,000
Shearman	440	563	281,000,000	575,000	800,000	83,000
Weil	391	522	200,000,000	340,000	385,000	83,000
Milbank	369	476	187,500,000	450,000	665,000	83,000
Simpson	448	457	201,000,000	525,000	1,015,000	83,000
White	304	422	144,000,000	388,000	425,000	83,000
Davis	351	415	240,500,000	630,000	1,125,000	83,000
Paul	377	410	195,000,000	535,000	915,000	83,000
Fried	256	397	213,000,000	580,000	815,000	82,000
Proskauer	325	392	120,000,000	355,000	360,000	82,000
Kelley	223	388	112,500,000	300,000	365,000	83,000
Dewey	278	386	139,000,000	410,000	465,000	83,000
LeBouef	211	384	117,000,000	330,000	305,000	83,000
Wilson	217	365	82,000,000	260,000	460,000	45,000*
Kaye	287	353	188,000,000	550,000	685,000	83,000
Willkie	279	347	142,500,000	460,000	805,000	82,000
Coudert	160	344	120,000,000	360,000	405,000	83,000
Sullivan	292	344	230,000,000	665,000	1,210,000	83,000
Stroock	245	339	120,000,000	365,000	460,000	82,000
Debevoise	274	338	147,000,000	485,000	655,000	83,000
Cravath	305	314	213,000,000	740,000	1,765,000	82,962
Rogers	223	307	99,000,000	355,000	320,000	82,000
Shea	262	304	123,000,000	405,000	345,000	80,000
Mudge	251	296	91,000,000	340,000	355,000	82,000
Cahill	273	290	146,500,000	575,000	1,515,000	83,000
Cleary	243	283	181,000,000	530,000	775,000	83,000
Cadwalader	197	279	96,000,000	355,000	410,000	83,000
Chadbourne	215	272	95,000,000	405,000	505,000	83,000
Winthrop	212	268	88,000,000	380,000	425,000	83,000

Rosenman	241	**247**	$80,000,000	$355,000	$360,000	$82,000
Brown	198	**244**	77,000,000	315,000	395,000	80,000
Whitman	141	**225**	NA	NA	NA	82,000
Bower	200	**206**	NA	NA	NA	NA
Lord Day	184	**196**	NA	NA	NA	82,000
Reid	152	**192**	NA	NA	NA	77,000*
Hughes	131	**191**	76,000,000	325,000	330,000	80,000
Epstein	80	**163**	48,000,000	NA	230,000	69,000
Patterson	154	**163**	NA	NA	NA	83,000
Donovan	103	**160**	NA	NA	NA	79,000
Schulte	156	**157**	NA	NA	NA	77,000
Curtis	104	**140**	NA	NA	NA	80,000
Kramer	140	**140**	NA	NA	NA	83,000
Parker	130	**134**	NA	NA	NA	75,000
Thacher	124	**134**	32,259,000†	NA	254,000†	83,000
Webster	108	**125**	NA	NA	NA	NA
Jackson	31	**121**	NA	NA	NA	65,000
Breed	109	**118**	NA	NA	NA	80,000
Phillips	109	**110**	32,000,000	285,000	240,000	75,000
Wachtell	96	**96**	115,000,000	1,225,000	1,590,000	NA
Hawkins	70	**72**	NA	NA	NA	NA

*1989
†1988 results

Gross Revenue (1989)

Firm	Total Number in New York	Total Number in New York and Branch Offices	Gross Revenue	Revenue Per Lawyer	Profits Per Partner	Starting Associate Salary
Skadden	550	1,085	$517,500,000	$545,000	$1,195,000	$83,000
Shearman	440	563	281,000,000	575,000	800,000	83,000
Davis	351	415	240,500,000	630,000	1,125,000	83,000
Sullivan	292	344	230,000,000	665,000	1,210,000	83,000
Cravath	305	314	213,000,000	740,000	1,765,000	82,962
Fried	256	397	213,000,000	580,000	815,000	82,000
Simpson	448	457	201,000,000	525,000	1,015,000	83,000
Weil	391	522	200,000,000	340,000	385,000	83,000
Paul	377	410	195,000,000	535,000	915,000	83,000
Kaye	287	353	188,000,000	550,000	685,000	83,000
Milbank	369	476	187,500,000	450,000	665,000	83,000
Cleary	243	283	181,000,000	530,000	775,000	83,000
Debevoise	274	338	147,000,000	485,000	655,000	83,000
Cahill	273	290	146,500,000	575,000	1,515,000	83,000
White	304	422	144,000,000	380,000	425,000	83,000
Willkie	279	347	142,500,000	460,000	805,000	82,000
Dewey	278	386	139,000,000	410,000	465,000	83,000
Shea	262	304	123,000,000	405,000	345,000	80,000
Coudert	160	344	120,000,000	360,000	405,000	83,000
Proskauer	325	392	120,000,000	355,000	360,000	82,000
Stroock	245	339	120,000,000	365,000	460,000	82,000
LeBouef	211	384	117,000,000	330,000	305,000	83,000
Wachtell	96	NA	115,000,000	1,225,000	1,590,000	83,000
Kelley	223	388	112,500,000	300,000	365,000	83,000
Rogers	223	307	99,000,000	355,000	320,000	82,000
Cadwalader	197	279	96,000,000	355,000	410,000	83,000
Chadbourne	215	272	95,000,000	405,000	505,000	83,000
Mudge	251	296	91,000,000	340,000	355,000	82,000
Winthrop	212	NA	88,000,000	380,000	425,000	83,000
Wilson	217	365	82,000,000	260,000	460,000	45,000†
Rosenman	241	247	80,000,000	355,000	360,000	82,000
Brown	198	244	77,000,000	315,000	395,000	80,000
Hughes	131	191	76,000,000	325,000	330,000	80,000
Epstein	80	163	48,000,000	NA	230,000	69,000
Thacher	124	134	32,259,000*	NA	254,000*	83,000

Phillips	109	110	$32,000,000	$285,000	$240,000	$75,000
Bower	200	206	NA	NA	NA	NA
Breed	109	118	NA	NA	NA	80,000
Curtis	104	140	NA	NA	NA	80,000
Donovan	103	160	NA	NA	NA	79,000
Hawkins	70	72	NA	NA	NA	NA
Jackson	31	121	NA	NA	NA	65,000
Kramer	140	NA	NA	NA	NA	83,000
Lord Day	184	196	NA	NA	NA	82,000
Parker	130	134	NA	NA	NA	75,000
Patterson	154	163	NA	NA	NA	83,000
Reid	152	192	NA	NA	NA	77,000*
Schulte	156	157	NA	NA	NA	77,000
Webster	108	125	NA	NA	NA	NA
Whitman	141	225	NA	NA	NA	78,000

*1989
†1988 results

Revenue per Lawyer (1989)

Firm	Total Number in New York	Total Number in New York and Branch Offices	Gross Revenue	Revenue Per Lawyer	Profits Per Partner	Starting Associate Salary
Wachtell	96	96	$115,000,000	$1,225,000	$1,590,000	$83,000
Cravath	305	314	213,000,000	740,000	1,765,000	82,962
Sullivan	292	344	230,000,000	665,000	1,210,000	83,000
Davis	351	415	240,500,000	630,000	1,125,000	83,000
Fried	256	397	213,000,000	580,000	815,000	82,000
Cahill	273	290	146,500,000	575,000	1,515,000	83,000
Shearman	440	563	281,000,000	575,000	800,000	83,000
Kaye	287	353	188,000,000	550,000	685,000	83,000
Skadden	550	1,085	517,500,000	545,000	1,195,000	83,000
Paul	377	410	195,000,000	535,000	915,000	83,000
Cleary	243	283	181,000,000	530,000	775,000	83,000
Simpson	448	457	201,000,000	525,000	1,015,000	83,000
Debevoise	274	338	147,000,000	485,000	655,000	83,000
Willkie	279	347	142,500,000	460,000	805,000	82,000
Milbank	369	476	187,500,000	450,000	665,000	83,000
Whitman	141	225	NA	NA	NA	78,000
Dewey	278	386	139,000,000	410,000	465,000	83,000
Chadbourne	215	272	95,000,000	405,000	505,000	83,000
Shea	262	304	123,000,000	405,000	345,000	80,000
White	304	422	144,000,000	380,000	425,000	83,000
Winthrop	212	NA	88,000,000	380,000	425,000	83,000
Stroock	245	339	120,000,000	365,000	460,000	82,000
Coudert	160	344	120,000,000	360,000	405,000	83,000
Cadwalader	197	279	96,000,000	355,000	410,000	83,000
Proskauer	325	392	120,000,000	355,000	360,000	82,000
Rogers	223	307	99,000,000	355,000	320,000	82,000
Rosenman	241	247	80,000,000	355,000	360,000	82,000
Mudge	251	296	91,000,000	340,000	355,000	82,000
Weil	391	522	200,000,000	340,000	385,000	83,000
LeBouef	211	384	117,000,000	330,000	305,000	83,000
Hughes	131	191	76,000,000	325,000	330,000	80,000
Brown	198	244	77,000,000	315,000	395,000	80,000
Kelley	223	388	112,500,000	300,000	365,000	83,000
Phillips	109	110	32,000,000	285,000	240,000	75,000

Wilson	217	365	$82,000,000	**$260,000**	$460,000	$45,000*
Bower	200	206	NA	**NA**	NA	NA
Breed	109	118	NA	**NA**	NA	80,000
Curtis	104	140	NA	**NA**	NA	80,000
Donovan	103	160	NA	**NA**	NA	79,000
Epstein	80	163	48,000,000	**NA**	230,000	69,000
Hawkins	70	72	NA	**NA**	NA	NA
Jackson	31	121	NA	**NA**	NA	65,000
Kramer	140	NA	NA	**NA**	NA	83,000
Lord Day	184	196	NA	**NA**	NA	82,000
Parker	130	134	NA	**NA**	NA	75,000
Patterson	154	163	NA	**NA**	NA	83,000
Reid	152	192	NA	**NA**	NA	77,000*
Schulte	156	157	NA	**NA**	NA	77,000
Thacher	124	134	32,259,000†	**NA**	254,000†	83,000
Webster	108	125	NA	**NA**	NA	NA

*1989
†1988 results

Profits per Partner (1989)

Firm	Total Number in New York	Total Number in New York and Branch Offices	Gross Revenue	Revenue Per Lawyer	Profits Per Partner	Starting Associate Salary
Cravath	305	314	$213,000,000	$740,000	$1,765,000	$83,000
Wachtell	96	NA	115,000,000	1,225,000	1,590,000	83,000
Cahill	273	290	146,500,000	575,000	1,515,000	83,000
Sullivan	292	344	230,000,000	665,000	1,210,000	83,000
Skadden	550	1,085	517,500,000	545,000	1,195,000	83,000
Davis	351	415	240,500,000	630,000	1,125,000	83,000
Simpson	448	457	201,000,000	525,000	1,015,000	83,000
Paul	377	410	195,000,000	535,000	915,000	83,000
Fried	256	397	213,000,000	580,000	815,000	82,000
Willkie	279	347	142,500,000	460,000	805,000	82,000
Shearman	440	563	281,000,000	575,000	800,000	83,000
Cleary	243	283	181,000,000	530,000	775,000	83,000
Whitman	141	225	NA	440,000	690,000	78,000
Kaye	287	353	188,000,000	550,000	685,000	83,000
Milbank	369	476	187,500,000	450,000	665,000	83,000
Debevoise	274	338	147,000,000	485,000	655,000	83,000
Chadbourne	215	272	95,000,000	405,000	505,000	83,000
Dewey	278	386	139,000,000	410,000	465,000	83,000
Stroock	245	339	120,000,000	365,000	460,000	82,000
Wilson	217	365	82,000,000	260,000	460,000	45,000*
White	304	422	144,000,000	380,000	425,000	83,000
Winthrop	212	NA	88,000,000	380,000	425,000	83,000
Cadwalader	197	279	96,000,000	355,000	410,000	83,000
Coudert	160	344	120,000,000	360,000	405,000	83,000
Brown	198	244	77,000,000	315,000	395,000	80,000
Weil	391	522	200,000	340,000	385,000	83,000
Kelley	223	388	112,500,000	300,000	365,000	83,000
Proskauer	325	392	120,000,000	355,000	360,000	82,000
Rosenman	241	247	80,000,000	355,000	360,000	82,000
Mudge	251	296	91,000,000	340,000	355,000	82,000
Shea	262	304	123,000,000	405,000	345,000	80,000
Hughes	131	191	76,000,000	325,000	330,000	80,000
Rogers	223	307	99,000,000	355,000	320,000	82,000
LeBouef	211	384	117,000,000	330,000	305,000	83,000

Thacher	124	134	$32,259,000†	NA	**$254,000†**	$83,000
Phillips	109	110	32,000,000	$285,000	**240,000**	75,000
Epstein	80	163	48,000,000	NA	**230,000**	69,000
Bower	200	206	**NA**	NA	**NA**	NA
Breed	109	118	NA	NA	**NA**	80,000
Curtis	104	140	NA	NA	**NA**	80,000
Donovan	103	160	NA	NA	**NA**	79,000
Hawkins	70	72	NA	NA	**NA**	NA
Jackson	31	121	NA	NA	**NA**	65,000
Kramer	140	NA	NA	NA	**NA**	83,000
Lord Day	184	196	NA	NA	**NA**	82,000
Parker	130	134	NA	NA	**NA**	75,000
Patterson	154	163	NA	NA	**NA**	83,000
Reid	152	192	NA	NA	**NA**	77,000*
Schulte	156	157	NA	NA	**NA**	77,000
Webster	108	125	NA	NA	**NA**	NA

*1989
†1988 results

Starting Associate Salaries (1990)

Firm	Total Number in New York	Total Number in New York and Branch Offices	Gross Revenue	Revenue Per Lawyer	Profits Per Partner	Starting Associate Salary
Cadwalader	197	279	$96,000,000	$355,000	$410,000	$83,000
Cahill	273	290	146,500,000	575,000	1,515,000	83,000
Chadbourne	215	272	95,000,000	405,000	505,000	83,000
Cleary	243	283	181,000,000	530,000	775,000	83,000
Coudert	160	344	120,000,000	360,000	405,000	83,000
Cravath	305	314	213,000,000	740,000	1,765,000	83,000
Davis	351	415	240,500,000	630,000	1,125,000	83,000
Debevoise	274	338	147,000,000	485,000	655,000	83,000
Dewey	278	386	139,000,000	410,000	465,000	83,000
Kaye	287	353	188,000,000	550,000	685,000	83,000
Kelley	223	338	112,500,000	300,000	365,000	83,000
Kramer	140	NA	NA	NA	NA	83,000
LeBouef	211	384	117,000,000	330,000	305,000	83,000
Milbank	369	476	187,500,000	450,000	665,000	83,000
Patterson	154	163	NA	NA	NA	83,000
Paul	377	410	195,000,000	535,000	915,000	83,000
Shearman	440	563	281,000,000	575,000	800,000	83,000
Simpson	448	457	201,000,000	525,000	1,015,000	83,000
Skadden	550	1,085	517,500,000	545,000	1,195,000	83,000
Sullivan	292	344	230,000,000	665,000	1,210,000	83,000
Thacher	124	134	32,259,000†	NA	254,000	83,000
Wachtell	96	NA	115,000,000	1,225,000	1,590,000	83,000
Weil	391	522	200,000,000	340,000	385,000	83,000
White	304	422	144,000,000	380,000	425,000	83,000
Winthrop	212	NA	88,000,000	380,000	425,000	83,000
Fried	256	397	213,000,000	580,000	815,000	82,000
Lord Day	184	196	NA	NA	NA	82,000
Mudge	251	296	91,000,000	340,000	355,000	82,000
Proskauer	325	392	120,000,000	355,000	360,000	82,000
Rogers	223	307	99,000,000	355,000	320,000	82,000
Rosenman	241	247	80,000,000	355,000	360,000	82,000
Stroock	245	339	120,000,000	365,000	460,000	82,000
Willkie	279	347	142,500,000	460,000	805,000	82,000
Breed	109	118	NA	NA	NA	80,000
Brown	198	244	77,000,000	315,000	395,000	80,000

Curtis	104	140	NA	NA	NA	**$80,000**
Hughes	131	191	$76,000,000	$325,000	$330,000	**80,000**
Shea	262	304	123,000,000	405,000	345,000	**80,000**
Donovan	103	160	NA	NA	NA	**79,000**
Reid	152	192	NA	NA	NA	**77,000**
Schulte	156	157	NA	NA	NA	**77,000**
Parker	130	134	NA	NA	NA	**75,000**
Phillips	109	110	32,000,000	285,000	240,000	**75,000**
Whitman	141	225	NA	NA	NA	**73,000**
Epstein	80	163	48,000,000	NA	230,000	**69,000**
Jackson	31	121	NA	NA	NA	**65,000**
Wilson	217	365	NA	NA	NA	**45,000***
Bower	200	206	NA	NA	NA	**NA**
Hawkins	70	72	NA	NA	NA	**NA**
Webster	108	125	NA	NA	NA	**NA**

*1989
†1988 results

Appendix B

....

Leading Law Firms Based Outside New York with New York Offices (1990)

(BASED ON NUMBER OF LAWYERS)

Firm	Base City	Total No. of Lawyers	No. of Lawyers in Base City	No. of Lawyers in N.Y.
Baker & McKenzie	Chicago	1,487	167	64
Jones, Day, Reavis Pogue	Cleveland	1,150	231	95
Gibson, Dunn Crutcher	Los Angeles	702	314	65
Sidley & Austin	Chicago	658	388	61
Morgan, Lewis & Bockius	Philadelphia	622	192	91
Fulbright & Jaworski	Houston	614	302	79
Latham & Watkins	Los Angeles	549	235	73
Morrison & Foerster	San Francisco	521	229	50
Mayer, Brown & Platt	Chicago	513	351	45
O'Melveny & Myers	Los Angeles	492	320	59
McDermott, Will & Emery	Chicago	462	271	22
Hunton & Williams	Richmond, Va.	434	227	43

Squire, Sanders & Dempsey	Cleveland	417	180	7
Dechert, Price & Rhoads	Philadelphia	384	260	33
Paul, Hastings, Janofsky & Walker	Los Angeles	382	215	30
Winston & Strawn	Chicago	357	265	79
Dorsey & Whitney	Minneapolis	356	273	37
Graham & Jones	San Francisco	350	119	38
Arnold & Porter	Washington	336	294	25
Bryan, Cave, McPheeters & McRoberts	St. Louis	326	169	22
Katten, Muchin & Zavis	Chicago	316	272	3
Seyforth, Shaw, Fairweather & Geraldson	Chicago	300	164	14
Gaston & Snow	Boston	270	172	68
Sonnenschein, Nath & Rosenthal	Chicago	265	194	19
Orrick, Herrington & Sutcliffe	San Francisco	261	173	38
Nixon, Hargrave, Devans & Doyle	Rochester, N.Y.	255	140	37
Schnader, Harrison, Segal & Lewis	Philadelphia	248	196	17
Oppenheimer, Wolff & Donnelly	Minneapolis	237	100	13
Drinker, Biddle & Reath	Philadelphia	227	175	3
Loeb & Loeb	Los Angeles	193	146	44

Appendix C

··

All Law Firms
Are Not Created Equal*

In his recent "At the Bar" column reviewing the recruiting brochures of a number of major law firms (NY Times: Dec. 23), David Margolick concluded that: "All [these major law firms] are 'full-service'; that is, if there's anything they can't do, they don't admit it. All are 'cutting edge.' All throw their young lawyers immediately into the fray. . . . All are both old-fashioned and forward looking. All have mushroomed, but without compromising quality. All have top clients, but aren't dependent on any of them. All are public spirited. All are meritocratic. Judging from the pictures, suit coats are superfluous. So are doors, since they are always open. In other words, all are unique, and in precisely the same way."

*This essay written by Erwin Cherovsky originally appeared in the January 18, 1989, edition of the *New York Law Journal*. Reprinted with the permission of the *New York Law Journal*. Copyright, 1989. The New York Law Publishing Company.

Having met the author and knowing something about his approach and attitude, I doubt he intended to imply that major law firms or law firms generally are in fact pretty much the same. After all, recruiting brochures are designed to entice and attract law school graduates to join the firms in question. They are not intended to be professional, economic or sociological analyses of these firms. Of all prospective targets, law school graduates are the least knowledgeable and the least able to secure reliable information on the firms which recruit lawyers on a regular basis. (If brochures ever were utilized to attract differing levels of associates and partners to make lateral moves, they most likely would be quite different in tone and content.) Moreover, it is not easy to convey to new lawyers what really matters in their efforts to discriminate among the law firms which they interview; neither lawyers nor Madison Avenue appears to have developed this particular skill or insight to a level at least equal to everyday commercial advertising.

Presentation is one thing. The reality of firms is another. For example: Some firms take pains in providing their associates with continuing legal education and in training, guiding and evaluating them; others evince only a modest interest; still others are barely involved. Some firms eschew sharp practices like the plague; some continually walk the fine line on the margins of propriety. Some firms maintain carefully monitored procedures to preclude at the outset conflicts of interest (and the appearance thereof); others are either lackadaisical in their approach or basically uninterested. Some firms have formalized oversight procedures before issuing opinions; the procedures of other firms are either haphazard or nonexistent. Some firms would as soon disclose a confidential discussion with a client as they would commit a crime; others act as if they at all times carry an implied waiver of the attorney/client privilege from their clients; still others are not terribly concerned about the issue. Some firms conduct painstaking research on important matters in a timely manner and reduce their research and analysis to writing; other firms are somewhat casual about the entire process; still others would have difficulty in finding the library or reducing their thoughts to writing. Some firms take pride in clarity of thought and expression; others are basically unconcerned; still others seem to thrive on imprecision and obfuscation.

Firms are different in other ways. Some firms are governed by partners who are selected by some form of democratic vote (whether by a majority of the partners or of their points based on profit participation or by a combination of partners and points); others, by an oligarchy; still others, by a benevolent despot. Some firms take their pro bono and charitable interest work very seriously; others become involved on an occasional basis; and still others basically have no interest. Some firms are headed by lawyers who are leaders of the bar and recognized authorities in their fields; others, by a few such lawyers; still others have no such lawyer at the helm. Some firms have uniformly strong departments in virtually every area of the law, and their departments have efficient cross-communication and coordination with each other; others maintain only a few departments with varying strengths and weaknesses.

Some firms enjoy an extremely diverse and long-standing base of significant clients; others have a substantially less diverse and time-tested base which is in jeopardy of significant adverse consequences if one or several clients are lost. Some firms are very stable and their growth is primarily internal compared to other firms which have become dependent upon lateral moves where, for example, entire real estate departments, bankruptcy departments and merger-and-acquisition teams with their stable of clients move en masse to shore up perceived weaknesses or enhance existing capabilities. The partners of some firms come exclusively or primarily from the ranks of their associates who, in turn, come from diverse backgrounds and law schools; other firms depend much more heavily on lateral moves and have a much narrower base of diversity. Some firms have a very steady and healthy financial growth and stability, well defined prospects and well and fairly compensated partners and associates; the financial health of other firms is basically unpredictable, is not monitored properly and has many weaknesses and vulnerabilities.

Some firms sponsor a full complement of lunches and dinners and cocktail parties (for particular reasons or no reason), outings, retreats, firm newspapers, basketball and softball teams, etc.; other firms either have an abbreviated schedule of social activities or by and large ignore them. In some firms there is civility and even affection and mutual respect among partners and associates who have a general sense of common purpose, community and trust; other firms exhibit substantial degrees of mistrust and hostility among both partners and associates, who function in separate fiefdoms for key partners and work at a frenetic and anxiety-ridden pace.

Although it may be entertaining to see lawyers with their suit coats removed and their galluses showing, it has no real relevance to the performance of their firms. What one really wants to know—and what is difficult after a few interviews to perceive and appreciate, particularly for young lawyers—is the mind, heart and soul of a firm.

Whether by pruning, osmosis or acculturation, lawyers in a firm, and the firm itself, take on distinctive features. These features are discernible to the experienced eye and form the basis of the reputation of the firm. Although it would be quite wrong to conclude that all lawyers in a firm resemble sardines in a can, or, to change the simile, a well-trained Marine corps color guard, they collectively take on, over time, a very particular and peculiar configuration which constitutes their reputation—or trademark to the world.

As firms are composed of many parts, some observers will perceive, like the blind men asked to describe an elephant, very different features. However, once those features are seen as a whole, it becomes clear that the firms themselves reflect distinctive characteristics which are very different from one another. While old firms change for better or worse and new firms are formed from time to time, all respond to the professional and market demands of the day. Whatever changes occur, they do not affect their performance or characteristics to any significant degree unless a substantial number of key lawyers arrive or depart. In any event, one should never confuse the outward similarities of firms with their inner reality which, in fact, determines their culture, reputation, and destiny.